WAGNER

Wagner

PHILOSOPHY AND REVOLUTION

BRIAN O'CONNOR

PRINCETON UNIVERSITY PRESS
PRINCETON & OXFORD

Published by Princeton University Press
41 William Street, Princeton, New Jersey 08540
99 Banbury Road, Oxford OX2 6JX

press.princeton.edu

GPSR Authorized Representative: Easy Access System Europe - Mustamäe tee 50, 10621 Tallinn, Estonia, gpsr.requests@easproject.com

ISBN 9780691246888
ISBN (epub) 9780691296814
ISBN (PDF) 9780691246864
Library of Congress Control Number: 2026944302

British Library Cataloging-in-Publication Data is available

Editorial: Ben Tate and John Drake
Production Editorial: Natalie Baan
Jacket Design: Chris Ferrante
Production: Danielle Capurso
Publicity: Charlotte Coyne and Natalie Zander
Copyeditor: Hank Southgate

Jacket image: Pierre Petit, *Richard Wagner*, 1860, photograph. Bibliothèque nationale de France, Département Bibliothèque-musée de l'Opéra.

This book has been composed in Arno

Printed in the United States of America

10 9 8 7 6 5 4 3 2 1

MIX
Paper
FSC FSC® C183721

In memory of John Aidan Proctor, my brother,
and my grandparents, Eileen Winifred and
the Reverend Ernest George Dixon

CONTENTS

ACKNOWLEDGEMENTS

WHILE WRITING this book I was very fortunate to benefit from suggestions and criticisms from an unusually high number of perceptive readers. For that invaluable assistance I want to thank Richard Bell, Ben Craik, John Deathridge, Owen Hulatt, Christopher Kimball, Wolfgang Marx, William Mulligan, Sean A. Murphy, Fred Rush, Hank Southgate (who copyedited the text), Tom Stern, Josh Torabi, Peter White, and Günter Zöller. Raymond Geuss was vital in encouraging the project along at every stage, and his willingness to look at different versions of the text is hugely appreciated. I am very grateful too to Anna Brennan O'Connor for her careful reviews of the translated material in this book. Ben Tate of Princeton University Press was an essential source of good advice. The Nationalarchiv der Richard-Wagner-Stiftung Bayreuth hosted a productive research visit. But yet again my greatest debt is to Eileen Brennan, whose interest and enthusiasm for this work mean everything to me.

ABBREVIATIONS

ALL REFERENCES are given first to an existing English version of the text, if available, followed by a reference to the item in one of the German collections specified below.

Collected Works

PW *Richard Wagner's Prose Works,* 8 vols., trans. William Ashton Ellis (London: Kegan Paul, Trench, Trübner & Co., 1892–1899). For the convenience of readers who prefer to work with English versions of Wagner's texts, references are given to the volume and page numbers of this collection, though its translations have not been used.

SB *Richard Wagner: Sämtliche Briefe,* vols. I (1970), III (1975), V (1993), ed. Gertrud Strobel and Werner Wolf, vol. VI (1986), ed. Hans-Joachim Bauer and Johannes Forner (Leipzig: Deutscher Verlag für Musik), vol. XIV (2002), ed. Andreas Mielke and Isabel Kraft (Wiesbaden, Leipzig, Paris: Breitkopf & Härtel).

SSD *Richard Wagner: Sämtliche Schriften und Dichtungen,* Volks-Ausgabe, 16 vols. (Leipzig: Breitkopf & Härtel / C.F.W. Siegel, R. Linnemann, 1911–1914).

Individual Works

AR *Art and Revolution* (*Die Kunst und die Revolution*), PW 1

AF *The Artwork of the Future* (*Das Kunstwerk der Zukunft*), PW 1

CF *A Communication to My Friends* (*Eine Mitteilung an meine Freunde*), PW 1

JM *Jewishness in Music* (*Das Judentum in der Musik*), PW 3

JN *Jesus of Nazareth* (*Jesus von Nazareth*), PW 8

ML *My Life* (*Mein Leben*), ed. Mary Whittall, trans. Andrew Gray (Cambridge: Cambridge University Press, 1983)

OD *Opera and Drama* (*Oper und Drama*), PW 2

This text observes the convention of referring to Wagner's musical and dramatic works by their original titles and to translated names for all others.

WAGNER

Introduction

IT WAS through intensive engagement with the political upheavals of 1848–1849 that Richard Wagner became a philosopher. Although as a younger man he had attended university lectures on philosophy, he was repelled by the academic obscurities of his teachers. As a consequence of that unhappy experience, the discipline left little mark on his early intellectual development.[1] In the decade or so that followed, none of his writings display an interest in speculative thinking, even if philosophical texts were sometimes among his private readings.[2] That began to change when, in 1848, the exhilarating and real promise of social transformation arrived in Germany.[3] Wagner enthusiastically involved himself in radical political conversations, writing short articles on the future of Europe and of Saxony, his home state. Those relatively simple contributions elevated his thought to a more abstract engagement with the social world than anything he had previously attempted in print. Over the following months, they grew in vision, vehemence, and complexity, culminating in a piece which called drastically for the elimination of every socially manufactured obstacle, including poverty, to human self-realization. For Wagner, that meant nothing less than the necessary downfall of the state. Soon afterwards, he collapsed the distinction between theorizing and activism when he joined the uprising that took place in Dresden in May 1849. It failed, inevitably, and Wagner went into extended exile to avoid arrest. He began, almost immediately, the substantial works that mark his great philosophical phase.

What Wagner left behind, as he started a new life abroad, was a secure yet artistically dissatisfying position as Kapellmeister to the Saxon court. It might be expected that the urgency of securing a means of living together with a space now free of official duties would have seen him return to his musical projects. Instead, he threw himself into a series of philosophical writings, declaring that it 'is most essential that I should accomplish this work and send it into the world before going on with my immediate artistic productions'.[4] The result was a quick succession of books of increasing size: *Art and Revolution* (1849), *The Artwork of the Future* (1849), and *Opera and Drama* (1851).[5] This set of works is sometimes labelled the 'Zurich trilogy' in reference to Wagner's main place of residence at the time the books were written (though they were all published back in Saxony). However, it might be more descriptive to call them the 'post-Dresden trilogy', since the bruising events of 1848–1849, together with Wagner's refusal to yield to the counterrevolution's triumph, can be detected in much of the theoretical thought its volumes contain. This was not a sublimation of revolutionary activity but, for Wagner, a new way of engaging with it. Given the overlap and complementarity of the philosophical content of the three books, they will be treated in this study as elements of a single synthetic project.

Wagner's achievements in the trilogy are both intellectually audacious and philosophically impressive. To support his conception of a truly free community, he developed a theory of spontaneous action that challenges rationalist notions of freedom. He added to the idea of what should motivate us to act with and for others by way of a deepened notion of need (*Noth*), a notion which will be interpreted here as needfulness.[6] This was the fulcrum for his many criticisms of the debilities that stem from the egoism of modern society. His revolutionary perspective also gave him a distinctive view of history. He rejected the notion of historical progress as promoted both by philosophers and writers of history, arguing that the progressionist model fails to break adequately with the impairing social practices of the present. Instead, a complete reconception of the human community is required. Throughout the trilogy, there are discernible lines of repudiation of precepts that are recognizable from Kantian and Hegelian idealism. Any theory which prioritizes spirit or intellect is condemned as inimical to vital human experience. That experience includes, importantly, aesthetic life, as well as affective and need-responsive social relations.

We can describe Wagner's philosophical project as *aesthetic materialism*. In arguing for the possibility of a world in which the richest capacities of human beings are realizable—a world without social or self-alienation—he draws from the example of aesthetic productivity, characterized as uninhibited, free, shared, yet truly directed action. He secures his project of freedom by way of something he could attest to from his personal experience of creative practice. By this point in his life, he had already accomplished a great deal artistically, having completed *Rienzi, Tannhäuser,* and *Lohengrin,* as well as numerous poetic texts. That practice provided him with a readily available exemplar of the experience of freedom, one that was so powerful for him that he was certain that ideas of community and morality should be shaped around it.

In the decades immediately following his death, there was within Germany, at least, a vibrant interest in the philosophical content of the trilogy, much of which was independent of the hagiographical mission headquartered in Bayreuth.[7] Outside Germany, however, there was largely indifference, and in more recent times that has given way to dismissiveness.[8] Disentangling the reasons for that reaction—expressed at times by some who should really have known better—is made all the more difficult when they are uttered as bare opinions that exhibit little or no evidence of engagement with Wagner's texts.[9] What value can there be in making a point of denying that some given writer is a philosopher without explaining where in their work they succeed or fail? It is even more puzzling that Wagner is pronounced unphilosophical even as, alongside that judgment, his dramatic creations—*Der*

Ring des Nibelungen (*The Ring of the Nibelung* or the *Ring* cycle) above all—are in some instances reverentially deciphered as texts of sublime human and philosophical wisdom. One reason to revisit the trilogy might be to see the interplay between its ideas and those of the *Ring* and other dramas. This book gives some space to that task without, however, losing sight of the keenness with which Wagner himself regarded theory and art as separable though not necessarily duelling endeavours. The first, in Wagner's hands, is essentially prescriptive, whereas the latter is experimental. Both should be studied by anyone interested in Wagner's intellectual commitments. Treating the dramas as though Wagner was otherwise silent on his opinions about human and social relations unmoors his work from the world in which it was created. Diligent negotiation of the trilogy—of Wagner's view of social reality, in particular—might end up dampening down the peculiar thesis that he is a thinker of transcendent meaning except when he is engaged in philosophical work.

Wagner himself might share part of the blame for the general disinterest in his mid-century philosophical writings. He put his books together at tremendous speed. None of them took more than several months to write, with little time evidently given to consideration of what makes a satisfyingly thematic volume. This is less true of the slimmest of the three, *Art and Revolution* (just sixty pages in its first edition). The other two contain material that is diverse not only in their range of topics but also in their methodologies. Invaluable insights on how words and music might work together in operatic composition, for example, sit together with theories of the state and ideas of human freedom. This is certainly unusual, but the product is not a jumble. Themes do not crisscross but are set out in different sections that the reader can readily isolate. No unprecedented level of patience is required. It would doubtless have been better had Wagner taken the time to make several books out of the brilliant but unwieldy *Opera and Drama* (a book of three parts amounting to about six hundred and forty pages). If, though, lapses of orderliness or thematic rigour legitimately exclude Wagner from the rolls of philosophy, we can only wonder at the inconsistent standards applied by the discipline's gatekeepers. That is not to say that Wagner's claims are always well supported by argument or that he successfully avoids contradictory commitments. But pointing out those places where his philosophy does not work is not the same thing as claiming it has no merit. Wagner had little conceit about his own abilities and was easily shaken by even the mildest of criticism. He did not enter into intensive theoretical activity with a view to arrogating a name for himself as a philosopher but simply because he believed that consideration of the post-Dresden situation necessitated it.

Some readers are doubtful about the originality of Wagner's philosophy. There is the untested conclusion that the Wagner of the revolutionary period was an unsophisticated follower of Ludwig Feuerbach. Wagner again may have contributed to this negative perception of himself when professing inspiration from the great philosopher in his (later dropped) dedication of *The Artwork of the Future* to Feuerbach. As we shall see, Wagner takes Feuerbachian ideas in directions that are not mere twists on what he found in the original. Rather, he produces innovative recastings of some of those ideas, resulting in a new and independent philosophical position that deserves evaluation on its own terms.

It is difficult to know how much Wagner's personal prejudices have contributed to the neglect of his philosophical writings. An essay of 1850 made it clear that he harboured antisemitic views, and as his career progressed, his confidence in that bias only grew. Some scholars have attempted to interpret the ideas of the trilogy (they overlap with the 1850 essay) as encoded expressions of exclusionary nationalism. The complex mixture of Wagner's prejudices, the pernicious delusions and neuroses of the Bayreuth circle, and, of course, the co-option of his art to the politics of twentieth-century Germany had for some time understandably brought into question the morality of staging his works, some of which are themselves thought to employ antisemitic motifs. Given the troubling association of Wagner with the European catastrophe, it is perhaps to be expected that his largely unheralded philosophical writings have slipped from view. The prose writings of Wagner's revolutionary period have, after all, considerably less cultural and historical weight than his operatic works or music dramas, as he preferred them to be called.

Finally, one might also speculate on the role played by the translations of Wagner's prose works into English, since it is predominantly within Britain that the most condescending reactions to his philosophical work are to be found.[10] Criticism of William Ashton Ellis's immense labours in translating, in the eight-volume *Richard Wagner's Prose Works* collection, almost every nonliterary publication by Wagner is often excessive. What he gives us is, as one scholar aptly puts it, 'by no means always misleading'.[11] Nevertheless, the voice he creates for Wagner's trilogy, at least, does not capture that of the original where we find Wagner speak, for the most part, with a relative plainness that is without stylistic flourishes and archaic locutions, though not at all times without some deployment of emotive rhetoric. In English he too often arrives with amateur and ornate exuberance. And there is the terminological challenge that few Victorian translators could satisfactorily negotiate. Wagner adopts terms that, although common to German philosophy, had until relatively recently no agreed-upon or stipulated English equivalent. This affected the early reception of all the notable thinkers of that era (with multiple renderings of words, such as *Vorstellung*, *Geist*, and *Moral*, leading to avoidable confusion). The absence of a shared vocabulary, even if it is a result of diverse and uncoordinated decisions among translators, may lead to the damaging consequence that ideas are not appreciated as part of a wider philosophical context of debate since they are not expressed in a common disciplinary language. The technicalities employed by Wagner are too often indiscernible in the translations—both because of the choice of word and inconsistency of choice within some of the texts—and his contribution to philosophy in the wake of the decline of German idealism, among other things, is lost to the English reader. In order, then, both to allow Wagner's seriousness to speak to us in the twenty-first century and to perceive his place within his intellectual context more readily, I have not used the translations found in the *Prose Works* (though references are given to it for the convenience of readers).

In considering Wagner as a philosopher of revolution, this book covers his thought up to 1852, the year in which the text of the *Ring*'s fourth and final part was essentially completed. Wagner famously agonized over the right ending to *Götterdämmerung* (*Twilight of the Gods*), the last part of the cycle, which though, confusingly for us, was the first of the four texts to be written, in 1848. He replaced the original in 1852. Several years later it too was revised in order to give voice to ideas drawn from Arthur Schopenhauer, a new philosophical inspiration (see chapter 6 below). However, he eventually settled for something that was more sympathetic to the 1852 notion of a new world for which human beings had responsibility, a notion that resonated with the revolutionary ideas of the trilogy even if they were no longer those that mattered most to him. The chronology of publications after 1852 shows a Wagner disengaged from the theory of revolution and philosophical advocacy for universal social emancipation. He did not constructively revisit the concepts he had developed to sustain a new notion of free human experience. The period essentially in view in this study is short yet astoundingly productive, beginning with spirited opinion pieces, advocating for political reform, moving on to quasi-insurrectionist literature, and culminating in the huge set of ideas contained in the trilogy. And alongside that work are not only the four parts of the *Ring*, with their historically embedded elements, but drafted texts for several other dramas, one on Jesus in particular, that voice lucid ideas of social revolution. Some level of sympathetic reconstruction is required simply to draw out the relevance of Wagner's ideas to the philosophical environment in which they were devised.

What should become visible in those ideas is the capacity of Wagner's aesthetic materialism to offer interesting and novel responses to the challenges posed by rationalism and idealism to how we are to understand social and individual freedom.

This study begins with a brief overview of the context and principal events of the 1848 revolution as they unfolded in Germany. We then move to a series of writings on various aspects of reform and revolution published by Wagner from June 1848 to April of the following year. His transformation across those pieces from constructive opponent of the existing regime to radical anarchist is discernible. The shift, as we shall see, was not the product of Wagner's abstracted theorizing about the future. It came in response to the evolving situation in which optimism for a new society drained away and was replaced by anger at the old authority's reversal of reformist concessions. These matters take us to the much-contested story of Wagner's role in the violent uprising in Dresden. Notwithstanding a defensible hostility to the heavy-handedness of the Saxon authorities as they sought to regain control of their capital city, Wagner's decision to involve himself in insurrection deserves some elaboration. It draws attention to a conflict between the peculiarly moral and abstract ideals that attracted him to revolution in principle and the reality of the violence in which his activism implicated him, even if his participation really was as minimal as he subsequently and controversially claimed. Wagner was profoundly troubled by the nature of the Uprising and quickly turned his revolutionary commitments to ever more purely philosophical reflections on what revolution involves and why it is required.

Those reflections are the main concern of chapter 2, where we will begin to see the core elements of Wagner's aesthetic materialism. His theory of revolution adopts a markedly unorthodox notion of history. Because he is committed to a framework which rests on certain ideas of the imperatives of nature, he does not see history as a progressive process, governed by extramaterial forces, which will result in the kind of free community he favours. Rather, freedom is a break with history as conceived by the idealist model, which he perceives as the validation of an overbearing and ongoing process of oppression. History, in essence, has taken us in the wrong direction. And as a philosophical device, history is, he believes, ideologically employed to bind the political imagination to nothing more than improved versions of the present. In opposition to this, Wagner references the untapped energies of what he thinks of as real material forces, namely, the natural tendencies of human beings both singularly and when constituted collectively as 'the people'. We shall see why Wagner believes those forces must eventually assert themselves.

Wagner's idea of need, *Noth* (see above), is identified as the natural basis of some of the capacities whose suppression has produced an unfree egoistical society and lifeless individuality. Since it is a feeling, Wagner takes it to belong to the same general source as the involuntary, that is, spontaneous character that he ascribes to aesthetic experience: both are reliably truth bearing and healthily productive. In setting out a conception of a society of feeling and creativity, Wagner develops the related notions of the Gesamtkunstwerk, that is, the total work of art, and the consummate work of art. The Gesamtkunstwerk is at one level an aesthetic ideal which urges the unification of the main artistic media in the creation of works of art. The notion of the consummate work of art indirectly implies that synthesis in that it refers to the great works of art of the Greeks, whose preeminent artforms, Wagner maintains, encapsulate the ideal of totality. The Gesamtkunstwerk, as we shall see, is not in its principal meaning, and contrary to much of the commentary, a pure theory of art as such. It is, in the specific context of Wagner's revolutionary theory, a vision of a society of aestheticized experience, involving cooperation towards shared ends and an intuitive sense of oneself as an individual and communal being. At the same time, Wagner believes that a new form of art practice will be characteristic of a genuinely free community, and it is in that space that his notion of the Gesamtkunstwerk as a theory of the artwork as such has purchase, notwithstanding some of the plausible criticism it has received.

It is in the context of Wagner's notion of an aestheticized community that a consideration of the implications of his essay on Jewish composers in music seems most appropriate. The essay infamously argues that the Jews as outsiders to German culture cannot contribute to its ongoing reproduction. That objectionable view is difficult enough on its own terms and may moreover undermine the universalism which is at the centre of Wagner's thoughts on revolution and the constitution of a single *Volk*, that is, 'people' (across the entirety of the trilogy). The striking set of recommendations that Wagner offers at that essay's conclusion points unexpectedly, however, towards an emancipated future as one in which all groups—*all* ethnicities—have, through some considerable labour, overcome the social conditioning which had once confirmed them in states of egoism and separation.

Wagner's thoughts on freedom are examined across two separate chapters. Chapter 3 looks at his strictly philosophical account of freedom, with particular emphasis on its material dimensions, that is, its sensual and aesthetic qualities. Since it is within this set of ideas that Wagner is sometimes perceived as helplessly indebted to Feuerbach, a detailed look at that connection is important. The differences between the two thinkers are, in fact, substantial. Feuerbach is famously motivated by a reappropriation of human possibility through the deconstruction of theology, whereas the question of God—though not religious authority—holds virtually no interest for Wagner. The metaphysical framework of religion is transformed by Feuerbach into the language of anthropology, but at its extreme it tends to generate its own new abstractions. The challenge of articulating the materiality of personal feeling, need, and creative freedom drives Wagner's divergence from Feuerbach's main theoretical lines. He subtly reconfigures a range of concepts he finds in Feuerbach, though others he adopts in their original form. What emerges from that complex engagement leads, among other things, to a critical alternative to the generalized version of Kantian rationalism that Wagner implicitly targets.

As the chapter shows, Wagner's use of the ideas of 'necessity' and 'control' stands in clear opposition to the Kantian usage where they serve as elements of reason's authority over human feeling. For Wagner, rather, necessity involves precisely that kind of responsiveness that is identifiable in creative aesthetic experience, and it is thereby a type of freedom marked by the absence of any notion of self-regulation or control. This radical notion of freedom is not intended as a recommendation for personal reform, nor is it just a different or competitor description of a thing that already exists. It cannot, Wagner holds, become a full reality without a transformation of the wider social world. At the same time, it stands as a critical model which philosophy can use against the counterintuitive artificiality of the idea of freedom as control or as the responses of necessity to reason's conclusions.

Examination of the characteristics of what Wagner understands as a positively transformed society, to some degree anticipated in the discussion of the Gesamtkunstwerk, brings the idea of the sociality of freedom into view. The fourth chapter sees Wagner grapple with the enormous challenge of developing an account of the relationship between the individual and the community in which neither is independent nor reducible to the other. His approach is based on a repudiation of the idea that either of these terms represents absolutes whose reconciliation is intractable in principle. Given his commitment to an aesthetic model of individual freedom, the role of the community must be accounted for in terms that are sympathetic to that freedom. Wagner develops a position not with a technical blueprint, with each part's individuation and dependency set out by argument. He turns, rather, to the force of the example given to us by what he regards as the so far unsurpassed arrangements for living enjoyed by the ancient Greeks. This example leans on a romanticized portrait of the Greek world as holistically comprising a set of dynamic principles which were geared towards the enhancement of individuality and the simultaneous preservation of the community as a democratic order.

While Wagner sees the Greek precedent as motivating evidence of what the freest human beings can bring about among themselves, he insists that we cannot simply imitate their world. The Greeks were not universalists, and Wagner even posits that the inhuman iniquity of their societies is the principal reason for their decline. This is an intriguing and useful contention, and in understanding it we gain further access to the role that Wagner thinks nature plays in the constitution of healthy communities. The latter can be contrasted with what Wagner takes to be the life-destroying character of the modern 'political state'. This is quite in line with the anarchist views that he nurtured during the Dresden events. Contrary not only to the reformists of that period but the constitutionalists of German idealism, he perceives the political state as, in essence, a device which is geared primarily towards the protection of private property. It is therefore of a piece with all systems that have gained some autonomy over human needs, among which the desire for permanent possession—that is, possessiveness without love—he maintains, will not be found. In explaining the persistence of these arrangements, Wagner develops a number of original ideas that, like others examined across this study, have been overlooked by scholarship on nineteenth-century German social thought. He is interested in exploring the role of habit as the means by which individuals lose their dynamic connection with life and recede into their own personal interests, a sphere Wagner captures with the expansive term 'egoism'. A society of habituated egoism inhibits any form of personal development that threatens its own self-preservation. Instead, it promotes, Wagner maintains, the lifeforms of fashion, money, work, and luxury. Wagner deserves recognition on these points as a philosophically minded social critic who understands the legitimating role those lifeforms play. He is not a moralizer who denounces shallow preferences. The chapter closes with Wagner's theoretical considerations of freedom as a reconciliation of individual and community and the destructive limitations of the idea of freedom as isolation from others. The political state upholds the idea of isolation, he argues, by encouraging and normalizing a condition of competition among individuals.

Chapter 5 departs from direct engagement with the theoretical writings. It offers a philosophical commentary on Wagner's completed and some of the unfinished dramatic works, covering the period from 1840 to 1852. The main objective, when considering the earlier pieces, is to identify the emergence of those ideas that later found expression in the trilogy. From the late 1840s, as this chapter will show, philosophical themes become increasingly important to core elements of Wagner's artistic creations. The musical and poetic characteristics of those works are not considered. The purpose of this chapter is certainly not to reduce the dramas to Wagner's philosophy or politics. The scope of his completed works, the *Ring* tetralogy in particular, is vast and spills beyond dramatized theory. That is to be expected of Wagner's uncompromising artistry. However, the usefulness of reading his philosophy as a way of understanding what he was thinking when devising some of the most significant of his dramatic figures should become clear. And to return to an earlier point, the idea that Wagner's dramas, rich in philosophy, can be cordoned off from the alleged philosophical emptiness of his theoretical work will be rejected. Wagner's embrace of Schopenhauer's philosophy just a few years after he had completed the last parts of the trilogy and the texts of the *Ring* might seem like a complete rupture with his revolutionary philosophy. However, part of the appeal of Schopenhauer, I will suggest in the concluding chapter, is explained by the affinities and compatibilities of some of the ideas of Wagner's revolutionary writings with those of his newly adopted philosopher.

This book, then, pursues a number of approaches that are not usually found in a philosophical monograph. Preceding the three central chapters on freedom in its many dimensions there is a compressed account of the political history of Wagner's time and a review of the facts of his personal involvement in the Uprising. And finally, the discussion turns to the dramas, without considering their dramatic effect. At all points the endeavour is to get as close as possible to an understanding of the motivations, modalities, and achievements of Wagner as a philosopher of revolution. Wagner's name might, in principle, serve to draw attention to his ideas. What I want to show here, however, is that they are not mere curiosities or novelties that survive only through fortunate association with someone more famous for other accomplishments, but deserve attention as intellectually sensitive and original responses to the philosophical and political contexts of mid-nineteenth-century Germany.

1

The Practice of Revolution

WAGNER WELCOMED the momentous political developments that in 1848 enveloped much of Europe. They aligned with his longstanding sympathy for deep social transformation first ignited by the events of July 1830, events which, as he later put it, had threatened to overthrow 'the old and outmoded.'[1] He enthusiastically supported the reformist movements that emerged across Germany and, in particular, in his home state, Saxony. Notwithstanding his ardent convictions about the inhumanity of society, he was not a natural militant. The reasons behind Wagner's conversion from benevolent liberal republican to defiant insurgent took place within the dynamic nexus of the turbulent political passions of the time, his implacable anger at the manifest duplicity of the old authorities, and his attraction to those of a more concretely activist and ideologically informed disposition than himself.

Context

A building resentment at absolutism, at the ruling classes' wilful disconnection from the democratic mood of the times, was widespread across the European mainland in the years leading up to 1848.[2] An obdurate old order faced ever-growing opposition by organized and popular political movements. Their pressure led to what seemed like a sudden collapse of unaccountable and unelected power and the beginning of lasting political renewal. The first and certainly most significant revolutionary advance saw France's king, Louis Philippe, abdicate in February 1848. He fled to England and was soon followed in that direction by Klemens von Metternich, the brilliant, once insuperable architect of conservative Austrian influence over the German world and beyond. Within the German states, reformists largely took the view that pressing changes could not be accomplished without the cooperation of the local powers. Their support was required for the sustainable enactment of new legal rights designed to provide unprecedented protections to all citizens. There would also need to be the correlative ratification of constitutions which specified the competences and limits of the state executive. The new constitutional order would include provision for parliamentary systems, with members elected by popular vote, empowered to hold the executive to account. The moderation of these proposals for change, as well as the largely constructive approach to achieving them, perhaps dilutes the usual sense that attaches to 'revolution', as the events of this period are collectively labelled. Their proponents had no intrinsic interest in 'revolutionary turmoil'.[3] The astonishing fall of the French crown, nevertheless, and fears of some recapitulation of 1789, encouraged the German princes to deal generously with the voices of reform. In retrospect, they appeared to believe that they could juggle concessions with the perpetuation of the old ways, hoping they might at an opportune moment recover everything they had merely temporarily surrendered.

The challenges to the ancient prerogatives of the German princes were pressing. Calls for a unified Germany were widespread, with obvious implications for the unchecked discretion of the ruling families in their separate regions. The predominant proposal envisaged a federation of states which would not subsume all aspects of the autonomy the states had secured through the foundation of the German Confederation in 1815. They would continue to have their princes, certainly. However, they would have to cede ultimate authority to a national parliament possessing preeminence on fundamental issues. The thought was that the deep structural reforms—liberty, governance, and economic related—required across the German states could only be justly achieved and secured on a pan-German basis. Martial ambition, it is worth stating for obvious reasons, was a minority interest with no reformist of stature fantasizing about a Germany that could compete with the large armies of her neighbours to the west and east. (The Wagner of 1871 who composed, with stirring intent, the 'Kaisermarsch' in honour of Prussian victory lies unrecognizably in the future.) By March 1848, the reformists had every reason for optimism, as all the major German states appointed liberal ministers to their respective administrations. It seemed that few further steps were required to move from a world crippled by inherited privilege to a modern one of democracy, freedom, and rights.

A notably violent episode occurred in Berlin at that time when police, who were dispersing a peaceful gathering, accidentally, it is reported, discharged two shots.[4] A skittish crowd, suspicious that the authorities were showing their true repressive colours and abandoning the spirit of reform, reacted aggressively. Brutal and wholly disproportionate force was used to quell the protests that followed. Hundreds of civilians died before calm was restored. In a conciliatory and potentially diminishing act, the Prussian king, Friedrich Wilhelm IV (an enthusiast, incidentally, of *Rienzi* and *Tannhäuser*),[5] attended the funeral ceremonies of those killed in his name. Saxony, in contrast, was among the most peaceful of all states when measured by confrontations between the authorities and reformers.[6]

On the surface, the pace of change was, for a while, sensational. Just weeks after the appointment of liberal ministers, an assembly—the so-called *Vorparlament*—of unelected representatives from across the German region took place in Frankfurt. Their purpose there was to discuss the terms of a constitution and formally elected parliament. Those elections followed soon after with over five hundred members taking their seats. Although reformist-minded, the assembly was by no means a monolith, and the diversity of views within it about what changes Germany needed necessarily involved negotiation. There were the radical democrats, who, in contrast to the moderate liberals, were not strongly inclined to sooth the princes' fears about what the future held for them. Also active were what were then considered extremes on the right and the left, with the latter demanding a reconstruction, if not elimination, of all those social institutions that had generated the deep iniquities of German life. The less compromising ideals of some on the left propelled them in particular to the centre of events the following year as revolution took precedence over the vain pursuit of reform. Different ideologies were in competition, then, but so too were conceptions of where Germany's problems lay, oftentimes informed by the very differing circumstances in the states from which the new members had been drawn.

The intricate work of establishing a constitution was a time-consuming process, hindering the reformists' capacity to seize that very moment when the existing regimes lacked the strength to reject the demands of the times. The very idea of unifying Germany was faced with the rather obvious question of which peoples it was to include, especially if Austria, 'an unnaturally thrown together mass of countries', as Wagner put it, was to be one of its constituent states.[7] A geographical area which was continuous with the old confederation, but without complicated Austria, was eventually adopted as the territory of what would be the new Germany, the so-called 'little Germany' solution. Peoples who formed substantial minorities in the existing separate states were expected to adapt to that new entity and forgo any national ambitions of their own.

Alongside these fundamental questions lay the less tangible task of establishing the parliament's authority, nationally and beyond, as the body that needed to be consulted before anything of consequence for Germany could proceed. The original authority of the parliament was moral: it was a kind of embodiment of the will for change felt across the country, a will the existing rulers recognized they could not withstand. A blow to its esteem came early, though, when it proved unable to direct the emotive events around the war with Denmark over ownership of Schleswig-Holstein. Its desire was to concede no territory to the Danes. It called upon Prussia, ever ready to mobilize, to intervene in support of that wish. Prussia, however, was forced to withdraw from the conflict, in spite of strategic success, by order of the Great Powers of Europe. Frankfurt was without a separate military option of its own and suffered the humiliation of having its instruction disregarded by one of the states. Furthermore, the Great Powers dealt directly with Prussia, effectively broadcasting their belief that it was beneath their dignity to speak with such a puny and inconsequential entity as Frankfurt. They preferred to negotiate with the traditional German states, not coincidentally those with a long history of militarism. This episode more than hinted that time was not yet up for old Germany. However, there was as yet no clear path back to the so-called *Vormärz* realities (the world before the concessions of March 1848).

The process of reform continued throughout the summer and autumn of 1848, though perceptive observers—Wagner among them—could discern a slowing of the very dynamism that had once made it seem irresistible. Its agents were up against forces that were deeply attached to power and had considerable dynastic experience of knowing how to hold on to it. The reformists entered the fray with high and modern ideals founded on their supposed truth alone, rather than on history, the tapestries of arcane interests and loyalties, and, indeed, the reassuring charms of stability and familiarity. By October 1848, the Frankfurt subcommittee was producing drafts of various parts of the constitution, which were then to be debated within the assembly. It framed a unified Germany as a constitutional democracy, with a continuing elected national parliament to be headed by one of the existing German princes who would act within stipulated constraints. The federal government would exercise control over foreign and transport policy but would have no direct tax-raising powers. Much, therefore, was left to the states themselves.

I have skipped over a huge array of details behind the events of 1848 and said nothing about some of the brilliant individuals who drove the German reformist project, including the tragic figure of Robert Blum, whom Wagner admired hugely. What I have tried to capture is the sudden birth of a possibility—a genuinely new Germany—which was not, in fact, to become a reality (not then at least). Wagner was actively contributing to the political discussions of those times, and the shape of his ideas changed as drastically as the political situation itself. His articles from June 1848 to April of the following year will be examined in what follows. What we will see unfold is a turn from constructive engagement with the existing powers to a passionate denunciation of everything they represented. It is not hard to see why Wagner's outlook evolved during those months. Simply put, the old powers, in what was suspected at the time of being 'a conspiracy of princes',[8] began to extricate themselves from the obnoxious constraints of liberal government. The greatest blow to reformist prospects came from Friedrich Wilhelm IV of Prussia who, in March 1849, refused the crown of a united Germany offered to him by the national parliament. A Germany created according to the imaginations of mere bourgeois lawyers or technocrats was an insult to the romantic patchwork of independent states that marked out the history of the region. He privately expressed the view that no noble German could accept 'a diadem forged out of the dirt and clay of revolution, disloyalty and high treason'.[9] He is also reported, though, to have disliked the exclusion of Austria from this new entity. This was a stunning disappointment to the moderates who had done so much to accommodate the entitlements of the princes while steering Germany towards modern standards of governance and law. The king could not have taken such a bold and haughty decision had he not determined—correctly, as it turned out—that his action would have no troublesome consequences for himself and the Prussia he would once again govern, divested of the unsettling and now nullified adjustments he had felt obligated to accept one year earlier.

Wagner's Writings Before the Uprising

The time reached by my summary of the historical background (March 1849) places us some months ahead of the point to which we now turn in a chronological analysis of Wagner's political writings. It is difficult to align Wagner straightforwardly with any of the standard categories used to group the various types of reformers of the revolutionary years. This has something to do with his shifting views and his relative indifference to the technicalities of state and law that distinguish one group from another. It is reasonably clear that his published commitments, at least, place him within the leftist cohort of the broader general political movement of which he was part, with radically democratic leanings winning out over some moderate liberal ideas. His writings in the lead-up to the Uprising track, in their own way, an initially mixed sense of hope with, eventually, one of a deepening outrage and further radicalization as reforms were rescinded. The autumn of 1848 saw 'a second wave mobilization of the left',[10] and it is clear that Wagner was in sentiment part of that movement. It was not the personal affront of impending defeat as such that pushed him in that direction. Rather, a Germany unable to move forward in reform would mean the continuation of the same dismal realities for those whose suffer. That concern is foregrounded in much of what he wrote at this time. The existence of poverty and cruelty disgusted him, and he believed the constitutional transformation of Germany could at least begin the process of alleviating the miserable conditions that had been inflicted for so long on his fellow human beings. He was affectively rather than intellectually democratic. Although he supported the Frankfurt reformers' endeavours, he was not properly of them. The parliament has been characterized, sometimes disparagingly, as a professors' club, an exaggeration which does, however, reflect something of its composition: well-educated professionals who were preoccupied with constitutional complexities and principles of justice. Wagner understood their approach simply as one not necessarily ideal way in which penury and degradation could be addressed. Its suffocation at the princes' hands would almost inevitably be interpreted by him as their callous disinterest in human welfare.

Preceding Wagner's writings on reform and revolution is a politically charged poem of May 1848, 'Greetings from Saxony to the Viennese' (Gruß aus Sachsen an die Wiener). It touches on some of the commitments he would later amplify in the trilogy. He sees the revolution in Vienna as an inspiring example to all within the German lands, speaking mockingly of the princes and speculators as well as those who urge caution at the expense of liberty. In light of Wagner's later developed criticisms of the intellect-first approach to action, it is interesting to see him target 'the bookworms'.[11] Their vice is the debilitating skill in finding any theory that will prove that movement against the current order is counterproductive. No particular accomplishment is attributed to the Viennese revolutionaries other than an honourable freedom. That generality might be expected of a poetic piece, but in the months that followed Wagner often struggled to specify what freedom was for and which arrangements could best guarantee it. The pamphlet-like journal contributions that followed show the limits of his willingness—or capacity, in reality—to narrow himself to that of practical reformer.

His first published discourse on the question of reform appeared in June 1848 under the title 'How Do Republican Aspirations Relate to Kingship?' (Wie verhalten sich republikanische Bestrebungen dem Königtum gegenüber?).[12] Here we find Wagner grappling with the challenges of refashioning Germany with the use of elements that might appear to repel each other. This piece is worth examining at some length since, peculiarly constructive in its approach, it gives voice to Wagner's sense of the renewal that might have been possible at that specific time. Some of his proposals are consistent with the demands of the reformist movement. He calls for the provision of 'unconditional voting and electoral rights for every adult born in the country'—that is, enfranchisement regardless of holdings—though it is unclear whether women are included in this demand.[13] This subverts the ancient thesis that only those with property have an interest in the state. In line with thoughts developed with less urgency just a few years later, he observes that property has taken on the power to determine who is of value and who can participate in public affairs, when it should rather be obvious that property is created by human beings. Adopting a further common demand, Wagner insists on the institution of a citizens' militia (the standing armies were too closely allied to the interests and authority of the old powers). It is the framework within which he places those proposals, however, that gives Wagner's position a distinctive quality.

The 'Kingship' piece was originally a talk given to the Dresden Vaterlandsverein, an organization whose political character has been interpreted differently within Wagner scholarship. Ernest Newman adjudges it a 'respectable' body 'inclining to the democratic right',[14] whereas Rüdiger Krohn describes it as 'left-wing' and 'republican'.[15] In fact, its complex history provides each of those options, since it encompassed figures from differing ideological factions.[16] Among its members was Wagner's friend, fellow conductor, composer, and activist, August Röckel, whose periodical, the *Volksblätter*, was discernibly left in its political leanings. Wagner's increasingly revolution-sympathetic reflections were published there until it was forced to shut down by laws designed to quash subversive expression. Röckel was one of the intellectuals of the Uprising of 1849 and an influential source of Wagner's education in political theory.

Wagner sets out a kind of romantic vision in which the king is elevated to an almost ethereal level of republican perfection while severed from every executive function. The model of kingship he offers is quite speculative in that it is not, as we shall see, a compromise in which both the regent and the proponents of democracy are left with something. Rather, what is offered utterly transforms the very notion of kingship, both stripping it of its traditional powers—'sacred and inviolable, unassailable and unaccountable', as a widely read text on political science put it[17]—while granting it a position merited by its exceptional virtue. Difficult though it might be to imagine this form of kingship in reality, Wagner is led to it by a very serious and, for him, worldly concern. He never believed that simple institutional reform was the lasting answer to the defects of society. What was needed, rather, was a refoundation of the entire nature of social relations. His extraordinary idea of kingship is therefore an attempt to conceive the nature of a wholly new political community—that is, not the present one somewhat improved—with its key member the mythic but living embodiment not of power but of morality and selflessness.

'Kingship' shows us that the Wagner of June 1848 occupied an emollient perspective that might at first glance seem oddly conflicted between opposing constitutional principles. He insists that a king is indispensable to any future political arrangements, even in a world without 'aristocracy', that is, where the special powers of 'feudal lords' no longer prevail.[18] His acid observations on the corruptions of palace life are remarkably contemptuous when we consider that, at this time, he occupied the position of Kapellmeister to the royal Saxon court. It seems clear, though, that Wagner did not especially value that role in spite of the musical opportunities, limited though they may have been, and financial security it afforded, and he expressed no regret at its loss when he was eventually and inevitably dismissed.

It would be understandably mistaken to conclude from the settings of *Tannhäuser* or *Lohengrin* (whose texts had been completed just several years earlier) that Wagner deemed the chivalrous customs of the Holy Roman Empire worthy of preservation. He later expressed his admiration for the readiness of the ancient Greeks to throw off any element of tradition the moment they perceived it as inimical to the fullest possibilities of their humanity. Wagner's retention of some role for the 'king', in 'Kingship', has therefore an altogether different basis than reverence. As one reads through Wagner's text, the question of whether he is wholly sincere or merely tactical inevitably asserts itself. To some degree, Wagner, perhaps with irony, exploits the lordly language that had previously flowed rather meaninglessly from the mouths of princely rulers. He suggests that the most loving thing of all would be for the king to become the first and paradigmatic republican and thereby an embodiment of the new state. The king enjoys an identification with the people that no other person can command (or so kings like to claim, Wagner seems to imply). If the king really is the state, that must mean that he expresses its republican values in full, and not, as the old thinking had it, that he can claim the state as his personal domain. He will happily bid farewell to privilege, to the 'pomp', of courtly life, and to a society where all but himself live as mere 'subjects'.[19] The 'love' that he shows the people is reciprocated.[20] As we witness Wagner quite possibly attempting to flatter the prince into self-destruction, it is hard to believe that he viewed any human being capable, most especially a scion of ancient privilege, of surrendering themselves to this peculiar role. His proposal, he explains, must entail 'the downfall of the monarchy',[21] yet it is also the emancipation of kingship. Wagner makes it clear that his proposal is not to be confused for some enfeebled version of constitutional monarchy. Nothing, he claims, is more humiliating for a king than to be constrained by law and parliament. There is, however, a future in which the dignity of the king is protected while a republic is established.

Furthering the image of a prince who will emanate perfection, Wagner envisages a Germany that will stand first among nations in achieving a fully human and humane society. By the force of its exemplarity, it can spread what Wagner marks out as German 'mildness' to those nations yearning for freedom, erasing the 'priestly abattoir' inflicted by the Spaniards on the new world and the tawdry 'pack of wares' of England's colonial endeavours.[22] As the very apotheosis of German republicanism—the king of a new Germany—the prince will serve as a compelling model throughout the globe. He will be 'the man of providence'[23] in that he has grasped the irreversible realities of the time where autocracy surrenders to constitutionalism. Wagner's reverie alights on Saxony's House of Wettin which alone, he maintains, can supply Germany with princes who possess those virtues required for this new and wholly selfless role. They stand in contrast with the 'blinded, deeply degenerate race' of nobles across the rest of Europe.[24] Wagner extolls the unique standing among the people of the local royals and declares 'Saxony a Free State'.[25]

At the time of Wagner's piece, Saxony was ruled by Friedrich August II, a man perceived within some quarters of the Vaterlandsverein as a man of 'excellent qualities'.[26] He was among the many German princes who appeared not to hesitate in appointing liberal, reform-minded ministers to their governments in March 1848 (the so-called 'March ministers'). Wagner may have genuinely entertained high hopes for him. It was, though, the very same king, just one year after Wagner's optimistic vision, who would trigger violent turmoil in Dresden, the May Uprising. Far from recognizing the necessities of a new era, he rejected the constitution that had been drafted in Frankfurt and dismissed those aforementioned ministers. He accepted Prussia's offer for military support in order to forestall anticipated reaction from the more radical movements. News of this alliance was perceived as an organized attempt at counterrevolutionary repression.[27] The king's incendiary decision brought revolutionary activists to the streets, with Wagner conspicuous among them.

An idea mentioned in 'Kingship' that would be carried forward into the more advanced theories of the trilogy is that of a cooperative community freed from the crippling 'power' of money and its 'demonic' capacity for dividing human beings from each other.[28] It is notable that Wagner wishes to leave no doubt that his position does not belong to what he calls the 'insipid and senseless doctrine' of communism.[29] His relationship with that concept is, in fact, rather tortuous. Sometime later, in the immediate aftermath of the Uprising, he would positively invoke the word 'communism', presenting it as the solution to social egoism.[30] His complaint in 'Kingship' is that communism rests on the notion of the equal division of property within a system that is not essentially geared towards the permanent elimination of hunger. It retains, as

Karl Marx would also observe of a particular version of it, the institution of private property. At the same time, Wagner warns that failure to act as he amicably advises will see the now dangerous system of communism inflict itself on those who resist. Wagner's position, by contrast, is committed to securing, as he sees it, a society in which each person is brought 'to full activity'.[31] He probably harboured the fear, voiced among radicals as well as more obvious opponents, that communism meant mediocrity and forced equality, a criticism he later openly voiced in *On State and Religion* (1864).[32]

In its concern for human capabilities, Wagner's thinking falls within a quite different space to forms of political radicalism that direct social transformation towards reconfigurations of wealth. The existing system creates conditions of physical and mental deprivation, and that remains the case even if the proceedings of that system are equitably distributed. What is required, instead, is a society where the many now-repressed dimensions of human nature—social affection and creativity in particular—are nurtured. Obviously enough, this vision lies outside the orthodox political reformism which had brought about exciting new prospects in Germany. Wagner never explained how he believed his wider vision of human freedom (self-realization) was to run alongside the liberties and rights sought by the broad reformist movement with which he had willingly aligned himself.

As noted above, an overriding motivation behind everything Wagner wrote during the revolutionary months, and much in the years that immediately followed, was an intense concern for the struggles of ordinary people. He had special contempt for those who refused to reconstitute society—something he considered within reach with enough good will—in ways that would erase basic need and grinding toil forever. This moral conviction drives the agenda of the essay 'Germany and Her Princes' (Deutschland und seine Fürsten) written by Wagner in October of the same year as 'How Do Republican Aspirations Relate to Kingship?'[33] It contains none of Wagner's conciliatory fantasies about a transcendent kingship. He points repeatedly to the absence of economic necessity in the present state of affairs. Those who work diligently to create Germany's wealth are, he observes, rewarded with 'worry' and hunger.[34] Their intergenerational experience of 'lack, need [*Noth*], misery, despair' voids them of any sense of a better future.[35] There is unvarnished disdain in Wagner's address to the princes who, he writes, 'have taken on responsibility for our weal and woe . . . *you who call yourselves the God ordained leaders of the destiny of peoples*'.[36] He reprovingly reminds them that they have long been '*warned and admonished*' about the hardships they have indifferently allowed to disfigure the lives of the many.[37] The notion of inherited merit is derided, and its beneficiaries are contrasted with those whose labour enjoys no recognition and little reward. Identifying with the industrious, he mocks the courtier who is 'honoured' for his idleness in doing 'what is of no use' and who 'creates nothing', while the workers, whose efforts are vital to all of society, are haughtily ignored.[38]

We can detect from this blazing series of accusations that by the autumn of 1848 Wagner was more than sceptical about the princes' commitment to reform. That may suggest at first sight that he was either impatient or naive about what it took to bring about the changes that had been promised. It was, after all, no more than half a year since some level of influence had been ceded to the modernizers. Wagner's criticisms had, though, some basis, not only in the decelerating developments of the day but also in historical experience. He points his readers back to the high-minded ideals professed by the princes at the founding of the German Confederation and has on his side considerable justification for the conclusion that those ideals did not make much difference in reality. It is fair to say that the regimes in their 1848 incarnation surrendered more than their recent predecessors were obliged to do, but they were worryingly far from proactive engagement with the reform process. The less sanguine among the reformers—Wagner included—did not rule out the possibility of a conservative counterrevolution.

We can, once again, wonder at Wagner's audacity in speaking so freely of that very class that provided him with relatively prestigious employment. 'Germany and Her Princes' finds no ingenious exemption for the House of Wettin from Wagner's scornful view of the ruling families. Yet his text appears to have caused him no immediate significant difficulties in his official position. His direct superior, August Lüttichau, was certainly aware of the 'Kingship' piece, and he indulged Wagner's explanation of its constructive intent. It is therefore likely that Wagner's ongoing involvement in the debate about republican reform was known to the court. Wagner's piece is certainly hostile to the German princes, sternly advising them to adapt to the times, though it is not technically a work of sedition precisely because it is, in Wagner's characteristic way, outside politics and uncoupled from praxis. It neither calls for revolt nor suggests any practical proposal for the abolition of the aristocratic order. It glows with morality but contains nothing that indicates any understanding of how power can actually be challenged. Ultimately, there is a real distinction to be drawn between a theory of insurrection and a theory of revolution, with the former focused on the practicalities of change and not, in contrast with the latter, an imaginary endpoint. A sophisticated society is capable of recognizing the differences between these two kinds of theory, though in times of crisis and raised existential sensitivities they are quickly conflated by those with some position to protect. Up until the momentous Uprising itself, Wagner benefitted, we might suppose, from the more forgiving interpretation.

Wagner's thinking became even more speculative as the months passed. He began to recognize that the princes alone could not be the reason for the dimming prospects for change. Those who were to be emancipated had yet to sense that the possibilities of freedom could be possibilities for them. 'Man and Existing Society' (Der Mensch und die bestehende Gesellschaft), which appeared in February 1849, is the first of his works to address that issue.[39] This essay might be considered Wagner's first real philosophical work, even if it is thin and rhetorical. Disapprobation of the aristocratic classes and emotive depictions of the good, beleaguered people of Germany are there, as expected, but they are joined by the question of the mechanisms of social progress. Wagner, even if speculatively, wants to set out a grounded explanation of how change, indeed revolutionary transformation, can and must take place. He aims to establish that 'existing society' rests on false grounds. It is therefore not merely morally objectionable. There are two dimensions to Wagner's thought. First, the false grounds of society mean that current society is, in essence, wrong—wrong in itself—in that it is a disordered version of how it ought to be. Over the next few years, Wagner put considerable effort into elaborating on that particular idea. It brought him to the notion of 'natural culture' which underpinned societies that by good fortune had found their way to some proper arrangement of their parts. The challenge for us would be recapturing the essence of that order, though not in its original form, as we shall see in detail in chapter 4. The second element concerns what Wagner saw as the unsustainability of falsely grounded societies: they inevitably fail since they deny what are ultimately the irrepressible forces of life. (In chapter 5, we shall see the presence of that idea in the *Ring*.) Wagner wanted to understand how, though, society appeared to be capable over generations of controlling, without overt or at least constant coercion, its members' capacity to improve their circumstances. It somehow prevented them from perceiving its antagonism to their needs. There would have to be an educational dimension to social renewal, where individuals learned to see through the supposed virtue of the world they were expected to preserve and respect.

Wagner maintains that each person must acquire a revolutionary 'consciousness'.[40] Genuinely emancipatory changes happen only when there is human action purposely directed towards the transformation of society. The notion of an autonomous historical process that drives humanity towards progress is rejected by Wagner. He elaborated insightfully on this anti-idealist thesis in subsequent writings, as we shall see in the following chapter. The volatility of the times is palpable, Wagner believes, but it must be productively grasped, and that can occur only when it is understood. This, for Wagner, will require a philosophical appreciation of the conflict between what existing society demands and the 'end' or intrinsic destiny—the *Bestimmung*—of human beings.

Wagner, at this point, was beginning to think his way, for the first time, into a conception of the nature of human beings. He is brought to that thought through his prior though underdeveloped notion that emancipation cannot be completed until a society that is responsive to the deepest human needs is achieved. The overarching end of human beings, he claims, is happiness, an end that is inscribed in us and therefore inexpungible, no matter how disordered social arrangements might happen to be. Happiness is the contentment that is gained when human beings are permitted to realize, as he puts it, their 'mental [*geistig*], moral, and corporeal capacities'.[41] These ends contrast with the experiences of hopelessness, disappointment, and violation that Wagner believes are characteristic of contemporary life.

A significant step in his argument is the move from a thesis about what produces happiness to the claim that happiness is a right. As a right, it is, he holds, something that cannot be privately secured. He believes that society must not simply abandon every practice and institution that is inimical to human happiness; rather, it must work positively to provide the conditions which allow happiness to be realized. Although Wagner does not elaborate on how he thinks this might be done, it is clear enough, from his general commitments, that he has in mind nothing as prosaic (or ridiculous) as the idea of a government constantly attending to the happiness of all. Instead, he was beginning to sense that happiness can occur only in a society that responds to the ever-changing needs of its members. These needs are born of our spontaneous nature. A society that accommodates our affective and creative dimensions cannot be structured by positive law and will be in no sense a version of the *Rechtsstaat* or constitutional state, an ideal that had inspired many of the reformers of 1848.

There are, we might observe, numerous forceful arguments against the idea of a natural right, and Wagner was almost certainly unaware of the complications claims like his carry with them. His thesis rests on a kind of simple primitivism that does have some persuasive force once negatively stated: how can the right to happiness be countermanded? (The idea that a state should remain neutral or indifferent to the happiness of its members would have struck Wagner as bizarre and indefensible.) Hence any new properly human society will understand that making good on the right to happiness is the basis of its only justifiable existence. In proposing the notion of a right to happiness, Wagner sees himself as confronting the attitude of resignation which accepts the limitations and life-sapping norms of the present. This idea is offered with heightened oratory as Wagner works to rouse the reader to indignation at the social conditions they have all too readily settled for. He is attempting to motivate our sympathies. And that implies a belief on his part that our capacity to regain a more human reality—notwithstanding the overbearing influence of present society—has not been lost entirely.

Happiness, Wagner suggests, is found in enriched forms of living. It is apparent that the individual can in some sense survive in a socially atomized environment, or one where community barely exists at all. But without the wider conditions that communities alone can create, certain human perfections, Wagner maintains, lie dormant. The human being remains substantially less than it might be and therefore not properly happy in some genuine or authentic sense, as he sees it. From the point of view of Wagner's intellectual development, this cursorily articulated perfectionism is notable since it will reappear, as a central concern, in the books that immediately followed his Dresden years. The general nature of this idea was not, of course, new. A substantially more complex conception of social perfectionism, encompassing a wide range of human competences, was set out almost a century earlier by

Jean-Jacques Rousseau in his *Discourse on the Origin of Inequality*. Wagner, though, had his own way into this notion. First, he began to focus on commercial society, with the particular inequalities produced by its obscene divisions of labour, divisions that condemned the majority of human beings to limitations in what they could experience. And, second, he took a prospective and revolutionary view of a future which would be marked by the conditions for social perfection.

'Man and Existing Society' makes the interesting claim, though certainly with far too little explanation, that morality lies among the perfections.[42] Morality, here at least, is not characterized as a system of alien regulation designed to stunt the fullest possibilities of human experience, a critical view that would become virtually axiomatic in the trilogy. Rather, it underpins both social cooperation and communal cohesion. In its truest form, it has no tendency to bring about conformity. Wagner suggests that it evolves in sensitive response to the increasing sophistication and diversity of developing social configurations. It protects those configurations, ideally at least, without at the same time closing off their potential to take new forms. Morality in this context, then, is responsive rather than stipulative. It provides intelligibility to social interactions while at the same time developing according to the needs of human beings in their changing circumstances. Although Wagner does not state it explicitly, he is suggesting that morality, as a perfectionist accomplishment, is at one with freedom.

Given, then, the significance of society in furnishing the conditions for human realization, it is clear that something of, what we might call, an ontological kind has gone awry. The being of human beings is now distorted precisely because existing society has no interest in establishing the conditions which would enable them to reach their perfection (and attendant happiness). As Wagner puts it: 'To *chance* it leaves the education, the growth of our corporeal powers, while its strivings are directed only to narrowing our needs, hence to reducing our capacity to satisfy them.'[43] The revolutionary consciousness, mentioned above, consists in knowledge of this very fact. Knowing how our 'right' to the happiness that comes with the pursuit of perfection is blocked means, at that very moment, recognizing that radical change is necessary. Once society 'is *recognized* it is then also *judged*', Wagner proclaims.[44] Wagner, then, is no pessimist about the realizability of a transformed world. The difficulties of existing society are not so deep reaching, in his view, that change is foreclosed.

At around the same time as 'Man and Existing Society', Wagner's poem, whose title I shall keep in the original German, 'Die Noth', appeared. Among other things, it contains an explicit criticism of idealist philosophy, one that is treated elsewhere in this book. It is a wide-ranging and remarkably coarse work, with its rough and ironic treatment of the rich, devout, and purely intellectual (the philosophers) who love falsely because they are detached from 'need', or *Noth*. It is Wagner's first significant deployment of the concept of need (we saw it in passing in 'Germany and Her Princes'), a concept that would become prominent in his future theoretical writings. Wagner exploits the various layers of senses of the word *Noth*. It refers to the needs necessary to sustain life and the sensuous needs that form our affective life (also a natural need). In this sense, *Noth*, as need, could be relieved through fundamental social rearrangements, where, for instance, no one wanted for nourishment or occupation. But it also references our capacity for misery and distress in the very sense that we are beings who are vulnerable to suffering. In this context, *Noth* is a term for our enduring *needfulness* as human beings. We see human beings rightly when we recognize their essential vulnerability. Wagner therefore is not advocating the elimination of *Noth* as such. Rather, he is urging his readers to see how the various parts of society err by failing to appreciate both our basic needs—which society could meet, notionally at least—*and* our very humanity as needful beings. His efforts, here and in later works, are directed towards bringing about a recognition of that human property and the consequences of a society that fails its members by prioritizing institutions that are disconnected from *Noth* in its various senses.

Wagner's last political publication before the Dresden Uprising is 'The Revolution' (April 1849), a short piece astonishing for its personification of the minacious spirit of the times. The influence of Mikhail Bakunin is manifest. Wagner had become acquainted with Bakunin during the weeks leading up to the Uprising, with a close personal bond soon forming between them. Bakunin was in Saxony where he sensed there might be opportunity for precisely the kind of political excitement that he like other 'ruthless men of action', as Wagner put it, favoured.[45] It is evident enough that his ideas and knowledge of radical theory and some of his temperament made their way into Wagner's thoughts. The startling extremism of 'The Revolution' gives voice to a kind of wrathful anarchy not present in the articles that preceded it. In his autobiography, Wagner observes that the 'annihilation of all civilization was the objective on which he [Bakunin] had set his heart'.[46] He illustrates this tendency with a vignette in which Bakunin, who had ordered some of the city's trees to be felled for use in barricades, shows his delight at the pain that caused the respectable townsfolk.[47] 'The Revolution' has a vehemence Bakunin must have welcomed. It is not, though, a manifesto for physical wreckage or bloodshed. Over a year had passed since revolutionary fears had hastened the princes into acquiescence with reformist demands. Wagner's text glowers at existing authorities and promises pitiless retribution at a time when it was plainly evident that the impetus towards change had not only stalled but was perilously close to slipping into reverse. The Frankfurt parliamentarians had moved things along to the best of their abilities, and impressively so, given the diversity of views that had to be mediated. The old powers had, though, quietly rallied, and in April a number of the represented states ordered the withdrawal of their elected members from the national assembly. No longer quorate, it was effectively dead as a political institution. Various states reverted to the comforts of the *Vormärz* arrangements and rejected key proposals for constitutional reform. Reformist ministers were simultaneously removed from governments across the country.

'The Revolution' invokes 'the sublime goddess *Revolution*', whose ferocity conjures up the archangel on the day of judgment.[48] Revolution, for Wagner, is something like a secular end of days, with the goddess set to erase every earthly endeavour connected with those distended institutions of state that exist only for the well-being of princes, courtiers, financiers, and state bureaucrats. As Wagner presents it, the revolution is transcendent in quality. It perdures even if each of its agents is silenced by the state. The authorities may flood the streets with their police and soldiers—Wagner presciently observes, just weeks before something close to that would transpire in Dresden—but a new phase of history is now in place that is irreducible to the physical forces of those who welcome it and is therefore inexpungible by whatever means. Some years earlier, Bakunin had written of 'the passion for destruction' as a 'creative passion too'.[49] Wagner likewise attempts to persuade his audience that revolutionary destruction—of institutions—is also an act of supreme renewal since it leaves the world open to possibilities where life can flourish and the ossified institutions of the present—'death'[50]—are overcome.

Wagner's vision is one of incendiary anger. As Newman has argued, there can be little doubt that the authorities who wished to identify the ringleaders of the May Uprising would have found much to trouble them in a text proclaiming the overthrow of the very institutions they were charged with protecting.[51] That it was written by a prominent citizen who took to the streets of Dresden in highly visible opposition to them surely added to its seditious qualities. The essay in some ways, though, floats over the political exigencies of the time. It is, in common with Wagner's typical approach, unburdened with arguments for constitutions or legal reform. It is a philosophically minded notion of revolution which gives no thought to the challenges of how its ideals might be practically realized. Some of Wagner's usual themes make fleeting appearances. There is the familiar complaint about private property. Furthermore, he also points to the dark capacity of industry to purloin human beings' joy in 'production' and to turn it against them by making the human being 'the slave of his own work'.[52] After the revolution, work should, he declares, lose its toilsome qualities and become a freedom and pleasure.

Wagner's thoughts on work in 'The Revolution' as well as in some later writings bear tantalizing resemblances to Marx's idea of alienated labour. That idea could hardly have been widely known given that it was developed by Marx in a set of texts he was never to publish. The longstanding question about how much Wagner knew of Marx's ideas remains unanswered since there is no documentary evidence in support of claims of influence.[53] It is not unreasonable to think that Wagner might perhaps have heard of Marx's ideas through intermediaries, with Bakunin, Röckel, and the poet Georg Herwegh significant among them.

There is something strange about the very existence of the 1849 pieces, not least 'The Revolution'. They might seem to come too late in the cycle: the chances of reform were fading at speed and no amount of polemics could do anything to change that, as Wagner surely knew. But we might also suggest that no matter what was to happen, Wagner would not allow the princes to escape his judgment. There is the last satisfaction of directing fearsome threats in their direction.

The Revolutionary Activist

As noted above, Friedrich August's decision to bring the Prussians into Saxony, in order to quell any unrest that followed from his ultimate abrogation of reform, led to the Uprising in Dresden. It began on 3 May, accelerated into a chaotic and ferocious urban battle, before being put down just several days later. Those confronting the forces of the crown acted under the auspices of a provisional government which sought to take control of the city. The question of Wagner's level of involvement in the Uprising and his place within the hierarchy of its leadership has animated his competing biographers. It was once a debate which at its extremes was largely between those who take Wagner at his word that his part in it was negligible and those who regard him as falsifying an unusually colourful record for merely opportunistic purposes. The so-called old Wagnerians—his original acolytes, the most effective of whom were Carl Friedrich Glasenapp and Wagner's English translator and editor, William Ashton Ellis—were so committed to the 'Meister' that they devoted themselves all too often to layering rather speculative defences on top of whatever stories Wagner wished to tell.[54] There is some agreement that discrepancies exist between what is known about Wagner's actions during those tumultuous days and his own professions of merely marginal participation when he came to write his autobiography. That book, *My Life,* is divided into four parts, with volume 2 containing the revolutionary period first printed in 1872. The suspicious assessment is that Wagner, by then a solid member of respectable society, enjoying a life lavishly funded by the Bavarian king, was uncomfortable with a past when royalty was considerably less dear to him. As we shall see, though, Wagner's deflated version of events appeared within just weeks of the Uprising, that is, at a time in which he could not have had the slightest anticipation of the patronage he would eventually receive. And within days of his flight he had written to a friend vehemently stating that he had taken no active part 'in the proceedings, either with weapons or with public oratory' and furthermore that he had no 'official' connection with the provisional government.[55] Perhaps he wrote in fear, with the weight of his actions now dawning upon him. But Wagner was not, we might suggest, habitually inclined to sanitize his actions. In his autobiography, for instance, he freely confesses to an act of drunken vandalism which he had committed in 1830 as an expression of solidarity with the revolution in France occurring at that time.[56] The possibility that trauma interfered with his ability to capture his recent experiences with accuracy cannot be excluded. It may be notable, to the benefit of those sceptical of Wagner's side of the story, that none of the fierier 1848–1849 papers devoted to political reform are included in the collected works Wagner himself edited over twenty years later. Ashton Ellis, however, regards it as 'foolish' to conclude anything from their absence.[57] Perhaps pieces, such as 'How Do Republican Aspirations Relate to Kingship?', obscurely published (Röckel's newsletter) were difficult to gather. The preface to the collected works (1871) does though emphasize Wagner's desire to bring together all his 'writings of every kind'.[58] Wagner's conservative and patriotic political texts from the 1860s onwards did after all find a place within the ten volumes. The composition of the collected works is therefore open to question on this complicated matter. By way of final observation, it should be said that by that point Wagner surely had no need to worry about his past. His position was more than secure, and the Germany he had once railed against no longer existed, at least at the constitutional level, following unity in 1871.

In *My Life*, Wagner readily identifies a problem with 'the forces of reaction' who, in the 1848–1849 period, had deserved his political opposition.[59] And, in 1851, he noted that he could 'fully recognize the necessity of the impending revolution of 1848'.[60] But he consistently presents his actions around the Uprising with the quality of passivity, undermining the very idea that he could ever have taken initiative as an activist. He was, he submits to the reader, 'inclined to let the tide of events' carry him 'wherever it might'.[61] This dilution of agency creates the peculiar sense of a man somehow present yet not really there where the Uprising was. He maintains that none of the actions he undertook in and around the Uprising had belligerent or revolutionary intent. For instance, he claims to have simply found himself on the street when the sudden ringing of church bells signalled the start of the insurrection. Glasenapp takes his cue by declaring Wagner 'a benevolent looker-on'.[62] Wagner's professed 'strangely impassioned interest as an observer'[63] never supposedly led him to much beyond spectatorship. An image is developed of a likeable though peripheral figure who could stroll through the chaos, occasionally meeting and conversing with key members of the Uprising, including the architect Gottfried Semper, whose professional aptitude was turned to the construction of barricades. Wagner appeared, even in his own words, free to come and go to the town hall where the leadership of the Uprising had based itself, stopping to enjoy long analyses of the unfolding events. Those liberties were surely not available to every citizen of Dresden. Perhaps, though, he was regarded as a harmless but trustworthy figure. It seems more natural to assume that he in some way belonged within the wider circle of the Uprising's key players. A piece of evidence uncovered by the Saxon police seems to support that interpretation. Just days before the Uprising, Wagner reported, in a letter to Röckel, the fear, which he seemed to share, that 'revolution may come *too soon*'.[64] Wagner is implying knowledge of what was planned as the most effective time for revolution.

A number of notably aggressive initiatives in support of the Uprising have been attributed to Wagner. Some of them are not mentioned in his autobiography, while the others are deflated and recast as the products of temperate civic mindedness. The following are the charges that Wagner himself addresses either against explicit accusation or with the accusation lurking in the background. Wagner was said to have acquired guns for the clear purpose of insurrection. He himself, however, tells us that he undertook a mission to a friend's house to advise them that their weapons should be secured lest they fall into the hands of what he called the 'mob'. He offered to take them into safe-keeping through arrangement with the Vaterlandsverein. This was, he explains, an 'eccentric whim' on his part that could only be construed 'in a most dubious way as a crime'.[65] A further contested episode is Wagner's decision to have posters printed, containing the words 'are you for us or against us?' which were directed at the Saxon police and soldiers.[66] His purpose was to discourage them from support for the Prussian foreigners who had been summoned by the king to assist in the suppression of protest. These posters were, he claims, placed at positions likely to be attacked by local forces. However, it was apparent to him that they were either unseen or ignored. In short, his brotherly effort was of no consequence. A different version of events sees Wagner solve the problem of the useless positioning of the posters. He is supposed to have walked calmly towards the forces of the state and distributed them by hand.[67] There was more to that than considerable coolness in the face of armed officers. Wagner would have known well that any attempt to induce an agent of the civic authorities to defy the order of the state would be considered among the more serious crimes. We can infer that easily enough from *My Life*. Just a few pages prior to discussing his semidetached involvement in the Uprising, he notes that his friend Röckel's 'appeal to the soldiers of the Saxon army' to resist reactionary forces who threatened the progress of reform—an endeavour that appears remarkably close to Wagner's own—led to the charge of 'high treason' for what Wagner himself recognized as so 'flagrant a misdeed'.[68]

A division of opinion is found around Wagner's decision to climb to the top of the Kreuzkirche's tower, a prominent building in the centre of Dresden. He states that he wanted to 'get the best possible overall view of the whole situation'.[69] This deed too he attributes to curiosity with his presence in the tower ambiguously disconnected from activist participation. He does not clarify his purposes there, referring to his position as, in a strangely neutral phrase, an 'observation shelter' (*Observations-Asyl*).[70] Biographers demur, with Martin Gregor-Dellin, among others, concluding that Wagner was in the tower in order 'to observe troop movements and report on them'[71] to the provisional government, that is, the executive established by the leading insurrectionists.

Those incidents are as far as Wagner's apologetic references to his involvement in the Uprising go. Others of an even more dramatic order have also been alleged, though their veracity is more doubtful than not. Glasenapp was not without success in his efforts to cloud questions of Wagner's guilt. He submits the plausible claim that the Saxon authorities who investigated the main actors were specialists in entertaining false and flimsy testimony. Hence any misdeed documented in the official files of the 'Saxon court of justice', which were typically stuffed with 'unverified statements', is factually compromised in principle. He speaks of 'trumpery' in the court's rough treatment of Wagner's friend, the singer Wilhelmine Schröder-Devrient, who had been heard to utter a 'cry for vengeance' against the authorities.[72] An entity so inclined to enthusiastic prosecution would have had no difficulty in exaggerating Wagner's innocuous presence at events into crimes of 'high treason'.[73] Famous among the lurid though now discredited allegations is that Wagner was centrally involved in the burning down of the old Dresden opera house. He was aware of that rumour, one which had sprung up almost as soon as the building was destroyed. It was subsequently listed among the charges against him, though Wagner himself in a letter to Franz Liszt appeared unworried by the attribution.[74] More diverse opinions surround the truth of the claim that Wagner, together with Röckel, had, sometime in early 1849, commissioned the manufacture of hundreds of hand-grenades for use by revolutionaries in Prague.[75] It would be an extraordinary piece of evidence in support of the portrait of Wagner's increasing aggression towards all authorities in 'existing society'. Ultimately, though, confidence in declarations by Wagner and his diverse biographers on the question of his guilt or innocence of involvement in some of the incidents discussed here is not easily won.

Once the Uprising had been subdued, the authorities issued arrest warrants for those who they determined had involved themselves in varying levels of sedition. Wagner was among the many listed as 'politically dangerous individuals'.[76] He enjoyed some good fortune in making his escape from Saxony, inadvertently avoiding the police who were sweeping up his associates, Bakunin and Röckel among them. He soon began his exile in Zurich, where his interest in revolution was transformed into a more speculative philosophical project, as we shall begin to see in the following chapter.

Why Did Wagner Turn to Activism?

Any effort to understand the motivations behind Wagner's involvement in the Uprising is faced with the curiosity of, what we might call, the two Wagners who are visible from this time. One is the moderate liberal for whom, as he put it in 1850, '*[r]eform and constitution*' were watchwords[77] (those very terms are, though, rarely present in his writings from those times). This captures the Wagner of the first part of 1848. He shared the widespread expectation that the old arrangements were about to give way. And then there is the firebrand who at the very least sought proximity to the physical conflict of the Uprising. That version took root in the autumn of 1848 and ended only with the suppression of the May Uprising. In choosing that path, he and his fellow-travellers were agents in the production of a new phase of events that departed in character and ambition from the reformist movement. Wagner was, though, as I have tried to show, responding to the succession of rapid political developments and the specific challenges that each of them posed. And despite his retrospective emphasis on his interest in constitutionalism, the Wagner leading up to the Uprising was, as we have seen, anything but conventionally political. He was not wrong to confess just weeks after the Uprising, '[m]y heart is greater than my sense [*Verstand*]'.[78] His later definition of real politics provides us with a helpful contrast to where he stood during his radical phase. In 1862, he wrote to Röckel, who had just been released from prison, having served a commuted death sentence for his role in the Dresden events, and shared the view that 'to be political means always to have nothing else in view but what is possible in the immediate future, for only then can you hope for results; and political activity, without results, is sheer nonsense', adding that '[i]deas belong to the domain of philosophy'.[79] But Wagner had been, as Bakunin described him, a 'dreamer',[80] who harboured improbable hopes for revolutionary outcomes, principally the eventual abolition of everything that hinders human happiness.

As we have seen from his writings of this period, Wagner had no toleration for the political structures that were stubbornly perpetuated by the German princes. Their very existence underpinned vast disparities and inverted the worth of human endeavours. Wagner, however, was not always precise in his identification of the causes of social suffering. Certainly, the princes possessed the power to make decisive improvements, yet the conditions of industry, which had not been caused by the princes, feature significantly in Wagner's images of a sick society. He was possessed by the inchoate idea that revolution would effectively undermine every cause of poverty and powerlessness in a single stroke. Whether that would immediately produce the best form of society is not something Wagner discussed. Of course, all of that appears to float above the issues on the ground. It seems that he was not particularly excited by the changes introduced in March 1848 nor by the further reforms that were to follow from the initial concessions by the old powers. He appreciated them as no more than beneficial to the democratic quality of German life, but he wanted something that was ultimately altogether more than politics could deliver. At the same time, the reformers opened up an opportunity—the only available one—for tangible improvement, targeting the hubristic authority of the princes and the states that seemed to exist simply to support their special status. As a member of the broad movement for change, Wagner, together with many of the more practical figures who belonged to it, felt compelled to respond to the outrageous duplicity of the Saxon king in the spring of 1849. The Uprising was a desperate counterreaction that few of its participants had sought. Wagner, it appears, was overtaken by the energy of the Uprising. He was carried by its momentum and adjusted to it in order to remain with it, but it took him to a disconcerting space. Once the shooting had stopped and he had taken refuge outside Saxony, he began to define himself as the type of revolutionary who has no desire to contribute to the kind of violence and destructiveness he had witnessed and perhaps been part of in Dresden. A more equable Wagner quickly reemerged. Just days after his flight from Dresden, he put the following thoughts in a letter to his wife, Minna:

> The Dresden revolution & all its consequences have now taught me that I am by no means made out to be a real

> revolutionary: I realized from the unhappy outcome of the rising that a true victorious, revolutionary must act in total disregard for others,—he must not think of his wife & child, nor of his hearth & home,—his single aim is:—annihilation. . . . But it is not people like us who are destined to carry out this fearful task: we are only revolutionaries in order to be able to *build* on new ground: what attracts us is not to *destroy* things but to *refashion* them, & that is why we are not the people that fate needs—these people will arise from within the lowest ranks of society;—we and others like us can have nothing in common with them. Look! *I herewith sever my links with the Revolution.*[81]

What Wagner is expressing here, in the immediacy of what he called the 'catastrophe in Dresden',[82] is that he did not quite understand what had attracted him to the Uprising. He assured Liszt, in a letter of June 1849, that it had nothing to do with the 'ridiculously fanatical notion' that every prince is worthy of 'active hatred'.[83] As we have seen, though, a dispassionate assessment of feudal power is far from obvious in the papers Wagner published in the *Volksblätter*. And while he was, as he further confided to a friend within days of that message to Liszt, 'in total sympathy' with the revolution 'right from the outset',[84] he concluded that the true revolutionary is driven by '*hatred*', rather than, as he put it, 'the *love* which guides us'.[85] That 'man of terrible energy',[86] Bakunin, whose magnetism had once captivated Wagner, now became, in Wagner's thoughts, emblematic of that hatred.

Wagner's distress at the violence of the Uprising speaks humbly of a self-confessed lack of revolutionary steel. An interesting retrospection is found in *A Communication to My Friends* (1851), where Wagner articulates, through his growing philosophical framework, what drew him to the revolution. Politics—though not abiding anger at poverty—recedes into near invisibility, and an aesthetic interest steps into its place. He wished, he claimed, only to create something that was sympathetic to what is authentically, naturally human. This is beauty in differing forms. Aesthetic action, he claims, was his mode of service to that cause:

> I had never really concerned myself with politics. I remember now that I paid attention to the phenomena of the political world only to the extent that the spirit of the revolution manifested itself in them, namely, when pure human nature rebelled against political-legal formalism. . . . I could only ever take the side of the suffering party, and indeed with the same level of ardency as that with which it resisted any kind of pressure. . . . My participation in the world of political phenomena had always therefore been of an artistic nature insofar as I looked beneath its formal expression to its purely human content. . . . [H]ere I then saw exactly the same urgent motive which drove me as an artistic man out of the bad sensuous form of the present to gain a new sensuous form corresponding to the true human being—a form which is to be gained only through the destruction of the sensuous form of the present, that is, through revolution.[87]

This, however, is a relatively unreliable retrospection in that it neatens up Wagner's driving impulses and ignores the wider range of motives that had been expressly present in his thinking in the period leading up to and during the Uprising. And if we take at face value his emphatically formulated claim that his main preoccupation was nothing less than 'the destruction of the sensuous form of the present', we are left to wonder how an objective so divorced from political action—'I had never really concerned myself with politics'—could motivate involvement with a more conventionally shaped revolutionary faction. However, what Wagner is telling us here does capture something of his fundamental disposition: a moralist whose hopes for a better society soared above ordinary politics. That society would not be realized through technical improvements, new and robust institutions, or even 'reform and constitution', the supposed 'watchwords' of 1848. It required, instead, the most humanly sympathetic of arrangements in which each part—that is, each individual—would feel perfectly at home and free yet form a cohesive and living complex collectively with others. This conception of social transformation draws on the practice of aesthetic production. Although Wagner may not have had exactly that in mind at the time of his political activism, it soon became a core theme of his post-Dresden writing: the revolution as creation and vice-versa.

2

The Revolution as Future

WE HAVE seen the unease with which Wagner viewed the Dresden destruction to which he had, in one way or another, given his services. Correspondence in its immediate aftermath shows us a chastened Wagner who now deemed himself quite unsuited to revolutionary political activism. This realization would also lead him away from crafting vituperative tracts against the 'princes' whom he had once implicated in many of the failings of existing society. However, a general desire for radical social transformation remained intact during his initial years of exile. That prompted him, for the first time in earnest, to immerse himself in the construction of a wide-ranging philosophical position. He hoped to find a new space within which to advance theories of a strangely apolitical kind on the necessity of revolution. The polemical writings that preceded the Uprising bore, as we have seen, little connection with practical politics. But after Dresden that gap widened yet further, even as Wagner's anger at the suffering caused by social arrangements remained intact. There may be something indicative in the fact that not a single item of his writings from this period—*Art and Revolution, The Artwork of the Future, Opera and Drama*—earned him the reputation as a dangerous subversive among the state authorities where he resided. Again, the distinction between theories of insurrection and of revolution should be kept in mind. As his thinking developed, revolution referred not to process but, exclusively, to outcome: the revolution is the future itself, not the fight for it.

Wagner was dedicated, over the span of the trilogy, to advocacy for the highest form of freedom, one which would allow each and every individual to realize and enjoy the human perfections. He increasingly understood these perfections as broadly aesthetic in character. (Little weight was given to what we might categorize as the intellectual perfections, for example, scientific investigation or philosophical reflection.) In a letter to Liszt of June 1849 (just weeks after Dresden), Wagner declares that 'art will not grow in the soil of the counterrevolution; initially, it may not even grow in the soil of the revolution, unless we take steps in good time to see that it does'.[1] Those 'steps' would turn out to be interventions in the argument about the kind of society a revolution worthy of the name should generate. Art, in a noticeably general sense, was foregrounded. In elaborating on those interventions over the following years Wagner lived up to the undertaking, which he had shared with Liszt in that same letter, to 'leave politics out' of his theoretical endeavours. The word 'art' is used with deliberate equivocality. He allowed establishment confidants like Liszt to presume it was meant in the paradigmatic and more innocent sense while Wagner himself also included in its meaning an ideal form of human activity that could be established only in a wholly new type of community.

The importance to Wagner of this new application of his energies should not be underestimated. It is seldom appreciated that this philosophical mission had at that time priority in his mind over a return to compositional work. This is extraordinary when we consider that in 1848 he had drafted in prose his idea for what would eventually take form as the *Ring* cycle. That, however, was set aside as matters in Dresden became more pressing. But while by the summer of 1849 the Uprising was now behind him, a commitment to the values of freedom, equality, and confraternity that had drawn him into it certainly was not. Once in exile, his choice of project was to design a new way of thinking about social emancipation rather than return immediately to the Nibelung idea. The trilogy contains an almost overwhelming range of topics, some of which are, at best, of marginal relevance to the question of revolution and others, particularly those on strictly musical issues, not at all. What unites them, in principle at least, is not that they happen to fall from the same pen. Wagner, rather, and in a pretty undisciplined way at that, believed he was indicating connections between each idea or thing he considered. He is given to the holistic view that all social phenomena are somehow related to one another in so far as they are marked by the historical environment within which they have appeared. He has partial success in making good on that idea.

We can, though, emphasize two main themes around which a great amount of Wagner's thinking on revolution, at least, coheres. (There are further uniting themes, and they will be considered in subsequent chapters.) The first is his antihistorical idea of revolution, and the second is his more famous theory of the connection between art and revolution. The latter involves complex considerations of the aestheticization of social life and the attendant superior form of artwork—the Gesamtkunstwerk—that such a transformed world could produce as the expressive act of its special unity. This chapter will now look at Wagner's theory of the conditions of revolutionary transformation. That will be followed by an examination of his views of how a society of the future will operate and be experienced. Since this chapter deals with material relating to both society and artworks as collective endeavours, it will be an appropriate place to consider Wagner's essay on the very idea of Jewish composers as contributors to music. And because the latter reveals that he placed limits on who might be included within an aesthetic community, its possible implications for Wagner's political universalism will need to be assessed.

Wagner's Conception of Revolution

Wagner, as we shall see in later sections of this chapter, turned towards an aesthetic model of experience as the desired endpoint of revolution, a theme at which he had barely hinted prior to exile.

But he was also interested in developing a theory of revolution per se, that is, in particular, of identifying its success conditions and its place—or otherwise—within the flow of history. This was effectively a speculative interest since he had no inclination, even at a theoretical remove, to return either in thought or deed to the field of concrete revolutionary activism. He nevertheless believed that his thoughts would illuminate the crisis of the contemporary human situation, as he understood it. In the course of this labour of reflection, distinctive and challenging philosophical contentions emerge.

Wagner's theory of revolution rests on materialist and strikingly antiprogressionist precepts. Revolution must, he contends, be understood as a process that is referenced only to the human beings who bring it about, and it cannot therefore be connected with any overarching historical process somehow standing above the wills of human actors. We find in Wagner's text, notwithstanding the surface confidence of tone, a hesitant theoretician too often inclined to express his claims at the level of proposals while leaving the tensions between them unaddressed. His materialism is itself presented ambiguously in that it encompasses both human action and the processes of nature (as opposed to spirit). Nonetheless, his quite innovative thoughts on the very idea of revolution motivate a number of radical propositions that have implications for much of what had been taken as settled in the philosophical thinking of his times.

In politics, conventionally, the word 'revolution' has tended to invoke images of the sudden ending of a particular set of entrenched arrangements and the appearance of new ideas that are supposedly free of the norms and practices of the system they have replaced. This conception of necessary change has, self-evidently, been exercised across recent centuries with varying degrees of rigour. It can take moderate forms, a paradigmatic case of which is the arrival, however briefly, of constitutional innovation Wagner himself had just witnessed. What the reformists sought was in some ways revolutionary—the old powers, as we have seen, certainly thought so—but it would have allowed much of what was in place to continue, albeit improved by a new legal and modern democratic order. It was a matter of reforming and augmenting institutions rather than of abolishing them. This contrasts with that extreme version of revolution (for example, that pursued by Bakunin) which adopts a methodical posture of suspicion of all existing institutions for their complicity in the arrangements that prompt the need for change.

Revolution may be defended by its proponents as an essential contribution to human progress. The idea of 'progress' comes, we might suggest, with narrower and wider senses. The narrower sense captures manifest improvement in some important aspect of social life. The wider sense connects progress with a historical process of which it is part. One version of the wider sense is found in a particular form of the writing of history, where events are lined up in an orderly way and not uncommonly structured like a novel of development where there is a narrative of inevitable growth within the main subject. But there is a more speculative sense—labelled 'universal history' by the German idealists—which grants the historical process an interest that seems to transcend the actions and decisions taken by human beings on, so to speak, the ground level. It has an end towards which it advances across time and which becomes apparent only when that end is reached. In this context, effective revolution is part of the historical process. It happens because it is required to do so by the reconditely inscribed ends of history.

Wagner's quite opposing ideas about revolution contain objections to the two senses of history implied here (narratives of progress and 'universal history'). They both, in his view, misunderstand what moves human beings to bring about social transformation, and because they decide in advance what progress amounts to, their narratives and theories have the effect of suffocating the open possibilities of the future. Based on some version of the story of humanity so far, they assume that the next steps will emerge from out of that story and must therefore be continuous with it. It is in rejecting that approach that Wagner understands himself to be an antihistorical thinker: 'history' is implicated in undermining what he sees as the prospects of a truly human revolution. History is either an authorly construction or a philosophical cage which is disconnected from life. Both worries are captured in Wagner's retrospective reflection on the failed basis of the revolution in Germany: 'a real revolution can never come about from above, from the standpoint of learned intelligence, but only from below, from the urge of purely human need', a zone of life that owes nothing to history in any sense, that is, to needs or values that have been produced by previous historical arrangements or by speculative planning.[2] (The exemplary Greeks, as we shall see, enjoyed a form of community that directly grew out of human need, rather than a conception of society.) Revolutionary 'power', he writes in 'The Artistry of the Future' (Das Künstlertum der Zukunft)—an unpublished text of 1849—is not generated by consciousness, that is, by sheer ideas, but by the forces of natural instinct and our response to the underlying material reality of our affectivity and needfulness.[3] He specifically rejects the idealist notion—expressed most influentially by G.W.F. Hegel—of a 'guiding world spirit' and thereby that history is driven by 'higher, inscrutable influences that predetermine' its 'course'.[4] He claims, in opposition, that 'the vital shaping of the future can, indisputably, only be the work of life itself'.[5]

The practice of history is guilty of the same authoritarianism as the philosophical construction of the historical process, Wagner maintains. It provides narratives of justification for 'bourgeois society' by means of 'retroactive expressions' of liberating purposes and intentions that are supposedly scattered across the past.[6] The narrative stance serves to inject the past with a structure—of conforming with some design that comes 'from above'—but which is prejudiced, throughout, by its effort to defend, as a beneficial outcome, the arrangements of the present.[7] What this complex of thoughts reveals to us, then, is that Wagner rejects the idea of revolution as progress along an inferable historical direction. It must instead be a rupture with the present. Proper historical life—life as unpredictable change—will begin 'when the previous so-called historical consistency comes to an end, which in truth and at core is founded on fable, tradition, myth, and religion, on origins and institutions, on justifications and assumptions which', he charges, are themselves based on arbitrary 'mythical, fantastical inventions'. Among the latter, he notes, are 'monarchy and hereditary property'.[8]

The decoupling of the idea of revolution from history has some significant consequences. Wagner is not at all interested in promoting his vision of a better world in the language of progress. He obviously hopes for a happier future, but he also appeals to goods that have already been naturally actualized by humanity, though lost to modern civilization. The radicality of Wagner's scepticism about the very idea of political progress has somehow gone unnoticed. The historical process, as he understands it, has been one of an ever-increasing repression of human capacities. Indeed, he maintains that that process has acted in the service of 'misanthropic' ends in that it has deformed human beings by according them alien purposes.[9] The historical process has advanced through the production of 'factitious' needs.[10] He claims, as he puts it, that 'the millennia-long revolution of humanity has proven itself almost solely in the spirit of reaction: it has dragged the beautiful, free man down to itself, to slavery'.[11] The influence of Christianity and modern industry are central to this debasement. Together they produce a culture in which human beings cannot perceive the constraints that are placed on their potential for the fullest forms of living.

We should note that in Wagner's writings, from this time, the word 'culture' generally signifies an artificial social environment which is insensitive to the true nature of human beings.[12] On distinctive grounds, Friedrich Nietzsche would later draw a similarly sweeping conclusion: 'These "instruments of culture" are a disgrace to man, more a grounds for suspicion of, or an argument against, "culture" in general!'[13] It is of course surprising that Wagner does not seem to think that culture or civilization have in any way improved human nature, given his considerable appreciation of the artworks of his predecessors. The consistency of his worry about the corruption of the human community over the course of modern history leads him to a judgment that is marked more by rigour than by subtlety. He does not believe that past and present should be carried forward into the future. They are deviations from the conditions of genuine human happiness and hence the importance of a complete revolutionary break with them.

As briefly noted above, rejection of history as a frame for human action also entails abandoning what Wagner sees as mechanisms of constraint on the future. The imposition of historical structure implies the projection of certain norms onto what must be done in order to bring about some preferred arrangement of the human community. Wagner warns against specifying the future because of the ways in which, as he puts it, our imaginations about human possibility can be crippled by 'arbitrary assumptions . . . taken from the present state'.[14] The historical mind tends to bind us manipulatively to what has gone before. In this way, the 'downfall of the state' is forever forestalled by the strategic use of history by its apologists.[15] The state 'imposes' on us, Wagner alleges, 'the experiences of history as a guiding rule for our actions', and history, in this way, becomes a potently conservative device.[16] It is, he charges, 'doctrinal calculation' in which some preferred pattern is to govern the unfolding of social development. His contrary position is, as he expresses it, that '[n]othing is made in history, but everything makes itself according to its inner necessity'.[17] In other words, there is no independent phenomenon of 'history' which of itself determines the course of the future. The historian of the state is involved, in effect, in suppressing what, Wagner believes, lies within the realm of necessity.

This idea of 'inner necessity', which Wagner proposes as an alternative to any supposedly autonomous mover of history, is not itself without complication. He thinks of the inner necessity of human nature as exercising an inevitable influence on the course of human affairs, but yet it is an influence that is not consciously channelled or endorsed by those who are its beneficiaries. He sometimes states this view in ways that resemble at a very general level a dialectical development in which the inner necessity of human nature, set in a social context, is to take human beings without their awareness of it to a point which 'is just the opposite of the present one'.[18] This deviates from his earlier thought that those who have been denied a properly human community must develop a revolutionary consciousness. What will be achieved through nature's ultimate assertion of its dominion, he claims, is the annulment of all those cultural excrescences that have repressed humanity up to the present, allowing it, indeed, to become 'someday so humanly beautiful and nobly developed'.[19] Human nature, as the driver of revolution has, then, an end inscribed within it which it cannot ultimately be prevented from realizing. What is absent from this account of revolution is a connection with human actors, and this may lead to echoes of the philosophical theories of progress that Wagner wants to reject.

That lacuna which is visible in *Art and Revolution* is, however, to some degree addressed in *The Artwork of the Future*, where Wagner introduces the notion of 'the people' (*das Volk*) who are put forward as the agents of revolution. This notion does not refer to everyone who happens to be in some given society. The group has not yet constituted itself: it does not exist as a cohesive phenomenon. At the present time, those whom Wagner derides as the elite see the people as merely 'the rabble'[20] and therefore inherently unsuited to a socially transformed reality. The 'people' will consist, he maintains, of those who 'feel a common need [*Noth*]'.[21] Once again, we are presented with the complexity of what Wagner intends by '*Noth*'. Its most obvious sense denotes the usual rudimentary existential wants, a concept also captured by the German word, which Wagner himself frequently uses, *Bedürfnis*. The latter is not itself without ambiguity, signifying both basic and nonnecessary needs.[22] This ambiguity arises simply because *Bedürfnis* is the name given, though unfortunately not invariably, to any need that is not at the level of *Noth*.

Noth, as discussed in the previous chapter, can refer to our sense of human vulnerability, of our needfulness and fragility, of our capacity for misery and distress, and our consequent mutual dependence. Those, therefore, who understand 'need' in that sense are oriented towards the development of a collective purpose which is responsive and protectively attuned to those very dimensions of human beings. If the people are to be a revolutionary phenomenon, it is because they will be, as Wagner describes it, 'the redemption from . . . egoistic enchantment'.[23] Egoism is the socially produced condition that prevents us from experiencing the human situation in terms of *Noth*.[24] Wagner goes on to say that the people 'will accomplish redemption by fulfilling itself and at the same time redeeming its own enemies'.[25] He expects that the people will 'tear apart'[26] existing nonnecessary—and thereby needs insensitive—societal arrangements. Wagner in this way avoids replicating the structure of 'universal history' by identifying the development of a natural and affective human capacity as the force that will produce a liberated society. That capacity is recognized and advanced by the people in their growing sense of unity and mutual concern.

The very idea of the 'people' as described in *The Artwork of the Future* is not, then, an exclusionary category.[27] It does not specify any ethnic, national, or gender-related qualities as essential for membership. Membership, indeed, is and must be voluntary, while those whose social actions are geared towards their own ends effectively exclude themselves. In Wagner's view of things, those who are 'egoistically' given to the accumulation of 'abundance' stand outside the people.[28] It is not the simple idea that their wealth represents an objectionably unequal division of goods produced by society as a whole. Rather, in the conduct of their lives, they are motivated by what Wagner calls 'a need [*Bedürfnis*] without the power of needfulness [*Noth*]'.[29]

Wagner is at pains to deny that he is proffering merely utopian fantasies. In fact, he sees himself as turning the table on his opponents with the argument that normative systems which rest on 'spiritual, supra-spiritual'[30] concepts rather than on the proper understanding of human nature—his theory—have repeatedly demonstrated their unrealizability over centuries of attempted enforcement. It is those systems that are irredeemably utopian since they require human beings to become what they cannot be, namely, beings who can finally renounce their sensuous existence and suborn themselves to a higher spirit, that is, to a model of humanity that is foreign to what they essentially are. Wagner's antihistorical notion of revolution is contrastively grounded, he believes, in nothing but what lies in human nature as it is and not in what we might prefer it to be.

What his theoretical efforts show us is that Wagner's desire for a wholly new society in no way receded after Dresden. At the same time, the content of his ideas was free of the type of provocative claim that could lead to a repeat of his troubles in Saxony. There is limited critique of the role of existing political power in perpetuating poverty. Politics in any usual sense really does disappear from his thinking. There are two main reasons for that change. First, his perspective is emphatically oriented towards the future and not the processes required to dismantle the present. And, second, politics, understood as the competition of entrenched factions for power and influence, is necessarily redundant within a proper human community. He claims that the 'driving force' of a radically transformed community is exercised through the people as 'an unconscious, involuntary one'.[31] By 'involuntary'—a concept that will be central to the ideas examined in chapter 3 of this study—Wagner means the productive impulses that assert themselves spontaneously as our wills. He believes that this is a more reliable source of motivation than 'spirit', favoured by philosophers, which, by its essence, has ends that are other than 'nature, reality, and man'.[32] Spirit has no connection with 'the social nature of man' whose affectivity involves that set of concerns that are found together under the idea of *Noth*.[33] The break with politics can occur only when we have somehow found the confidence to turn towards 'involuntary action'.[34] Involuntary action is obviously free of the structures that are given to experience by, for instance, the curated history mandated by the state. What Wagner must have recognized, though, is that this precept has implications for the realization of the revolutionary society of the future he regards as possible. It will have to emerge from a widespread and spontaneous desire among the people. They cannot be led 'from above'. What they produce in this way will be post-ideological in principle since it is sentiment and not theory that leads them to their own emancipation. The apparently necessary absence of any mechanism of transition is what, in the end, makes Wagner's theory a matter of thought, but not of political action.

The ideas about the necessity of nature, the problems of history, and involuntary action operate at a conceptual level that is not easily connected with the concrete human situation that Wagner wishes to rescue from the supposed realm of spirit. He has, though, a second approach that takes us to a more tangible space of experience.

Aestheticized Experience

Wagner holds that an emancipated future will be one in which experience will be aesthetic in its qualities. The very idea of aesthetic experience encompasses a range of differing types of behaviour. It can refer—as it most often does in philosophical discussions—to what we undergo when we are actively and positively engaged with artworks. Wagner, in fact, largely emphasizes its other main sense, the experience of creation. The significance of that sense, as we shall see, is that it captures a certain kind of spontaneity and also—and this is a claim of particular meaningfulness to Wagner—of cooperation, two qualities that are repressed, as he sees it, by the circumstances of life within the political state (whose destructive characteristics will be explored further in chapter 4).[35] Cooperation will, Wagner thinks, be realized through the practice of dynamic interactions between individuals who work together towards the production of complex artworks. And it is in that activity that the unique qualities of the richest form of aesthetic experience are found. The analogies with anarchist politics are obvious and appropriate to Wagner's wider commitments.[36] Each project is self-governed and involves the voluntary participation of each of its members.

Wagner thought of a socialized form of that artistic creativity as the purpose, not the means, of social renewal. This new idea gave some degree of retroactive structure to the untidy passions of his revolutionary past. It is a mistake to think, as some believe, that Wagner was drawn to revolution purely because existing society could not give life to true art.[37] The efforts to pull down the old order were egalitarian in intent, but the world needed to sustain that egalitarianism had yet to be justified in theory. The idea of an aestheticized human being now emerged as the enabling principle, though it is to some degree already gestured at in 'Man and Existing Society'.

The idea of the Gesamtkunstwerk, usually translated as the 'total work of art', forms a significant part of Wagner's vision of an emancipated future.[38] As I shall clarify shortly, that term is not restricted to the sphere of art. It is often observed that the fame of this idea vastly outstrips Wagner's use of it in his writings. That is literally true, though it does not give due recognition to a phrase to the same effect that Wagner quite frequently employs, namely, the idea of a completed or consummate work of art, *das vollendete Kunstwerk*. Like the phenomenon intended by the Gesamtkunstwerk, it refers both to a future artform and to the accomplished dramas of the Greeks. And since Wagner characterizes those dramas as instances of the great unity found only in a total work of art, its proximity to the idea of the Gesamtkunstwerk should be self-evident. Those ancient dramas were total in the two senses of the term 'Gesamtkunstwerk': they involved the entirety of the city in their production and audience appreciation, and they drew together the various artforms. In just a few places, the term 'consummate work of art' is, it should also be said, simply one of praise and carries no special technical weight.

The very idea of the Gesamtkunstwerk / the consummate work of art encompasses dual points of reference. First of all, it signifies a work of art that contains each of the art media. But it is also, secondly, designed to capture the practices of an aestheticized society which can implement itself through the actions of *all its members*. Society is the artefact, as Wagner seems to say when he speaks of '*the common work of art of the future*'.[39] The term *gesamt*, in this context, refers to the involvement of a community in its own collective self-realization. Understanding the relationship between these two senses of the Gesamtkunstwerk—a type of artwork and the activity of producing a community—takes us to the centre of Wagner's position. They stand together without referring to the same thing. What combines them is a reimagined notion of creativity. Wagner believes that a particular kind of sensibility is required for the creation of the Gesamtkunstwerk in the artistic sense, but it can be actualized only when human beings have learned to live in a new communal way, where each individual sees themselves as enhanced in the exercise of their powers in that shared endeavour.

The order in which Wagner lines up the two dimensions of the Gesamtkunstwerk is important here: a society with aestheticized social practices is one that can produce consummate works of art. The correct social and political arrangements have primacy, then, in the logic of the Gesamtkunstwerk. And that, it seems to me, is largely to be expected once we appreciate that Wagner's thinking in the trilogy is as continuous with the stimulant that led him to revolution—social change—as he could make it. In what follows, I shall separately consider, as far as is possible and for the sake of conceptual accessibility, the two main aspects of the very idea of the Gesamtkunstwerk even though Wagner had no such clear separation either in mind or in the architecture of his arguments.

The Gesamtkunstwerk as Aestheticized Politics

Wagner's reflections on the artwork of the future are almost invariably indexed to a conception of the kind of society that is supposed to nurture it. Although that idea looks forward, beyond the present age, it draws some confidence from Wagner's view of the Greek past. He maintains, based on what he takes to be the paradigmatically unified nature of the Greek world, that there is an isomorphism between the fundamental arrangements found in particular societies and the artforms they are capable of producing. Their 'consummate' artworks represented to them 'the nation itself, in intimate connection with its own history'.[40] That is, it expressed their intuitive sense of both their being in the world among others within a specific community—the values of the polis—and the inscrutable forces of life that exercised themselves upon them. Art, in this way, is no sui generis product, linked solely to individual genius, nor is it pure inventiveness whose structure and content is hermetically untouched by prevailing cultural values or the wider normative environment of the society in which it is produced.

Wagner is evidently aligned in a general way with historicism. That commitment perhaps explains Nietzsche's bare observation that until 'the middle of his life, Richard Wagner let himself be misled by Hegel'.[41] That is not, though, straightforwardly correct. He is no kind of Hegelian if endorsement of the thesis of the progress of history is a qualifying commitment. At the same time, he is no relativist either, since that variety of historicism would be patently incompatible with his notion of revolutionary reform, be it in politics or art. The Gesamtkunstwerk is for him the exemplary expression of a society that experiences freedom in its fullest possibilities. Wagner thereby believes that there are more or less realized types of art, but certainly not a diversity of equally valuable types. Hence, historical circumstances (with the exceptions of the Greek past and a notional future) inhibit the full realization of art. The deficiencies we can find in the forms of art that prevail in particular societies are the result of the negative pressures of the social arrangements within which they are formed. This is instanced in the parallels Wagner draws between the individualism and egoism of modern society and the convention that artists are 'egoistically isolated' (sole operators) and therefore practice only within a single artistic medium.[42] Hence 'the artist of today' produces work which reflects 'only an egoistic, self-satisfied activity' that is 'entirely for himself', that is, for his own ends.[43] There is no attempt to express the needs of the community, for example, or the broader struggles of humanity. Rather, the artist seeks, Wagner's cynical view holds, fame and dazzling success.[44] And it is for these reasons that contemporary society cannot give life to consummate art.

Wagner tempers this view when commenting on the incomparable brilliance of particular figures, perhaps Ludwig van Beethoven above all. He seems, in those instances, to detect no imperfections that might be traced back to the historical limits of aesthetic possibility (to any variety of egoism). Indeed, and contrary to his usual principle, he implicitly intimates that some artworks overcome the normative limitations of their times. He holds that Beethoven's ninth symphony represents an enormous development in the history of musical art but, as he puts it, '[a]fter it no progress is possible, for it can be immediately followed only by the consummate work of art of the future, the *universal* drama, to which for us Beethoven has forged the artistic key'.[45] It is obvious enough that Wagner's efforts to accommodate Beethoven places some strain on his general view of social reality as an essential condition of aesthetic excellence. And it complicates his dismissive assessment of culture. His contention has two aspects. First, it seems that, in *The Artwork of the Future,* Beethoven is, in fact, an artist who advanced the musical range in a way that could be seen, within his context, as futural. (The discussion of Beethoven in *Opera and Drama* is, by contrast, discernibly less interested in the question of historicality, and more with musical evolution.) But those advances can be absorbed into the ongoing development of music. Beethoven, then, may not be an artist of the future in the strict sense—that is, as futural for us—but, nevertheless, the formal achievements of his work cannot be fully explained by reference to the aesthetic norms of his times. The second and related thought, as Wagner attempts to resolve the tension between his notion of the determining effects of the social situation and Beethoven's apparent freedom from it, is the identification of Beethoven as a bridge figure whose genius allowed him to create works as though the general circumstances required for them existed.[46] And those circumstances implicitly include a sense of humanity that is free of egoism, reaching its expressed apotheosis in the final part of the ninth symphony. Indeed, a sensibility that is capable of thinking of a world that has not yet been realized must be possible if any emancipatory vision—Wagner's included—is to be considered grounded rather than mere fancy. There is a specific cost to the futural artist, however, Beethoven specifically. It positioned him outside the conventional aesthetic community—aesthetic form tracks our fundamental intuitions about humanity—and this explains, as Wagner frames it, the perplexity Beethoven faced in the contemporaneous appreciation of his work.[47]

Wagner may be an antirelativist historicist with regards to art, but that standpoint is founded on his vision for the perfectibility of communal life and not primarily a theoretical concern for art's ultimate self-realization. The practice of aesthetic cooperation as the highest form of creation, even if it is a largely notional idea, gives shape to Wagner's ideal community. Artistic genius in the future will be located not in individuals, but in a shared enterprise.[48] The most useful idea he can produce in support of this contention draws, once again, on the case of the Greeks. He maintains that in their great dramas—the tragedies—they created unified works of art that were expressive of the deeper unity in diversity that underpinned their society. They enjoyed the 'highest common formation [*Bildung*]'[49] but not merely in the superficial sense of being subject to the same education or training which the word *Bildung* might also imply. It was, rather, a formation which encouraged individuality—the very 'essence of the human species'[50]—one which found itself most fulfilled when working with others to maintain their shared society. They appreciated, and not necessarily consciously, that the very life of the community was furthered only where participation was broadly based—the practice of democracy, such as it was—and outcomes thereby jointly achieved. The eventual 'dissolution' of the Greek state, Wagner claims, saw 'the common spirit splintered in a thousand egoistic directions'.[51] As a consequence of this, 'the Gesamtkunstwerk of tragedy also dissolved into the individual artistic components contained within it'.[52] And we who are formed within that fragmented world are incapable—the privileged critic excepted, it seems—of appreciating 'the great Greek Gesamtkunstwerk' since it is essentially a production of quite differing people and circumstances.[53] The fate of drama and art in general is, then, always an effect of a wider political and moral environment.

Although Wagner points us with distinct reverence towards the Greeks, his objective is not to leave us with an impotent nostalgia. Rather, the example of the Greeks provides a precedent which, he believes, can instruct a future age. We recall that for Wagner revolution means a break with history, and he is consistent in adhering to that point in rejecting the idea that we should adopt the experience of the Greeks: such an imitation would be external to the processes that originally motivated that experience. Their world simply provides some sense of the fundamental constitutive elements for any society which can transform itself into an aesthetic community. Wagner uses the term *Allgemeinheit* to refer to the most fundamental of those elements. With the connotations Wagner attaches to that word, we might translate it as 'a community of all'. That captures his intended sense of a group that is aware of itself as a group, a property that is less obvious in the word's more neutral renderings: 'the general public' or 'public at large'. He repeatedly argues that art in the modern world is necessarily deficient precisely because it is not grounded in *Allgemeinheit*. It does not operate with the influencing intuition of *Allgemeinheit*, and hence it is narrow and, at best, incomplete. At worst, it stems from the selfish motivations of its creators (a selfishness he sometimes benevolently sees as necessitated by circumstances beyond their influence) and is directed to the entertainment of its individual consumers. Because those are the qualities of the modern situation that Wagner interprets as inferior to what is ideally possible, the idea of *Allgemeinheit* functions here as a normative concept. It does not refer merely to the totality of individuals who happen to be in a given society and whose needs—in the sense of *Bedürfnis*—must, on some formal principle, be met equally. The latter is sufficiently present where individuals see their interests extending only so far as their self-preservation within the specific challenges of their societies. Those challenges may, as noted above, include the obvious mortal ones, but they can extend to the preservation of status. *Allgemeinheit*, by contrast, is found where there is a kind of affective sensibility of interest towards a wider human reality. That sensibility, Wagner maintains, disappeared with the fall of Greece. From that point onwards, political arrangements and the aesthetic endeavours that follow them structurally have necessarily floundered—though evidently not failed entirely—because there has been no *Allgemeinheit* that might sustain them on anything other than a basic level of mere individual need.

Wagner maintains that the disappearance of *Allgemeinheit* led to the supersession of art by the asocial discipline of philosophy.[54] This idea is perhaps a precursor to Nietzsche's thought that a society that loses its vitality—that is, one that is decadent—turns to the psychologically distorting practices of creating moral principles and philosophical theories that are prejudiced against experience. A future in which the deepest capacities of human beings are exercised is one,

Wagner suggests, when states and indeed philosophy—a symptom of isolated activity—have come to an end. At that point 'the artist begins again'.[55] And, as the context here seems to imply, this is the artist who will be the creator of society and of artworks.[56] This reading of Wagner's intention is corroborated by his claim that the artist of the future will be 'the people',[57] a role they take on both in the formation of their communities and in the creation of artworks. That will be a future in which human beings are released from the misuse of their 'vital forces'[58] and elevated thereby to an aestheticized disposition which works in the first instance on the generation of a new social environment. Consequently, a form of art practice that is in sympathy with that environment will emerge.

The texts of this period are thin enough in ideas about how we might move from the debased modern world to a future of vibrant aesthetic individuals. Wagner was not an impractical person, as his abilities to stage operatic works and his intensive involvement with the design of the Bayreuth Festspielhaus amply demonstrate. During the revolutionary years—when still a court employee—he had compiled a detailed report containing concrete proposals on the reorganization of the theatres in Saxony, a piece which he later prefaced as a contribution to the prevailing spirit of 'reform'.[59] Unsurprisingly, given its intended readership, the report's connection with revolution is not explicitly made and probably does not, in any case, exist. Generally, though, Wagner was not, as we have seen, a thinker of what might be called 'real politics', not least because of the aestheticized version of human interaction which moved him. The mechanisms of revolutionary transition that would take us to that future are characteristically skipped over. Much of his discussion takes place as though from the perspective of a future barely recognizable from the perspective of present society. The very notion of the Gesamtkunstwerk speaks in that manner to the end of social fragmentation and the transformative possibilities of a community in which affective connection and common purpose are central to the free decisions made by each individual.

The Gesamtkunstwerk as Politicized Aesthetics

The societal meaning of the Gesamtkunstwerk does not disappear once we consider that idea within the directly aesthetic senses with which it is usually associated. It continues to retain essential sociopolitical dimensions, though they are translated into the register of aesthetic practice. In this context, in which the Gesamtkunstwerk is conceived as the art form of a revolutionary future, a range of conventional assumptions about both the nature of artworks and their production are challenged:

(i) The artist is a creative individual. Wagner proposes, instead, that we begin to adopt the idea of the artist as a creative collective. All those involved in the production of an artwork are united as a single artist. And, relatedly, Wagner hints through the precedent of the Greeks that the artwork expands to include the audience. Their spontaneity is engaged in its performance as cocreators, of a certain kind, of the singularity of the living artwork in a time and place.

(ii) Art talk appeals to shared norms about beauty or recognized aesthetic experience. The properties of the Gesamtkunstwerk, however, do not follow existing standards of aesthetic worth (and yet we are supposed to anticipate it as supremely valuable as art). Its qualities will seem elusive to those to whom Wagner is directing his challenge. This is a troubling thesis in that it depends on the very existence of a tradition of art for its intelligibility and yet it projects the meaning of art into a future that has overcome tradition.

(iii) Art operates unproblematically within distinct and often irreconcilable media (as G. E. Lessing argued in his *Laocoön*). Wagner opposes this with the notion that future artworks will—indeed must—combine the different art media. While this may seem like an

> extra-aesthetic stipulation, contrived merely to parallel the social idea of cooperation, Wagner's contention is that the Gesamtkunstwerk has unparalleled expressive possibilities. This, nevertheless, defers the measure of what the standards of the richest expressivity really are to the standards of the future.

When comprehended as the '*total* work of art' the Gesamtkunstwerk tends to invoke the idea of an artform which, in a sense peculiar to Wagner, represents the final culmination of the aesthetic innovations of Western culture achieved by the unification of the separate arts: principally, dance, sound, and poetry. This general idea is captured in a locution, the consummate work of art, which Wagner uses, as noted earlier, in apparent preference to that of the Gesamtkunstwerk:

> Only when the defiant independence of all three arts breaks down in order to merge into the love of the others; only when each is able to love itself only in the other; only when they themselves cease to be individuated arts, do they all become capable of creating the consummate work of art; yes, their cessation in this sense is already of itself this very work of art, their death directly its life.[60]

Wagner's holistic standpoint entails the view that *separateness* is a kind of lesser or merely preliminary condition to a cohesive totality in which each element, at last, will realize its potential (in some specific sense) by finding its proper place in harmony with every other element. The political ideology often inferred from theories that regard unity as more important than individuation is a conservative communitarianism in which idiosyncrasy and difference are discouraged by a supposedly purposeful and somehow authoritative whole whose integrity has overarching value. If, however, Wagner is successful in holding political and aesthetic considerations in sympathetic relation to one another, we should hesitate in ascribing a 'totality first' perspective to him. It would, after all, hardly be conducive to genuine artistic endeavour to suborn it to a collective end where individual expression was curtailed.

It has been suggested that the Gesamtkunstwerk should be grasped alternatively along the lines of a gathered work of art. This is proposed on the basis that *gesamt* is a derivative of the verb *sammeln*, meaning to gather or collect.[61] We might build further on that connotation and suggest that a 'gathered', as opposed to 'total', work of art is characterized by cooperation, an idea that resonates with the anarchism that is discernible in Wagner's view of a revolutionary society. It is an assembly that respects the integrity of each part and therefore does not require any irreversible surrender to the whole. There is much from the wider context of Wagner's writings from this period to recommend that more dynamic model over the totalistic image. It is sympathetic to his notion of the flourishing of diverse individuality. But yet, and against that suggestion, the specific notion of the Gesamtkunstwerk as an ideal artwork seems less amenable to the 'gathered' connotation. Wagner usually intends something altogether more reconstructive: an artwork in which each medium has been constitutively recast through its involvement in that product.

It is reasonable to again worry that that aesthetic precept is isomorphic with a politics that runs contrary to Wagner's views of a dynamic society of vibrantly free individuals. That worry, however, is the expression of a view about individuality that Wagner outrightly rejects. It supposes that the concept of individuality that has valence in modern society is essentially complete in form and simply in need of a kinder social environment (that is, the transition from corrosive competition to cooperative egoism). It does not recognize that the connectedness, discussed above, that is found in a condition of *Allgemeinheit* is an enhancement of individuality. Wagner believes that this is freedom proper. And, in fact, there is not the slightest implication in his writing that he wishes to reconceive individuality as an element or moment of a social totality that has a value that transcends the irreducible diversity of a vital community.

A quite different objection to the very idea of the Gesamtkunstwerk is that it lies uncomfortably distant from serious thought. When we look at some of the details of how that artform is to be developed, it is not hard to see what prompts that concern. A 'total work of art' involves, as Michael Tanner sceptically highlights, the 'redemption' (*Erlösung*) of individual art forms as they are transformed into elements in the great totality.[62] That transformation, as noted above, involves a reconstruction of their existing determinations in such a way as to increase their capacity for even greater expressivity. Outside the *Gesamtkunstwerk,* they can achieve that only partially. 'Redemption', indeed, is the weighty and unattractive word Wagner attaches to the transformative process, though what he attempts to gain by it is less exotic than its religious and metaphysical resonances perhaps lead us to fear. Using it across a wide range of contexts, it refers in his work to any kind of deep change that brings a society, a group, an individual, or an artform to find its proper meaning and significance through a willing act of self-transcendence. The object concerned is rescued from incompletion, distortion, or isolation, and brought by itself to its truth, that is, to its best form. The following three are representative examples, found in *The Artwork of the Future,* of what Wagner understands as the process of redemption that transforms specific art media.

(1) The development of the folk song into advanced musical form:

> The *folk tune,* which had remained true to itself in its undistorted gracefulness, the *song* that was intimately interwoven with poetry, united and securely bounded, raised itself on its elastic wings into the regions of the learned [*wissenschaftlich*] musical art world in need of beauty, announcing joyful redemption.[63]

(2) The appreciation of the human form expressed in sculpture transformed into drama in which it is placed within the living present:

> the redemption of sculpture is precisely that of *the disenchantment of stone into the flesh and blood of man, from the motionless into motion, from the monumental into the present.* Only when the urge of the artistic sculptor has passed *into the soul of the dancer, the mimic performer,* the singing and speaking one, can this impulse be thought of as truly satisfied.[64]

(3) The overcoming of poetry's supposed detachment when embedded in drama:

> a poetry turned away from life must remain eternally barren. . . . From this state of misfortune, the poetic literary drama can redeem itself only by becoming a living real drama.[65]

We are likely to want to resist some of these proposals while also finding ourselves quite unmoved by the emotive language in which they are partly conveyed. But we might try to rescue Wagner's thinking on this point by suggesting that disputes over the redemption of specific media do not warrant dismissal of the project entirely. Wagner is attempting to capture speculatively the idea of the greatest possible version of each of the separate media, an idea which we need hardly frame in terms of redemption, with all its distracting resonances. Media that have reached the extremity of what they can express have somehow run their course. That is not to say that they cannot advance technically, but that kind of improvement, Wagner perhaps maintains, does not track or generate greater expressivity. Their future development can be found only in the new configuration Wagner is proposing. No existing art medium can develop 'consummately' from within itself alone. What Wagner is reaching for is, plainly enough, a synthesis of the arts for the purposes of aesthetic possibilities. He anticipates that through this synthesis '[n]ot a single richly developed capacity of the individual arts will remain unused in the Gesamtkunstwerk of the future; only through the latter will it come to full realization'.[66]

We can, then, perhaps accept that there may in principle be some aesthetic advantages (as well as losses, at least by the measure of our aesthetic prejudices) in the aesthetic evolution Wagner envisages. It may, though, be a matter of taste that words that skilfully interact with complex and dynamic music and are played out on the stage are found to be more aesthetically or emotionally affecting than words alone, that is, in poetry. A familiar criticism of Wagner's proposal is, to cite one commentator, that 'the great achievements within the individual fields [of art] cannot simply be added up'.[67] It is indeed more than difficult to accept the idea that a well-crafted poem or piece of music for solo instrument suffers from an intrinsic deficiency because the genre within which it exists has yet to be redeemed. Wagner is driving at the idea that the exemplary future will be marked by entirely new and significantly more ambitious aesthetic criteria than those of the present. They will influence the artworks of the future and serve as a standard from which to judge retrospectively the artworks of our present. Those artworks, notwithstanding the excellence they have achieved within their historical contexts, may be appreciated as preparatory (the case of Beethoven again). As mentioned above, however, Wagner leaves us with a problematic break with tradition, with its precedents and canonical standards, as we embrace on a theoretical level an aesthetic paradigm which can only be realized in the future.

A further issue of concern is found in Wagner's regular conflation of aesthetic and moral norms. He presents the inherent failings of separate artforms as structurally and normatively equivalent to egoism. That thought gratingly introduces to aesthetic production an alien grammar. To cite just one instance of this association, where Wagner speaks of an inferior form of opera: it 'becomes the joint contract of the egoism of the three arts'.[68] If there is merit to aesthetic synthesis, it cannot be because the separate artforms otherwise languish in a stunting and narcissistic self-regard. At the same time, Wagner's fundamental point would not have been lost had he chosen to argue for his aesthetic ideal without the language of morality. Perhaps Wagner, to now give Nietzsche's observation its due, is drawing on a Hegelian idea in which a society's normative environment—its practices of freedom specifically—inform its expressive activities. Hegel's analysis of the background conditions is immense and complex, whereas Wagner tends to find holistic associations in contemporary society that are reducible to the supposedly all-pervasive influence of egoism. And, of course, Hegel speaks from the standpoint of his own time, adumbrating the developing forms and phases of human self-consciousness, in society and its most advanced self-expressions, in the course of reaching the culminating moment of the present. Wagner, in addition, however, anticipates the future. That is, he is trying to anticipate the form in which that art—both practice and product—will take root in a society that is based on a dynamic, cooperative anarchism. He claims that 'a free, self-conscious community of all [*Allgemeinheit*]' will provide the conditions for the consummate work of art.[69] Under those conditions, the Gesamtkunstwerk will be the product of 'the necessarily conceivable common work [*gemeinsames Werk*] of the people of the future'.[70] If that is the emancipated future, then the present age is, inversely, one of egoism both in social and aesthetic life. The worry remains, though, that a conceptualization of anti-egoistic practices of art production cannot without contrivance apply also to the basic materials of art itself (its media).

Wagner's thoughts on a post-egoistic world of artistic practice and production may be fanciful, but they are central to his outlines of a revolutionary future. By way of clarifying that point a little further, we might contrast it with Howard Becker's similar-sounding thesis of 'art as collective action'. That thesis identifies art production as the outcome of a 'network of people, however large or extended, whose collective activity made it possible for the event to occur as it did'.[71] Wagner, at one level, seems to say something along these lines too, where the focus is placed on the conditions that are conducive to artistic production. However, the vital difference is that for Wagner that network supports not simply art as such, but the emancipated practice of art creation. And, as we have seen, that practice itself rests on the background condition of a particular kind of revolutionary social reality. Wagner, moreover, ties art to a specific idea of freedom which involves willing participation in a cooperative aesthetic project which both unifies the separate arts and unites the artist with others. As he puts it: 'The artistic person can be satisfied completely only in the unification of all the kinds of art into a *common* work of art: in every *isolation* of his artistic ability he is *unfree*, not completely that which he can be; whereas *in the common work of art he is free*, and completely what he can be'.[72] And for that very end, the artist of the future will place themselves within '*the cooperative* [Genossenschaft] *of all artists*'.[73] It is not then a network in which each element serves its own interests. It occurs only where the shared undertaking is consciously coordinated towards the achievement of a specific end.

Given the unsurpassed attention Wagner gave to each dimension of his art and to the staging of his music dramas, there is a suspicion that he quietly believes that his work, in fact, exemplifies art's redeemed unification and that he is thereby an individual forerunner of the cooperative of artists. This cannot be ruled out as his private intention of course, though it is not a claim he actually makes. We can find several statements that might suggest, however, that some artist—if not Wagner himself—can achieve that great artistic unity. In *Art and Revolution*, he notes that the 'true artist' may already begin to create the artwork of the future since, by virtue of their artistry, they can occupy a standpoint that has transhistorical validity.[74] In the very final paragraph of *Opera and Drama*, though, a conclusion arrives with no preceding justification: '*[t]he creator of the artwork of the future is none other than the artist of the present*', an individual who has an intimation of the future.[75] Although these statements may be misleading, they are, however, little more than exhortations to innovate and thereby advance beyond the present, in a manner Beethoven had shown to be possible.[76] This does not imply that the Gesamtkunstwerk can be a production under current historical circumstances. Such a claim would undermine the social criticism on which Wagner's notion of revolution is founded: the prevalence of egoism necessarily excludes the kind of artwork which involves collective, co-operative, and socially oriented action.

Unfortunately, Wagner's well-stated and adequately reasoned position is regularly overlooked, with grandiose personal ambitions instead attributed to his aesthetic motivations. Among the most prominent of the critics is Theodor W. Adorno. Adorno cites Thomas Mann's assessment of Wagner with approval: 'His relationship to the individual arts from which he composed his "*Gesamtkunstwerk*" is worth pondering; there is something peculiarly dilettantish about it'.[77] Adorno finds a range of reasons to explain what he sees as the practical failure of 'Wagner's intention of integrating the individual arts into the *Gesamtkunstwerk*'.[78] The core problem for him is that the senses which have primacy in each of the media have developed with different histories, and their separation, he revealingly acknowledges, is the result of 'reification'. Any proposal for their unification rests therefore on the imposition of a spurious identity.[79] We have seen, though, that Wagner's view of the Gesamtkunstwerk is prospective, even if it is, as one interpreter puts it, 'the central directing inspiration of his music'.[80] What Adorno puts forward as a fundamental criticism is actually in line with Wagner's assessment of the present. He did not have a theory of reification, of course. What Adorno might have acknowledged, however, is that Wagner had much to say about the damage to our aesthetic capacities that can be traced to contemporary social conditions, even if the analysis falls short of the insights of critical theory. The reality of the unification of the arts belongs, for Wagner, to a future in which the dehumanization that fragments experience has been displaced. And in further response to Adorno, we can counter that it is important, and surely not difficult, to separate what Wagner notionally envisages for the artwork of the future from his searing criticisms of those composers—Gioachino Rossini most brutally, in whose hands 'opera died'[81]—who failed in his view to integrate words and music, drama and action. Those critical observations emerge from within Wagner's accounts of the development of opera by reference to its own inner formal demands, namely, that of bringing voice, music, drama, and staging together into convincing cohesion without necessarily reaching the ideals of the Gesamtkunstwerk. Culpability for confusion on this point does not, in this instance, lie with Wagner since, as I noted above, he did not declare his own works to be cases of the Gesamtkunstwerk. Indeed, he himself was irritated by the narrowing of what he meant by the term as it took on a reality, contrary to his intention, as a label for everything he was attempting to achieve.[82] And, really, it can only be by ignoring Wagner's thoughts about cooperatives—however blurry they may be—that he can be tied to the complementary allegation that as the creator of a Gesamtkunstwerk he implicitly crowns himself as the artist of the future.

Wagner's futural perspective also explains why he does not suggest that we should now adopt the kind of art practice required to produce the Gesamtkunstwerk, or something of that sort, in order to prefigure the future.[83] Wagner was often confusing when representing the thinking of the revolutionary years, with most of his muddled retrospections appearing in an introduction added to the self-edited *Gesammelte Schriften und Dichtungen*. Following a quote from Thomas Carlyle, who speaks stirringly of a world without government and a millennium-long reign of anarchy to follow, Wagner explains that in full agreement with Carlyle he interpreted his task as that of holding 'this work of art up to life itself as a prophetic mirror of its future'.[84] His earlier commitment to anarchism is faithfully recalled, but the 'mirror' motif is nowhere to be found in the works that are reprinted in the volumes (3 and 4) in which that introduction appears. What is evident in the trilogy, rather, is that no work of art capable of casting critical light on the present could then be created. It could at best be set out in purely speculative terms as a description of future practice.[85]

Correlatively, Wagner did not propose that art has efficacy in bringing about a revolutionary transformation of society. The principal reason against the idea of art as a revolutionary force should by now be obvious enough. The Gesamtkunstwerk—the truest art—and the practices required to create it do not exist prior to revolution. Those practices are not autonomous: they will become possible only when transformed social conditions allow. As Wagner forcefully expressed it in private correspondence (in December 1849), after the publication of *Art and Revolution* and completion of *The Artwork of the Future*, 'works of art cannot be created at present, they can only be prepared for by means of revolutionary activity, by destroying and crushing everything that is worth destroying and crushing. That is our task, and only people utterly different from us will be the true creative artists'.[86] (Wagner, we recall from his letter to Minna, did not see himself as one among those destructive activists.)

Wagner remains largely consistent with the thought that the aestheticization of experience is the fundamental condition and that what follows from it, among other things, is artwork of a special kind. Virtually all that is difficult to follow in this corner of his writing arises from the changing vantage points from which he makes his pronouncements: sometimes it is from the perspective of an anticipatory present, and at other times from a fictional point in a future in which a revolution has brought about a new society. A conflation of these two perspectives, which Wagner's presentation might sometimes inadvertently invite, produces the unsatisfactory impression that the right kinds of aesthetic practice and of art production are already at hand.

As we have seen, a systematic reciprocity exists between the conditions of a genuinely free and spontaneous community and the renewal of aesthetic productivity. They imply each other, with Wagner maintaining that a community of that sort would necessarily feel urged to express itself through the form of aesthetic activity that leads to the creation of a Gesamtkunstwerk. Likewise, aesthetic activity that does not lead to the shared creation of artworks, which also involves bringing the major art media into union, is symptomatic of the wider prevalence of societal egoism. The qualities of the world Wagner envisages are not obviously objectionable, given his insistence that it accommodates individual freedom, a sense of community (*Allgemeinheit*), and the dynamic remaking of society by its members. This is ultimately, obviously enough, and perhaps unavoidably an inexact prospectus.

What Wagner is proposing here may, nevertheless, be open to the charge of historical closure. That is in spite of its benevolent intentions and its deliberate strategy—motivated by his worry about the ideology of historical narratives—of underspecifying the future. We might, for instance, accept Wagner's contention that modern life is characterized by egoism and commercialism and that a truly free society would have overcome those debilitating forces. But it is not strictly the case that what Wagner proposes is the only emancipating possibility, that is, the only way beyond those negative conditions. Wagner's solutions are aptly derived from the very problems which he himself thematizes (of which we shall see a great deal more in chapter 4). A world of social fragmentation, as Wagner diagnoses it, violates our affective needs, and the direct consequences of that violation are the loss of creativity, community, and spontaneity. Set out in this way, it seems obvious, Wagner believes, that the Gesamtkunstwerk must be the redemptive art of the future. Alternative prospectives, however, can be—and have been—conceived for artworks and styles which may be very different to the Gesamtkunstwerk in type, production, and appreciation. Wagner's theory is a holistic conceptualization of the mutual determination of communal and aesthetic action. The reciprocity is so tightly designed that any artwork which falls short of the principles of the Gesamtkunstwerk can be accused of carrying forward traces of an imperfect social order. But this will have to be to the exclusion of aesthetic possibilities that are not directed by a Wagnerian communal ideal. Challenges to Wagner on this point can therefore be raised in the name of competing social visions and, correlatively, of aesthetic plurality and diversity.

Jewishness in Music as a Question for Revolution

Wagner's notorious 'Jewishness in Music' appeared in the autumn of 1850, falling chronologically between *The Artwork of the Future* and *Opera and Drama*.[87] A question about the relationship between that essay and the very project of the trilogy—*Art and Revolution* included—quite understandably presents itself. If Wagner's antisemitic prejudices are a determining element in that project, then all surface claims to universality and the emancipation of humanity as a whole are undermined from the start. The task of determining where 'Jewishness in Music' departs from or complements the political agenda of the trilogy is intricate as well as joyless given the noxiousness of much of the essay. It requires closer textual analysis than some of Wagner's more trenchant critics have perhaps accepted. Among the most prominent of them is Paul Lawrence Rose, who writes: 'Wagner never subscribed to the modern Western liberal idea of revolution of the British, French or American variety. He believed, rather, in a peculiarly German form of revolution in which the sacred German race was to blaze a path to freedom. This would emancipate the whole human race from a loveless and irrational way of life, symbolized, and at the same time, made practical by the Jews'.[88] This potently expressed charge is, in fact, defied by an absence of evidence in the contents of both Wagner's Dresden political writings and the post-Dresden trilogy. Indeed, there is virtually nothing to support the idea that at this phase of Wagner's life—what was to come later was a quite different story—he was committed to a 'German form of revolution'. Certainly, there is that risible reference to German mildness in the essay on Kingship, but Wagner's intentions are quite transparent and were soon after abandoned. Nevertheless, terminological similarities can be found between the trilogy and Jewishness essay which, prima facie, sustain the charge that Wagner's revolutionary vision is contaminated with exclusionary prejudices.

'Jewishness in Music' was first published under a pseudonym, K. Freigedank, that is, K. Free-Thinker, a decision that is revealing in itself. Wagner knew that what he had to say would be perceived by many among his cultivated readers as distasteful, but his choice of moniker suggests he considered himself to be courageously engaged in a dangerously countercultural yet necessary task. The essay appeared in a musical journal founded by Robert Schumann though edited by a successor at the time of Wagner's piece. His essay was a contribution to a debate that had recently begun in that journal concerning, as Wagner noted, 'Hebraic taste in art'.[89] He throws himself into that discussion with disturbing bigotry. The essay may have been written as an occasional piece, sandwiched between much greater artistic and philosophical projects, yet Wagner was happy to return to it when he defiantly republished it in 1869, this time under his own name. For the sake of historical contextuality, I will quote from the original 1850 text when discussing its contents.[90] The lightly revised though no less venomous later version was accompanied by a justification which artfully took the form of a letter to an admirer. The essay was also included among the collected writings that appeared several years after the second publication.

Much has been said about Wagner's motivations for writing that essay. Alongside some element of romantic nationalism, which is not a detectable feature of the trilogy, there was the prompt of rage at what he saw as attempts by Jewish figures with influence in the European musical scene, either connivingly or as a consequence of other aims, to prevent his work from receiving the recognition he believed it deserved. What the essay attempts, precisely in response to that perception, is to delegitimize Jewish expertise in matters of aesthetic judgment.

The essay has several dimensions, none of which fit particularly well together. The first concerns Wagner's view of Jewish people, whom he chooses to characterize in the most offensive of ways. In the introduction to volumes 5 and 6 of the *Gesammelte Schriften und Dichtungen*, Wagner makes the incredible claim that he had intended no insult in those characterizations.[91] He believes it is quite natural for non-Jewish people to experience aversion towards the Jews. The 1869 edition implausibly claims, in the accompanying letter, that Wagner was merely uttering a view that if left unvoiced would remain a silent barrier to the real challenges of Jewish assimilation. The essay also contains the thesis, built from a mix of elements, that Jews are incapable of producing authentically German art, literature and music specifically. A reason for this, he proposes, is that they are not at home in the German language and hence do not have the necessary intuitive rhythms required to connect creatively with it.

Rather than leaving the point at that—easily dismissible though it might be—Wagner decided to explain the sounds made by speakers of something he refers vaguely to as the 'Jewish language'. It is unknown whether he is adverting to the language of religious worship—the synagogue is mentioned—or to Yiddish. One way or another, he finds in it only ugliness and unmusicality.[92] (Those imaginary sounds are widely thought to have been captured in the unpleasant singing patterns Wagner assigns to the role of Mime, the devious manipulator of Siegfried, and also to Sixtus Beckmesser.[93]) It is quite impossible to follow Wagner's weak reasoning when he turns to particular instances of those whose aesthetic impairments have been supposedly caused by that language or indeed the religious identity of those who speak it. Felix Mendelssohn is identified and Giacomo Meyerbeer is implied, yet both were German born, culturally refined, and socially elevated.[94] The thesis is empirically empty. And it should also be recorded that Wagner, not so many years before the essay, had been delighted to have the company and good opinion of both composers.[95]

Wagner then moves on to a second element, as he attempts to capture the incapacity of Jews to engage authentically with art, in which he maintains that cultivated Jews enter the world of art with an eye primarily for what is profitable. They are thus disposed towards the production of commercial entertainment that skilfully passes for true art, a process Wagner corrosively terms the 'jewification' (*Verjüdung*) of art.[96] He hinges this thesis, with all its extraordinary ramifications, on the implied case of Meyerbeer, whose spectacular operas gained him enormous celebrity. This leads Wagner, in effect, to set up a criterion of authenticity which he takes as licence to attack a social group somehow considered to lie outside the bounds of those capable of making art of a particular kind. Whatever they produce will therefore be culturally suspect or fraudulent. Wagner's dark ingenuity in pushing the discussion in that direction expanded the scope of antisemitism, one scholar observes, into 'the field of culture' and into music above all.[97]

What we should now return to is the question of whether 'Jewishness in Music' has debilitating implications for the very meaning of Wagner's idea of revolution. Two strands of the essay may appear to tie its claims with that larger project: money and the idea of the people. As we shall see in detail in chapter 4, Wagner, throughout the trilogy, maintains that money is responsible for a range of deficits in contemporary social life. It supplants, in short, genuine human interactions, becomes the only means of freedom in a society structured around financial capacity, and it distorts our urge for self-realization by narrowing it to activities that can contribute to the forms of self-preservation required by present society. 'Jewishness in Music' draws a number of hackneyed connections between money in contemporary society and the power of the Jews. As numerous commentators have pointed out, these views can be found in roughly similar formulations in Bruno Bauer and Marx, among others. Wagner puts the claim in this way: 'The Jew is, according to the present state of the world's affairs, really already more than emancipated: he rules, and will rule as long as money remains the power before which all our acts and endeavours lose their power'.[98] And he also observes, with a thought that may seem to connect with the writings on revolution, that the Jew stands in 'relationship only to those who need his money: but money has never succeeded in securing a revitalizing bond between people'.[99] Money may therefore be understood as a key source of social fragmentation or egoism.

Commonplace though this type of lazy social commentary might have been among Wagner's contemporaries, we should be clear on the boundaries of what he is alleging. It is his view that contemporary society is dominated by the logic of finance and, furthermore, that the Jews have a particular place of importance within its flow. It is of critical significance to state this clearly because of the potentially persuasive charge made by some scholars that the critique of money power is encoded antisemitism.[100] Similarly, there is no reason to accept that Wagner's comments on egoism carry an antisemitic agenda. We have seen Wagner identify egoism as a symptom of a society void of the affective aesthetic capacities he believes can be regained in the future. The writings of the revolutionary years, however, do not identify the Jews as the source of this deficit. As a point of broader relevance, it may also be important to reject in principle the idea that the lament over the power of money and the phenomenon of egoism is essentially a veiled complaint about Jewishness, as otherwise the critiques of capitalism and social alienation—which remain essential—will be disreputable in principle.

A more obvious worry belongs to the category of the people (*das Volk*). We recall that in Wagner's view the people consist in all of those who 'feel a common need [*Noth*]'.[101] 'Jewishness in Music' claims that the Jews are unable to create authentic German art because they are not grounded in the 'spirit of the people [*Volksgeist*]'.[102] The juxtaposition of these bare statements may seem to unlock a less innocent idea of the people than the version visible in *The Artwork of the Future*. The matter, however, is not quite so simple. After all, the people, as we have seen, have yet to constitute themselves. Hence the very idea of the people is one that looks forward. A revolutionary future does not rest, therefore, on whatever currently exists within the 'spirit of the people'. The notion of the spirit of the people, as it appears in 'Jewishness in Music', is antisemitic in intent, but it quite obviously belongs to a reality that Wagner necessarily holds apart—because it is the society of the disordered present—from a future society of the 'people' where each and every individual is transformed and emancipated.[103]

What is perhaps most surprising of all is that, after ten or so pages given over to the justification of an exclusionary theory of aesthetic activity, Wagner, in the essay's final two paragraphs, reconnects his thinking with the agenda of his post-Dresden revolutionary writings. As Dieter Borchmeyer puts it, Wagner 'appears to return by a mysterious route to the liberal position he had earlier abandoned'.[104] The appearance of those thoughts within the essay's context is indeed difficult to explain. Because they do not address the material that precedes them, they actually leave the contemporary situation untouched in that they radically depart from it. What Wagner has to say in the concluding parts of the essay does not bear upon the place of Jews within authentic German art. Rather, and irrelevantly to the essay's main agenda, they anticipate a future in which it is perfectly possible for a Jewish person to become one of the people.

Wagner cites the case of a writer whom he greatly admired, Ludwig Börne, who was able to cast off his Jewish background. At first, Wagner's interest in Börne's example seems to be of a piece with his antisemitic views: 'Becoming human together with us means for the Jew', he claims, 'to cease being a Jew: that had Börne ceased to be'.[105] This is identified by Wagner as 'redemption', a crystallization of the thesis, as Saul Friedländer puts it, of 'the redemption of the Jews from Judaism' (in the sense primarily of Jewishness).[106] Where Wagner's universalism asserts itself is in the claim that each and every person must undertake some relevantly similar act of self-overcoming in order to prepare for a future society. The arduousness of Börne's transformation—a process requiring 'sweat, adversity [*Noth*], and an abundance of suffering and pain'[107]—is, it seems, a model not only for the Jews but for

Wagner's 'us' too. And it is reasonable to infer that Wagner includes under 'us' anyone whose identity-formation is marked by, among other things, commercialism, egoism, and Christianity (Wagner's criticism of the latter's life-destroying norms will be examined in subsequent chapters).

The example of Börne is not though without complexity, since he was an historical individual who in some sense or other severed himself from his original identity: he is not an individual of the future. He became German, in Wagner's stipulative sense, by some ideal of perfect assimilation, not a postrevolutionary citizen. Wagner's point, though, coming from a form of analysis that places a great deal of significance on precedent, is that the cultural determinations of ethnicity, faith, social actor, or occupation, can be overcome. In a fragment from this period, Wagner speaks resonantly about the 'annihilation [*Vernichtung*] of sexual and national barriers and proclamation of the necessity of the individual's redemption into the community of all [*Allgemeinheit*]'.[108] This is consistent with what he envisages as a shared endeavour of individuals who are 'united and inseparable'.[109] Of course, it will mean the end of Judaism and Jewishness, just as it means the end of all existing identities. As such, it outruns the idea of assimilation.[110] Wagner is not, that is, involving himself here in a discussion of civil emancipation or in the question of assimilation within, for instance, the spirit of the people as currently constituted. He is addressing his pseudonymous self, in what is certainly an unattractively high-handed manner, to a notional Jewish reader who, like Börne and Wagner himself, understands that we are generally conditioned for the worse by a second nature which is complicit in the deficits of the modern world.

The evils of the Holocaust have given the language of the essay's final sentence an unsettling association. It is evident, though, that Wagner's terminology is metaphorical and explicable through the general meaning of his idea of redemption. He speaks about the redemption of the Jew as a 'self-annihilating, bloody battle', but it is one in which each and every individual must 'take part'.[111] He symbolizes the specific challenge of the Jews in this process through the figure of Ahasuerus, the wandering Jew, who suffers the 'curse' of enduring exclusion. The Jews must bring about their own 'downfall' to allow them, as renewed individuals, to enter into the wider human community.[112] The word Wagner uses for 'downfall' is *Untergang,* and because it contains connotations of 'destruction' may hint alarmingly at physical elimination. That is not, though, Wagner's intention. We should note that he employs the word *Untergang* in *Art and Revolution* to capture the idea of the irretrievable decline of Greek tragedy. In *The Artwork of the Future,* though, it has two senses. The first arises in the context of Wagner's claim that we will only appreciate how human freedom really operates—in sympathy with our sensuality and our spontaneity—with the decline of rationalist philosophy.[113] The second relates to what he foresees as the eventual redundancy of sculpture. The latter is an artform that gives shape to imaginary and perfect human beauty, and it lives on only because the reality, which we evidently desire, is absent under current historical circumstances.[114] The word appears with greater frequency in *Opera and Drama,* that part of the trilogy that followed 'Jewishness in Music', where its most significant sense is found in Wagner's discussion of 'the downfall of the state' (discussed in chapter 4). There he also speaks of the 'annihilation [*Vernichtung*] of the state', an endpoint reached by its own necessary collapse rather than violent intervention.[115]

Wagner's closing thoughts hardly count as an inspiring call for confraternity given the nature of the language used and the invocation of Ahasuerus. However, it is apparent that Wagner understands himself to be expressing a position that demonstrates that the current state of social relations between Jews and non-Jews is contingent and can be superseded through a radical social transformation that is for the benefit of all. Nevertheless, the essay is intellectually awkward in that it evidently contains two quite different commitments: the first and dominant one is a romantic nationalism whose central concern is qualification for cultural production, while the second restates his distinctive revolutionary universalism, albeit from a new angle. Over the course of the 1860s, Wagner's beliefs in the latter had all but disappeared, and he therefore had no higher principles with which he could correct the other side of himself. 'Jewishness in Music' does not, however, leave us with any sound reason to see the revolutionary project itself as implicitly motivated by prejudice. That is the important point and as much as this study has claimed. There is nonetheless something dissatisfying in this conclusion, and I think that rests on the searing impression left by the unpardonable presence in the essay of a prejudice that he consciously—not blindly—nurtured with some degree of pride. The ignoble reputation it has earned him is fully warranted, even if a final paragraph or two tell a more complex story.

3

A Philosophy of Freedom

WAGNER'S VARIOUS thoughts and arguments about the very idea of freedom are complementary elements of an intricate story about an emancipated world in which human beings live without coercion, realize themselves as individuals in their actions, and act in unforced harmony with others where the highest ideals of their community are concerned. His position is, then, a tight weave of abstract theoretical claims and an analysis of freedom's social dimensions. It is evident that he believes that these thoughts belong within a single philosophical space. That would not be wrong: after all, the division between the principles and social function of freedom is a matter of academic convention and not reflective of the complexity of social reality. There are, nonetheless, advantages in treating the philosophical and social dimensions in separation, as I shall do here and in the following chapter respectively. That approach will allow us to draw out the lines of justification that support the specific claims that make up his contribution to the question of how we might understand freedom and, furthermore, why we should endeavour to realize it in the world.

I have already suggested some possible reasons for the neglect of Wagner's ideas by the history of philosophy. In considering why his innovative conception of freedom in particular has been ignored, we might return for some explanation to Wagner's ill-advised self-criticisms. After all, if an author with a generally fervent readership—as had become the case by the time Wagner wrote against himself—seems embarrassed by an earlier effort, it is likely that his loyal supporters will not be disposed to contradict him. There are the opening comments in *Music of the Future* where he declares, almost a decade after the trilogy, that his efforts to engage in a 'labyrinth of theoretical speculation in a purely abstract form' plunged him into 'an abnormal state' from which he had since implicitly recovered.[1] And in the *Gesammelte Schriften und Dichtungen* he went further in his self-denigration. His retrospection was sparing but damaging. The introduction to volumes 3 and 4 of those writings speaks of 'a certain passionate confusion which manifested itself as haste and lack of clarity in the use of philosophical schemata'.[2] Wagner confessed to worries about his inadequate grasp of the meanings of specific though quite fundamental philosophical terminology. He may have been attempting to avert criticism through a strategy of touching humility, softening the reader's desire to argue with the text or to react uncharitably to what might have been perceived as his philosophical presumptuousness. Wagner castigated himself for what he now regarded as his misrepresentation of the concepts of 'sensuality' (*Sinnlichkeit*), 'arbitrariness' (*Willkür*), and 'involuntariness' (*Unwillkür*).[3] (He also lamented his use of the term 'communism'.) These three notions, as we shall see in some detail, are central to his notion of freedom. If Wagner was encouraging scepticism about the ways in which he had once handled them, the implications for the reception of his earlier philosophical project could only be destructive. And yet, it should be stated from the outset, there is, in fact, nothing notably awry in Wagner's original grasp of those terms. They are employed according to his own novel purposes, certainly, but not at the expense of intelligibility or at jarring odds with the philosophical conversations of the times in which he was writing.

The years between the early works on freedom (and other matters) and the preparation of the collected writings had, I suggest, rather tempered his philosophical acuity. By the 1870s, he seemed unable to recognize, never mind defend, the real achievements of his earlier theoretical efforts. The threads of argument that had generated the writings of that period were evidently now lost to him, leaving him in doubt about the coherence of what he had been thinking at the time. Perhaps that is not surprising when we consider the suddenness with which he had originally turned in his thirties to abstract philosophical writing, the rapidity of his production—again, weeks or months alone for each book of the trilogy—and the abrupt silence from 1851 onwards on the most distinctly philosophical of his earlier concerns. His involvement with philosophy, at least as a writer, became increasingly occasional, leaning ever more on the authority of Schopenhauer. In a new register, his intellectual exertions were given mainly to essays and books on music, some of which, though, contain the most lasting contributions to the philosophy of music of his career. When he turned to philosophical—that is, philosophically inflected—politics, he sought, in the main, to articulate a particular set of thoughts on nation, patriotism, and culture.

There are, as mentioned above, two broad categories into which his thoughts fall. First there is what I will call the purely philosophical conception of freedom. In this conception, Wagner holds that freedom is properly experienced through the involuntary, that is, spontaneous, processes of deciding and acting. Aesthetic experience is an inspiration for this model. Wagner speaks aptly, in another context, about the artists' surrender to the impressions that prompt their sympathies.[4] By 'involuntary'—*unwillkürlich*—he does not mean action performed against our will, as the perhaps misleading English word might suggest. We feel compelled to act, rather, on urges that originate in us. It is a nonrationalist yet meaning-producing spontaneity. There is thinking, certainly, but it underdetermines the actions that follow. Involuntariness does not include in this context actions that arise from our bare biophysical nature. Rather, they stem from who we are as *persons*, engaged with the world with the fullest of our humanness. The notion of involuntariness may nevertheless sound odd as a designation for motivations that are free in nature. However, it draws its meaning from its contrast with what it negates, that which is arbitrary, *willkürlich*. Arbitrariness is synonymous for Wagner with imposition. Imposition takes various forms. It can be found in oppressive situations or, less violently, in a life of habitude within the wrong kind of society. More deeply, moral or legal systems that are insensitive to our nature and which insist on a uniform model of human behaviour are arbitrary. A further feature of the involuntariness idea of freedom is that it does not attach to an 'I' or 'ego', that is, a distinctive self that stands apart both from a human life in the full and the outer world. Nor is freedom in evidence in some process of general reasons-based justification: we are not made free by argument with or against ourselves. That would be, from the point of view of Wagnerian thinking, the self-infliction of something that stems only from ratiocination, not from the 'involuntary' which alone expresses our individual dispositions.

The second conception of freedom focuses on our sociality. Its interest is freedom as a way of life. The free person lives with a sense of well-being in creative relationships with others and is uninhibited in the expression of their own individual personality. Freedom cannot, in Wagner's view, be compatible with narrow individual self-interest—competitive self-advancement—or a purely personal view of what is good. It is present only where all are free and, at the same time, motivated by shared collective goals and projects that are not directed from any source other than the wills of each individual. This notion of freedom owes much to the example Wagner detects in a rather partial way among the ancient Greeks. Freedom will mean liberation from manifest political oppression and restrictive institutions in the first instance. It is therefore not some enhancement of the existing legal-political form licenced by existing society. It involves, again, the radical and revolutionary transformation of communal life itself, a break with history. This chapter will concentrate on the philosophical conception of freedom, though its separation from the social aspects that Wagner considers—examined in the following chapter—is far from rigid.

I will begin with some consideration of Wagner's complex connection with the philosophy of Ludwig Feuerbach. Feuerbach's ideas make their presence felt in Wagner's work, particularly in that space in which he is developing a philosophy of freedom. With some delineation of the content of that influence, we begin to see the independent and creative differences between Wagner and his inspirational source. Feuerbach obviously gave Wagner access to a philosophical lexicon. However, Wagner adjusted what he discovered there, sometimes by placing Feuerbachian-sounding ideas in striking new configurations. His quite differing intellectual commitments also played a role in shaping the senses of what, at a superficial level, seems in his texts like merely secondhand ideas. His interest was in what he could do with ideas, wherever he encountered them, not in how, in some scholastic manner, he could be faithful to their original meaning. This is not to downplay Feuerbach's significance: he is a necessary condition of the philosophy of the trilogy, but he is only one of its conditions.[5] This chapter will then develop some illustrative contrasts between Wagner's materialist idea of spontaneity and several core elements of Immanuel Kant's practical philosophy. Its final part examines the special sense of necessity at work in Wagner's notion of the 'involuntariness' of genuine freedom.

Feuerbach as Educator

Wagner retrospectively doubted his grasp of what had once been, for him, pivotal philosophical concepts, as we have already noted. But he went so far as to arraign himself for what seemed to him, by the 1870s, to have been a failure of intellectual independence by allowing himself to surrender 'without critical consideration' in the trilogy 'to the guidance of' Feuerbach.[6] He had, in fact, dedicated the original edition of *The Artwork of the Future* to Feuerbach, claiming in hugely deferential if not, indeed, inaptly self-abnegating language, that the work in the pages that followed was effectively Feuerbach's 'property', albeit channelled through the quite different standpoint of an artist.[7] That crucial distinctiveness of purpose, one shaped by an aesthetic sensibility—that is the point of Wagner's qualifying comment—is easily overlooked.[8]

Wagner reports that he first read Feuerbach when he was presented with a copy of the latter's *Thoughts on Death and Immortality from the Papers of a Thinker* (1830). He was immediately impressed by the freshness of Feuerbach's approach since his enquiries assumed no deep acquaintance with the specifics of any of the positions he attacked. This was philosophy Wagner could appreciate. As a 'layman', he admired the 'widely praised, very stimulating, lyrical style of the writer'.[9] With a degree of interpretative conjecture we can detect in Feuerbach's book several themes that reappear in some form in Wagner's work. But it should be noted, first, that these are themes that Feuerbach himself refers to only passingly and, second, that they are, as far as he is concerned, problems that stem from the purely theological conception of humanity. When, for instance, Feuerbach observes that the 'modern age' is one which understands the individual as radically individuated and self-contained, he is not referring to the phenomenon of social individualism or egoism—one of Wagner's abiding concerns—but to the religious tenet that declares that each individual is 'divine and infinite'.[10] And his claim about the intersubjective processes of love might seem to reappear within Wagner's developed philosophy. As Feuerbach puts that idea: 'When you love, you no longer exist in the connections and associations with things and humans in which you previously existed and which alone constitute particular existence; you no longer exist in your particular interests'.[11] The person who loves takes on a higher form of being through union with another.[12] However, the metaphysical language Feuerbach uses to frame this new reality and the dialectical arguments he deploys to sustain it are not echoed in Wagner's work.

Wagner spoke accurately when he described Feuerbach as 'useful support' in rooting his aesthetic conception of the world in the 'purely human'.[13] Feuerbach, it seemed to him, had turned towards, as he put it, 'a conception of the human being in which I believed I clearly recognised the artistic human being I meant'.[14] *Thoughts on Death and Immortality* might contain few themes that are directly adopted by Wagner. However, his approach to the idea of the 'human being' may owe something to the general philosophical intention of Feuerbach's book. Feuerbach is relentless in his efforts to tear down the notion of each individual person as most truly a divine and disembodied entity. Human beings must, rather, be understood as temporal and finite. It is only under those conditions that the idea of death can remain intelligible.[15] He assails the idea that the language pragmatically used to articulate the things of the material world can also be effective in capturing a world of supposed pure essences where anthropomorphic qualities are falsely given metaphysical reality. His atheism is confrontational and uncompromising and was, in its time, scandalously antireligious. What he offers here, at least, is not, though, a philosophy with a social dimension, remaining largely abstract in its sense of what it means to appreciate the essentially embodied nature of human beings. And in this way, it is, again, of a fundamentally different character to the very motivations of revolution that drive the philosophy of Wagner's trilogy.

Outside Theology

After *Thoughts on Death and Immortality,* Wagner turned to Feuerbach's more famous work, *The Essence of Christianity* (1841). He later alluded, fairly enough, to its 'unhelpful prolixity', but some of its language nevertheless found its way into Wagner's own thinking.[16] Feuerbach reverses the ancient story about the order of the universe, arguing that the entity we call God is nothing more than the hypostatization of human qualities. As he puts it: 'Man has given objectivity to himself, but has not recognised the object as his own nature'.[17] Theology, the study of God's attributes, must therefore give way to anthropology, since 'the knowledge of God

[is] nothing else than a knowledge of man!'[18] The division of the universe into a God with his perfect attributes—all-loving, knowing, and powerful—and his creations, who are in all respects his inferiors, immediately voids the human world of confidence in its special qualities: 'The impoverishing of the real world and the enriching of God', he writes, 'is one act'.[19] Feuerbach sees his anthropological deflation of the existence of God as producing two essential outcomes. First is the de-alienation of the human essence. God is denied and the qualities that were once ascribed to him are restored to humanity. The second involves an appreciation of what he calls 'real man'.[20] The concrete, physical reality of human beings supersedes the 'mere abstraction',[21] a being without physical needs, devised by religion. From this stems Feuerbach's vision for a new community that is appropriate to our 'real' human nature. Its realization requires a supersession of the lower forms of living that are imposed on us by the theological worldview as it prevails in modern societies. There are obvious parallels between Feuerbach's notion of 'real man' and Wagner's notion of 'the purely human', a phrase that appears throughout *The Artwork of the Future* and *Opera and Drama*.[22]

It is also important to note, though, that Wagner does not adopt the neat inversions—in which the categories used to frame theological qualities are reconstructed as anthropological, human qualities—that drive Feuerbach's transformative world view. His focus is on the degrading practices demanded by Christianity as an earthly institution rather than the alienation of the human essence produced through theological constructions of the perfect being, God. The question of God was not, in fact, of any great consequence for Wagner. That in itself is an interesting point when we contrast him with his contemporary, Marx, who, at least in his earlier days, followed Feuerbach in drawing a direct connection between the content of the theistic notion of the universe and the correlative degradation of humanity.[23] Wagner, the artist and son of artists, unlike the scions of religious households (including Nietzsche with his Archimedean 'death of God' thesis), did not see the meaning of God as bearing in any way on the confidence of human beings to create the conditions for their freedom, happiness, or social order. His nonexistence was not a giddying opportunity, but, for Wagner, an irrelevance. Feuerbach's place in Wagner's philosophy is therefore attenuated from the very start precisely because the supposed nature of God is, for Wagner, no purloined source of human excellence. Wagner appropriates Feuerbach from within a framework that has no prior sense of a metaphysical entity that needs to be given material reinterpretation. His approach is, rather, social. Once Christianity, as well as industry and feudal rule, are abandoned, human beings will begin to see their emancipation from the miserable practices that prevent them from attaining their ends.

More specifically, we might see traces of Wagner's key notions of involuntariness and need in Feuerbach's work. Close textual examination reveals, though, the degree to which Wagner had developed those concepts on his own terms. Feuerbach speaks frequently, especially in *The Essence of Christianity,* of the 'involuntary'—*unwillkürlich*—forces that underpin our actions. It is not, as he uses it, a term of art, but an ordinary-language word designed to capture the immediacy of feeling. Furthermore, it has, for him, no positive or truth-revealing status: we might have involuntarily immediate responses to religion, due to our formation, or to sensuality. As we shall see, Wagner, by contrast, tends to identify involuntariness as a meaning-producing freedom and therefore as a good which must be nurtured by revolutionary social arrangements.

We can also discern a difference in the grammatical forms this concept takes in both thinkers. We find it in adjectival and nominal form in Wagner's texts, as both *unwillkürlich* and *Unwillkür,* but only as the former in Feuerbach. This indicates the status Wagner grants it as a kind of property of human beings, a faculty, so to speak, and not simply a quality of actions. A further important divergence is visible in the connection Wagner discerns between necessity and the idea of the involuntary. The notion of necessity is frequently in use in Feuerbach's texts, but it is never connected, as it is by Wagner, with involuntariness. The difference can, again, be explained by Wagner's interest in finding in involuntariness the ground of a humanly worthy freedom. And as freedom it has—as has yet to be explained—the force of necessity.

It is possible that Wagner's key idea of need, *Noth,* also bears some level of Feuerbachian provenance.[24] That very idea is, as we have seen, caught up in a range of everyday usages that are resistant to philosophical authority. The word—though not necessarily as a concept—appears with some frequency in *The Essence of Christianity*. In many instances, it is a synonym for ordinary need (in the sense of *Bedürfnis,* as discussed earlier).[25] At other times, it carries the sense of urgent necessity (connecting it with the etymologically related word, *Notwendigkeit,* necessity).[26] However, *Noth* is also used in that text in ways that carry the existential and experiential connotations found in Wagner. It may be notable that where this occurs Feuerbach is usually drawing on scriptural and theological sources. In this context, *Noth* connotes trouble or crisis, and God is identified as the relief to that suffering.[27] What is of particular interest, notwithstanding Feuerbach's atheism, is his claim that '[i]f the personal God has a true sympathy with distress, he must himself suffer distress [*Noth*]'.[28] What this introduces is the importance of a capacity to be affected as the basis of a concern for others. In this vein he also claims: 'Where there is no pressure, no want [*Noth*], there is no feeling;—and feeling is alone real knowledge. Who can know compassion without having felt the want of it? justice without the experience of injustice? happiness without the experience of distress [*Noth*]?'[29]

It will be clear enough that Wagner's attacks on the philosophers and pedants, launched in but not confined to the two revolution-themed poems we touched upon earlier, invoke the dispositions required to feel distress, to be attuned to needfulness. What must be said, though, to problematize the conclusion that Wagner may have just copied this idea is that in Feuerbach's hands it is not a technical term, a critical concept, nor even a thematized and identified idea. It is used (again) by him as a piece of ordinary language in the course of his critique of the hypostatized entity called God. If Wagner is influenced by Feuerbach on this point, he must be credited with a reconstruction and conceptualization of the idea of *Noth*—of turning it into a tool for social criticism—rather than the importation of a ready-made idea.

Wagner's commitment to the concept of a broadly sensual human being, in contrast with a rationalist one, more clearly owes its origins to the Feuerbachian philosophy that he had read. Feuerbach understood that a materialist philosophy must place the idea of sensuality, *Sinnlichkeit*, at the centre of its accounts of experience and of freedom. It is the location of each human being's fullest connection with others and with the world. The intellect, so often the faculty lionized by philosophy, narrows experience to what is available only to itself. This general perspective was quite congenial to views Wagner held before the beginning of his philosophical phase. His adoption of the idea of sensuality as the fundamental disposition, orientation, and need of human beings required no revision of his previous commitments. Feuerbach, however, gave authority to those commitments. In *The Essence of Christianity*, he rejects the notion of 'transcendental subjectivity',[30] an abstract disembodied something, since it extricates human beings from contexts of sensuous interaction. The 'sexual instinct'[31] is discounted as an important feature of human beings and, as a consequence, a mode of connection between the sexes, as Feuerbach sees it, is diminished. The 'denial of sexual love'[32] succeeds therefore once human beings are removed from nature. Wagner was certainly aware of all of that, but we also need to mark the limits of where it determined his own thinking. Arthur Drews concludes that Wagner 'condemned every belief in an abstract truth and, with Feuerbach, intoxicated himself on the cult of the senses'.[33] However, 'the senses' are just one part of what Wagner includes within his aesthetic materialism. Alongside it stands the disposition to feel the needs of others and the quite different capacity to respond to the inner necessity of our involuntary expressivity.

Those Feuerbachian overlaps and distinctions may be relatively decipherable, but they are thrown into confusion by Wagner's later view of what his use of the idea of sensuality actually was. In the revisionary introduction found in his own collected works, he writes:

> that word [sensuality] is understood in common parlance in the evil sense of 'sensualism' or even of surrender to sensual pleasure, but in and of itself, however common it has become in the language of our philosophy, it would be better to replace it with a less ambiguous designation in theoretical presentations of such warm excitement as mine.[34]

We might dwell on the oddness of this piece of circumspection. Kant, among others, gives *Sinnlichkeit* a central philosophical place though with little fear of indecorous implications. Especially curious, though, is that the younger Wagner—a man in his late thirties—was manifestly happy to allow the ambiguity to dance its way through his thoughts on sensuality. The older and perhaps Schopenhauerian Wagner—the editor and judge of those early works—suffered an apparent and exaggerated discomfort with its connotations of sexual experience. There is nothing objectionable about radical shifts of view. The problem is that Wagner was entangled in the twin and contradictory project of both criticizing his earlier self while also denying that he was saying the things he was now disavowing.

His retrospective claim that *Sinnlichkeit* was never intended to convey anything connected with sexual pleasure is at odds with the work he had originally asked the concept to do. Rendered purely as a term for sensory life, it loses its power as a device of criticism of, for instance, Christianity's imprisoning lionization of chastity. That effort was plain for any reader to see. His interest in the moral condemnation of sensuality impressed Nietzsche who, some years later, resonantly derided Christianity's fear of sex and exposed the moralist's 'radical antagonism, a deadly hostility, to the senses' (*Sinnlichkeit*).[35] We should, then, set aside Wagner's late prudishness and recognize a fully exploited ambiguity in the very notion of sensuality: it refers both to material experience and the full range of embodied expression.

By the time Wagner came to prepare his collected works, much had changed in him. His earlier texts ripple with insinuations of the liberating significance of sexual experience, while his operatic work—*Tannhäuser*, obviously enough—sympathetically dramatizes his interest in rescuing sexual love from the chaste legends of hypocritical Christianity and of chivalry.[36] Indeed, one may well applaud Wagner's willingness to draw out and augment the significance of the anti-idealist 'sensuality' theories that happily opposed 'the intellect', abstraction, and so on, but never quite dared to invoke sexual passion or erotic connection. It would have been obvious to the younger Wagner that what was important to him about sensuality could appear to be an unseemly focus on the indecent in human nature even if he never wished to take a defiant or publicly polemical stance on its behalf.[37]

The Question of Being

The very title of Wagner's *The Artwork of the Future* is an intentional reference to Feuerbach's *Principles of the Philosophy of the Future* (1843). Although the latter is a more technical and abstract work of philosophy than *The Essence of Christianity*, its central intention seems to have given Wagner the confidence to dismiss, in like manner, the claims of idealist philosophy to have accurately conceptualized 'being'. It develops the agenda of the book that preceded it, arguing that a new philosophy, as Feuerbach puts it, must think 'in harmony and peace with the senses'.[38] This is perhaps the part of Feuerbach's philosophy that is found with the least amount of constructive revision in Wagner's work. The implications that Feuerbach believes follow from his critique of idealism are mirrored in various parts of the trilogy.

Feuerbach rails against those contemplative philosophies that have turned 'being'—to which we humans also belong—into a cold abstraction.[39] He urges that we instead recognize the human capacity for affection that gives living vibrancy to the world around us. That attitude demands a new philosophical stance, one which aligns itself with an affective connection with being. It will enable us to orient ourselves towards '"this person" or "this object", that is, the particular'.[40] Love directs us towards what is real and other than ourselves. It involves a relationship with something we do not want to reduce to our interests or ideas. Philosophy in its present condition cannot be the vehicle of access to what is genuinely valuable. It lovelessly and thereby falsely apprehends the world: 'In feelings—indeed, in the feelings of daily occurrence—the deepest and highest truths are concealed. Thus, love is the true ontological proof of the existence of an object apart from our mind'.[41]

Idealism, Feuerbach maintains, replicates the theological perspective, taking on, as it were, the point of view of God, though without his supposedly caring interest in his creations. It operates with the assumption that things are in some sense dependent on thought. What exists is indexed to the capacity of reason to validate it. In this way, being is dependent on the immanent processes of reason, that is, on the operation of philosophical judgment. Feuerbach is thinking here of Hegel's dialectical system of thought in which the totality of 'the real' is mapped out in a finite set of interconnected concepts. Idealism, detached from being proper, misses the very basis of human interactions which should, he thinks, be understood as both sensuous—in that we can see and indeed touch one another—and affective. In its blindness to these aspects of human experience, idealism forecloses the possibility of noncontractual or extralegalistic social relations. The truth of human needs, and what motivates them, is neglected.

What Feuerbach proposes here appealed to Wagner's natural affinity for materialism. We will see it echoed in a number of ideas he develops in his efforts to expose the corrupted conditions of modern life. It is worth noting, at the same time, that the criticisms of idealism put forward by Wagner, including the critique of universal history, cannot be explained by a Feuerbachian influence alone. The aesthetic dimension is distinctly his own, and it, if anything, sharpens the existential significance of what is found in Feuerbach's dismantling of the idealist notion of being. And, as we shall shortly see, Wagner's identification of a tendency in idealism—the Kantian one—is without obvious precedent in Feuerbach's texts.

On the transformative objectives of Feuerbach's work, then—the anthropological turn and the critique of philosophy—we can detect pivotal differences in Wagner. His 1850 dedication is as admirably humble as it is confusing, emphasizing overwhelming indebtedness while, at the same time, subtly hinting at an aesthetic agenda not found in Feuerbach. Philosophers more seasoned than Wagner tend to display less candour when acknowledging the influence of others. Wagner, by contrast, exhibited the enthusiastic appreciation of a literary man. Elements of Feuerbach's thought are certainly present in Wagner's reflections on the ends of life and freedom, but it is clear enough that he largely grafted pieces of what he found in Feuerbach onto his own efforts to construct a philosophy for revolution and that itself incorporated commitments that long preceded his acquaintance with Feuerbach's ideas. Wagner's intuitions were enhanced and philosophically educated by the work of Feuerbach. Rudolf Louis nicely observes that Feuerbach provided a 'maieutic service', which is, of course, a significant though quite different relationship to the paternal one too often assumed.[42] Wagner was therefore not wrong to suspect, as he put it in his dedication, that his theory 'does not perhaps at all correspond' to the appropriate use of Feuerbach's original intentions.[43] That is evident, as I have suggested, in the way he develops the concepts of involuntariness and *Noth*. And Wagner's preference for a social theory rather than one driven by a programme of antitheological redemption sets him on independent ground. The primacy of what he understood by the freedom of flesh and blood and feeling creatures determined every decision he made about what exactly in Feuerbach he wished to adopt and how he would reconstruct it.

Kantian Contrasts

Much of what Wagner has to say about freedom reads as though targeting Kantian rationalism above any of the other enemies of expressive spontaneity, including Christianity, he has variously in mind. Although it seems quite unlikely that he had heard nothing of Kant's ideas at the philosophy lectures he had attended, Kant's name is never actually mentioned in this context. That is surprising because the motivations behind many of his critical interventions are elusive without Kantianism as their implicit referent. We know that in 1869 he received a gift of Kant's collected works.[44] Perhaps they replaced an older set or individual volumes, but that addition to his library obviously occurred long after the texts concerning freedom had been written and published. Most references to Kant appear in Wagner's later writings, where he is approvingly, albeit fleetingly, identified as a precursor to the great Schopenhauer. We may assume that Wagner was eventually to become acquainted with Schopenhauer's sympathetic and elaborate treatment of Kant in volume 1 of his *The World as Will and Representation*.

One highly polemical and significant characterization of Kant appears in 'Die Noth' (the poem mentioned in chapter 1). In the fourth of its sixteen verses, he derides 'Hegel and Kant' for promoting the world of spirit and turning scornfully away from 'all earthly excrement [*von jedem ird'schen Kot*]'. They, he apostrophizes, 'know you not, need [*Noth*]'. This judgment is of enduring relevance to Wagner's worries about the rationalist notion of freedom. In the latter, in Kant's version specifically, human beings, as we shall see Wagner argue, are decontextualized and converted into thinkers who operate according to some 'higher rule' quite disconnected from what is properly human.[45]

Kant's theory of freedom is demandingly rich in detail and systematic complexity. Among its core principles are several which can serve us at least as critical foils for Wagner's thoughts on free human action. It is important to stress that Wagner's position is not reducible to anti-Kantianism. It is actually more ambitious in its scope than that. Its achievements, however, are easier to appreciate once set in contrast with Kant's main theses, particularly those on the nature of necessity, self-control, and happiness. I will defer discussion of happiness to the chapter on the social aspects of freedom which follows from this one since, for Wagner, happiness is a condition of the free person in an affective, expressive, and morally excellent community.

Kantian Necessity

Kant writes that '*duty is the necessity of an action from respect for law*'.[46] He connects duty in his specific sense—acting according to the moral law—with freedom. The law is what is sanctioned by reason, and obedience to it is therefore not a matter of unquestioning acquiescence. Reason involves deliberation on whatever idea we might feel inclined to act upon. Through that process, an obligatory course of action is identified. It will be devoid of all motives of self-interest, including love and happiness. It will also be logically consistent with itself in not recommending any universal principle for action—a law—which annihilates itself (for example, it is contradictory to make a law of theft since that would thereby negate the very idea of property whose positive status is required for the practice of theft).[47] Underlying this description of the rationality of the moral law is Kant's assumption that human beings are, as he puts it, 'determinable by reason'.[48] What he means is that we human beings are capable of acting according to the purest reasons and of setting aside motivations that come from other features of our humanity. The moral law—as noted, sanctioned by reason—'represents a possible action as good and thus as necessary' for rational beings.[49] As the famous dictum of moral philosophy puts it, 'ought implies can'. Necessity means that the moral law is non-optional, that is, binding for rational beings. Rational beings freely choose the moral law as necessarily action guiding. The very act of accepting the necessity of what reason presents to us as a law—by means of our deliberation—is the supreme act of freedom since it is the very moment in which we place ourselves above the compulsions of nature. To allow, by contrast, our passions to govern us is to surrender to nature and therefore to unfreedom.

An early though longstanding objection to that position is that human freedom should involve the whole human being, not simply that part that can engage with convincing abstractions and in emotionally detached refection. Is there not, to put it another way, freedom in acts that are sensuous and expressive of who we individually are? Kant of course recognizes the force of that dimension of our nature, but freedom—which is present where we act through 'duty'—requires that we subdue it under what he calls 'necessitation'.[50] Necessitation is burdensome, even if it is on the side of the good, of morality. And precisely because it is motivated by a rational preference for the moral law, it is an act of freedom. Something, though, appears to be lost here, particularly when we consider a distinction Kant makes between the response to the natural law by a 'holy' will and the will of creatures like us: 'The moral law is . . . for the will of a perfect being a law of holiness',[51] that is, it commands the perfect being who will respond to its demands without reluctance or hesitation. But, he continues, 'for the will of every finite rational being' the moral law is 'a law of duty, of moral necessitation'.[52] The rational character of a finite being—namely, an adult human being—entails the ability to recognize the necessity of the moral law: again, it is not optional. For the nonrational side of our humanity, however, it is a different matter. It may attempt to defy the rational motivations of our higher selves, but at that moment necessitation ought to make its presence felt. We do what our rational will commands even though our creaturely being continues to urge otherwise. Necessitation seems, though, to fall short of the quality of freedom that is ascribed to perfect beings: spontaneity. What is displaced here, when we think of moral action as necessitation, is the paradigm of spontaneous rational response to reasons that seem wholly part of us. It is, rather, a complex experience of struggle. Kant insists, nevertheless, that this is no less a freedom than the happily experienced freedom of spontaneous rational response: both are grounded in respect for the moral law. One must wonder whether Kant is really speaking about freedom and not simply morality if discipline is demanded of those whose dispositions do not orient them freely and readily to aligning their wills with the law. These worries—the tensions between freedom and discipline and the restricted sphere of freedom's interest—have shadowed Kant's theory from the very start. Even though, as we shall see, Wagner is quite opposed to the notion of rational freedom, he is, in fact, a proponent of the notion that spontaneity is a key quality of freedom.[53] The challenge he faces, as we shall see, is in advancing that notion while eschewing the principle of the priority of reason.

Kantian Control

In contrast with the concept of necessity, 'control' (*Gewalt,* also to be understood in the sense of having power over something or someone) is not an idea that Kant formally thematizes. It is mentioned only in passing yet has an implicit underpinning role in how we are to think of the operation of moral agents. A significant statement of its function occurs in his *Metaphysics of Morals.* There Kant writes:

> Since virtue is based on inner freedom it contains a positive command to a human being, namely to bring all his capacities and inclinations under his [reason's] control [*Gewalt*] and so to rule over himself, which goes beyond forbidding him to let himself be governed by his feelings and inclinations (the duty of *apathy*); for unless reason holds the reins of government in its own hands, his feelings and inclinations play the master over him.[54]

This claim lucidly foregrounds what a rationalist notion of freedom demands. The key idea is that human beings have the power to bring their inclinations 'under their control'. And elsewhere Kant states that acting in the right way presupposes 'the idea of a reason having complete control over all subjective motives'.[55] Kant does not explore the psychological dimensions of this notion, but it is apparent that control of this kind requires a particularly powerful self, an ego that can take possession of itself according to directives it takes to be supreme. It involves the ego's capacity and willingness to police what moves it. The absence of control—or self-rule—will mean surrender to 'feelings and inclinations', and therefore the absence of the power to respond to the kind of rational necessity we saw in the previous section. Under those conditions, freedom is essentially impossible. Much of the substance of this position is directly challenged by Wagner's idea that freedom does not consist in—implicitly—the ego-control of experiences.

Another feature of Kant's notion of control emerges from the question of what purpose it is to serve in the actual world of human interactions. Although not an explicit commitment, it can be interpreted as containing a sociopolitical dimension that is not immediately apparent when the discussion seems to be focused on the narrow practical question of self-regulation or self-control. Kant's position, in fact, presupposes—even if he does not acknowledge this—a social order of a particular kind, one from which his idealized model of human capacities follows in a derivative way. It is the modern state where behavioural expectations are based on certain assumptions about the ability of each individual to regulate their actions—that is, a disposition of self-control—according to authoritative norms and, strikingly, to show the reasons for their actions. Wagner's position, by contrast, projects quite different sociopolitical arrangements together with an accompanying notion of freedom that is appropriate to it. The latter comes with no criterion of control simply because it is not a notion freighted with the need to make freedom accountable to authority, a need which itself generates reasons-giving practices.

Wagnerian Necessity

Wagner uses the word 'necessity'—*Notwendigkeit*—in various ways. It is not, however, a fatally equivocal concept, in that its different though complementary connotations are generally kept separate from each other in specific discussions. Alongside the meaning we are exploring—its connection with the experience of freedom, where Wagner holds that the essence of 'free individuality is necessity'[56]—Wagner also speaks about the necessity of nature and of human necessities as authentic need. By the 'necessity of nature', Wagner intends the processes naturally inscribed in things. We have seen the force of that claim in some of Wagner's thoughts about the inevitability of revolutionary transformation. There is a familiar version of normativity accompanying this thought: Wagner believes that what nature ordains is essentially right. This natural order can, nevertheless, be violated by the false values, unsympathetic socialization, and practices found within certain contingent historical configurations. Those are artificial, the thought goes, because they stem from processes that are quite independent of nature's laws.

'Die Noth' derides what Wagner sees as the contrived assemblage of 'higher rules' and 'mental whistles' at the centre of rationalist philosophy.[57] The latter purloins the idea of necessity, connecting it exclusively with the directives of reason which Wagner consistently interprets as secondary to the truer motivations of our natural wills. In the arrogated role given to it by philosophy, it is an imposition that distorts our capacities to respond affectively, and thereby spontaneously, to ourselves and to others. Necessity must, he maintains, be extricated from that rationalism. If Wagner was self-consciously attempting to remodel the very meanings Kant had given to the terms surrounding the idea of necessity, he again did not say so. And nor does he reference Friedrich Schiller—another artist-philosopher—whose *Letters on the Aesthetic Education of Humanity* were an earlier effort to articulate an idea of freedom that both opposes Kant's version while remaining overtly indebted to the Kantian terminology of 'necessity'. Like Wagner some half a century later, Schiller rejects the idea that rationality has primacy in action we call free. A sensuous dimension is indispensable to any viable theory of freedom. Schiller famously develops a notion of emancipated human action based on the model of play, an essential human activity that, he maintains, can encompass both rules—any playful activity operates under norms that make and limit it to the specific form of play it is—and sensuousness in that it involves physicality, that is, purposeful bodily movement, adjusting to the singularity of the situation. As he contends: 'Man only plays when he is in the fullest sense of the word a human being', and freedom is the quality of actions marked out as playful.[58] Schiller is uncertain about how the phenomenon of free play is to be captured as one of necessity. He is troubled by the pains of 'necessitation' connected with moral duty. Yet play is identified as a higher form of necessity which somehow reconciles and transcends the dismal necessity of dutifulness and the wanton necessity of physical compulsion.

Wagner travels in a similar direction to Schiller in that he holds that 'necessity' captures something of the quality of genuine freedom. It is involuntary 'inner, free necessity', not the product or perhaps process of deliberation.[59] This necessity is incompatible with that necessitation which involves a disciplined subjection of the self to a principle it does not experience as especially appealing. Freedom is a wholly positive experience, in Wagner's view. I have noted that Kant's idea of necessity can be understood as the non-optionality of a good reason presented to a rational being. To disregard the reason would be to disavow one's rationality. Wagner's use of the concept of necessity works within an entirely different conception of the human space. Freedom, for him, is experienced where action has been produced by our authentic impulses, impulses that stem from our needfulness as individuals and communal beings, but also as creators. To deny those impulses is somehow to disfigure oneself. And most importantly of all and contrary to the necessitation thesis, the suppression of those impulses is not an act that can glorify itself as 'freedom'. This is the basis of his claim that we must 'free ourselves into the necessity of nature' because we have come to understand that it—in contradistinction to the artifices of reason—is the real basis of our humanity.[60] As he also puts it:

> To overcome these errors, to recognize human life according to the necessity of its individual and social nature, and ultimately *to give shape to it* because it lies within our power, has been a drive of humanity ever since it gained the capacity to understand the essence of natural phenomena; for from this understanding we have won the measure for understanding the essence of humanity itself.[61]

Nature will not, then, simply assert itself to defeat the distortions which history has imposed on it. It is impossible to refashion nature permanently against itself, indeed, but our *knowledge* of what our nature consists in is the key to releasing the forms of life and freedom most appropriate to us.

It is Wagner's thought that we cannot, as noted above, advance any plausible account of freedom that excludes the powerful, deeply human reality of sensuality. Some story about the connection of freedom and, in particular, necessity with sensuality needs to be offered. Sensuality, as we have seen, is not to be confused for that bare passive capacity philosophy has labelled 'sensibility'. The word *Sinnlichkeit* covers both sensuality and sensibility. Used in the latter sense, it belongs to the mechanics of those theories that wish to explain knowledge as something we gain 'through the senses'. Sensuality, by contrast, is dynamic, unpredictable, and creative. We might say that for Wagner philosophy fails because it falls into what could be called the Beckmesser problem: it sees freedom only in adherence to formal principles, to laws and not to spontaneity.[62] The mistake of 'our metaphysicians'[63]—who indeed equally exclude sensuality and sensibility—Wagner claims, is to appropriate the necessity that underpins life-based freedom—freedom in our sensuous existence—and to grant it instead to 'conscious arbitrary thought'.[64] 'Thought' in that way attempts to predetermine what should count as valid experience. It thereby denigrates what sensuousness urges, while promoting the distinctive medium of philosophy itself, so-called pure thought, as the essence of human freedom. Wagner writes: 'If the spirit is necessity in itself, then life is what is arbitrary, a fantastic masque, an idle pastime, a frivolous whim, a "*car tel est notre plaisir*" of the spirit'.[65] He regards the edicts of the spirit as mere philosophical confabulations. When imposed on human beings, they are arbitrary, an attempted arrogation of necessity. Human beings are creatures for whom life is the totality of their material activities, and that essentially places them in a realm that is not subject to the supposed governance of spirit.

Although Wagner does not use the terms of art found across scholarship on German idealism, it is apparent that he has an interest in exposing the idea of a supposed 'autonomy of reason'. There are two core elements to that idea. First, reason is autonomous in the sense that it is not a part of the causal processes of nature. It is therefore thought to be capable of asserting itself—of being operationalized, so to speak—in our reflective moments without interference from our biological urges, selfish needs, or conventional habits. Second, that separation from nature somehow affords reason a valence that means it has authority over human affairs. It is supreme in directing moral action and may not therefore be overwritten by considerations not originating in reason itself. Reason, in this way, is thought, again, to have necessity. What ought to happen in human affairs must be produced by or be consistent with reason. Actions not grounded in reason, by contrast, are arbitrary. (Reason—in this autonomous sense—is also said to be evident in the structure of history in which social evolution tends towards a rational society in spite of the selfish intentions of human beings.) Fully autonomous reason does not claim that it discovers the laws that should govern human beings. Rather, it commends itself for giving rise to those laws. Reason is sovereign in determining what is lawful and therefore necessary. There are two dimensions of operating according to reason: (i) *submission* of what is not reason—that is, nature—to reason; and (ii) the *construction* of laws for us that are consistent with reason and nothing outside reason.

Wagner responds critically to the elevation of reason through a counterproposal which reconceives the relationship between freedom and necessity such that acting out of nature becomes the essential quality of what we think of as freedom. His anti-idealistic claim is that the capacity for thought has been mistaken for a constitutive force, and this has licensed it to rewrite the very idea of what it means to be a human being. In Wagner's view, the very ideas of necessity and arbitrariness have been inverted. As he satirically puts it:

> But where thinking leaves behind this connecting chain, where it, after double and triple self-objectification, finally grasps itself as its own ground, where spirit does not see itself as the final and most conditioned, but as the first and most unconditioned activity, and therefore as the ground and cause of nature—then the bond of necessity is also broken, and arbitrariness rushes without restraint—without limit, freely, as our metaphysicians think—through the workshop of thought, pouring itself as a stream of madness into the world of reality.[66]

The view against which Wagner is arguing here is that the autonomy of reason authorizes itself to order whatever it is not (to submit to it). But since, in Wagner's view, reason has misappropriated this authority, its regulations are arbitrary, capricious (*willkürlich*). They have no proper connection with the thing they attempt to govern. It is interesting that Wagner speaks of this process as madness. He understands madness as the violent implementation of rules that are not inherent in what it is that is to be governed by them. Indeed, Wagner distinctly connects the very enterprise of philosophy—again, rationalist idealism implicitly—with that madness: of making nature subordinate to thought. Once thought—'the unconditioned'—is posited as autonomous, he argues, nature becomes unnecessary in principle, and reason takes on the authority to construct, to create new forms of life and of values from its own independent standpoint. It is a standpoint which is defined as separate from nature. But nature, Wagner maintains, does not simply vanish with the elevation of reason: it becomes something to be controlled. Its existence is then interpreted as 'superfluous, even harmful' to the pretences of a self that encompasses itself fully through its own thinking.[67]

Wagner's positive project adopts the contrasting approach. And it does so with direct rejection of the submission and constructivist principles. Against the *constructivist* principle, Wagner maintains that adopting a priority of nature perspective means that human knowledge is—in this sphere at least—the capacity to uncover though not to determine nature. What was unknown or unconscious (*unbewußt*), as Wagner puts it, is brought to knowledge.[68] And Wagner understands that knowledge to have ramifications for the emancipation of human actions, ramifications that directly deny the *submission* principle.

The Aesthetic Model

Wagner models the notion of a sensuously grounded freedom on the experience of necessity within the processes of aesthetic production. This is perhaps the central element of the materialism that underpins his philosophy for revolution. It is a new conception of human action, and he takes it to be wholly consonant with aesthetic freedom. Wagner understands necessity in the sphere of aesthetic production as a decisive criterion in determining the authentic qualities of a work of art. The artist succeeds if they have responded to what is aesthetically 'necessary' rather than to what is dictated by exogenous factors that Wagner labels 'arbitrary', factors that have come from without the aesthetic process.

Wagner's first published discussion of this notion of aesthetic freedom as the ideal for human freedom occurs in *Art and Revolution*. The poet, he claims, creates 'without behest [*Geheiß*], by himself, and out of inner natural necessity'.[69] Wagner then connects this thought with freedom: 'art is the highest freedom, and only the highest freedom can make it [i.e. art] manifest; no command [*Befehl*], no prescription [*Verordnung*], in short, no extra-artistic purpose can give rise to it'.[70] As Wagner claims, the artist relies on 'involuntary' and 'unforced [*unerzwungen*]' inspiration. (We might note contrastingly the significance of the negative feeling of compulsion in Kant's notion of necessitation.[71]) Authentic artistic production is, in this way, a process of necessity. The artist moves, as Wagner also puts it, from arbitrary choices towards a necessity in which we arrive at 'the eradication of the last traces of creative arbitrariness'.[72] The necessity here is the non-optionality of what presents itself to the artist within the process of aesthetic production. To reject what is presented amounts to withdrawing from one's very identity as an artist, a decision analogous to the rationalists' notion of our self-denial as rational beings when we reject what is determined by reason. Wagner does not consider this necessity to be an external force which somehow inflicts a creative duty on the artist. It was perhaps as a consequence of his extraordinary facility for production—in music, drama, poetry, prose, and correspondence—that Wagner did not dally with the image of the tormented artist. Creation, rather, is joyous and free, with the artist experiencing the process as their own. Importantly, it is unprompted by 'arbitrary' considerations (the nonnecessary ones noted above). The connection between freedom and *Unwillkür* is thus established: aesthetic necessity is involuntary yet free and is not experienced or produced by calculation or detached deliberation. What is not excluded here, though it is not stated, is the artist's awareness of their own process, their sense of their unfolding project, its missteps and the corrections required to bring it forward. There is therefore judgment, an assessment of each step, but it is not, and this is Wagner's point, strictly determined by or loyal to any preconception of the final product.

This 'involuntary' freedom is tied harmoniously to nature. That connection will at first seem obscure. It starts with the idea that freedom is a process within the sphere of material action. As such, it is, Wagner believes, indissociable from nature's processes. There is a great deal more to this than the notion that action is empirical or takes place within the material world. Indeed, that is the wrong way entirely to frame Wagner's thinking. And that is because nature is not, for Wagner, an abstract noun encompassing the totality of causal processes recognizable by science. Nature is, rather, a source of order, though it, obviously enough, does not hold unwavering dominion over actual human choices. Countervailing influences may always assert themselves, giving us responses that *seem* to be spontaneously experienced but are the product of, for example, a false morality. Wagner maintains that the integration of our sensuous drives with our natural order will see us cast off the arbitrary antilife prescriptions of 'religion, nationality or the state'.[73] And this is because, he argues, nature—'true human nature'[74]—has in some way implanted in human beings a capacity for life which they can realize once they cease to place themselves outside or in opposition to nature. The variety of freedom Wagner attributes to us involves recognition and endorsement of our natural dispositions. In that space, the human being, 'joyfully conscious' of their 'connection with nature', 'becomes free'.[75]

Wagner, then, is unsympathetic to those conceptions of nature that are produced by a dualistic thinking which tells us that there is simple nature on the one hand, fully governed by causality and therefore devoid of spontaneity and freedom, and, on the other, nonnature—spirit, mind, intellect—which is the locus of freedom because it stands apart from the space of causes. The notion of nature produced by that dualistic division of life is burdened with assumptions about a world that is fundamentally mechanical in structure. And it leaves 'spirit' in some special space that is fantastically untouched by nature, particularly by sensuousness. Wagner's primacy of the aesthetic—directly opposed to the idea of the autonomy of reason, as discussed earlier—provides a fruitful way of thinking of freedom that is not distracted by that peculiarly modern dualism. Aesthetic creation is fully experienced as freedom, yet its basis is sensuous, that is, feeling located in time and space. Creativity is a matter of responding to impulses that seem welcome, compelling, and absolutely right for the work in hand. Rightness here has nothing to do with any correctness predetermined by rules of production. This is the ideal of freedom more generally: it does not operate according to rules that are preestablished, nor can it be guided by what simply appeals to others. When Wagner connects freedom with nature, then, it is not the nature of causality, but the nature of 'life'.

The freedom experienced through the 'necessity of individual involuntariness [*die Notwendigkeit der individuellen Unwillkür*]' is the necessity of doing what we ought to do once our wills and our needs are aligned.[76] That is a situation in which we can trust our impulses, knowing that what we want is what we should pursue. Clearly, this is not a matter of appetitive instincts and animal impulses: that would be to surrender to the dualism of free spirit and indifferent nature. Rather, Wagner's thoughts are oriented once again towards 'the purely human', the human being with the totality of their competences, humanity with its distinctively rich form of nature.

Although his emphasis is on our affective qualities, Wagner does not eliminate thought from the stock of distinctive human traits. By 'thought' he means our conceptual capacities particularly, our ability to abstract, identify differences, synthesize, and cognize the relations between things within the order of nature.[77] Thought is hardly to be denied its reality as a significant feature of human beings, but it cannot supplant the primacy of sensuousness—of our responsiveness to spontaneous feeling—as the basis of freedom. The characteristic error of philosophy is to confuse the freedom of its own reflective space for freedom in the wider existential and embodied context of full human life.

Wagner Against Control

We have seen Kant's declaration that the exercise of morality through 'inner freedom' commands that we bring all 'capacities and inclinations under . . . (reason's) control'. Although penned by Kant, this thought does not fall far from everyday conceptions of what is involved in the proper conduct of life. Authors before him, for instance, speak about the task of 'self-governance' as a feature of virtue. However, there is something quite particular in the association of self-control with freedom (as opposed to virtue). They become synonyms: to be free is to exercise control over what one decides to act upon. The very idea of freedom as involuntariness may seem nonsensical from this perspective. Vast swathes of the theoretical literature promoting the specifically philosophical idea of autonomy, up to the present time, continue to adhere to the principle of self-control. Without it, individuals are thought to be unable to act as effective agents in developing or protecting their legitimate personal interests. In the autonomous person, two things are controlled: first, internal motivations—a capacity to resist impulses—and, second, susceptibility to outside influences. There is, of course, a freedom not to bother with self-policing. However, those who promote autonomy as a kind of human excellence deplore declarations of apathy (see Kant above) towards taking oneself seriously or vigilantly assessing what one will be moved by.

The very different conception of necessity we have seen in Wagner's philosophy is, obviously enough, incompatible with the autonomy model of control. In *The Artwork of the Future,* he effectively rejects the control criterion of freedom by aligning freedom with 'recognition of the unconscious, the involuntary, and therefore the necessary, the real, the sensuous'.[78] This will distinguish his position from the brutal version of freedom he finds in rationalist and Christian acts of self-denial. We may be inclined to see this as outlandish, a flamboyant and illiterate way of thinking of freedom. The question really, though, is why the notion of freedom should, rather, be grounded in 'reason'. Self-evidently, discussions of freedom allow for both. Each, though in differing ways, latches onto something recognizable in human experience: the feeling of being in control of one's actions and the experience of being at one with one's spontaneous directives. How, though, is freedom without control supposed to work in societies like ours? Wagner maintains that we have no prospect for the 'involuntariness of individual action' until we can somehow bring about the 'downfall of the state',[79] a phrase he employs in *Opera and Drama*. That downfall has a necessary connection with the supersession of a control-based society. This has purchase, yet again, in the context of the rationalist notion of freedom. That theory's true commitments are all too human in that they serve to underpin a quite distinctive function of modern societies: the need for each of us to justify ourselves to others who have the authority to seek our reasons. Involuntariness, *Unwillkür*, as a quality of freedom, is radically opposed to the rationalist—deliberative—model. The implications of this difference spill beyond abstract theoretical accounts of what is the case.

A significant absence in the *Unwillkür*-based theory of freedom, then, is a mechanism for the justification of behaviour. It does not appear to entertain the question of how actions that operate without the primary guidance of reason, settled convention, habit, or simple adherence to authority are to be defended. The very question of why someone chooses one action over another assumes a shared understanding of why some things might be intelligibly preferable. That understanding will be based on existing expectations that are part of the everyday lifeworld or perhaps tethered to systems of law which for the sake of social order require obedience. Wagner's theory simply does not acknowledge this issue, but that is not entirely because of negligence on his part. What he does reflect on, taking it to be the real issue, is the difference between the abstract justification of moral action and the real feelings that give rise to benevolence. He refers critically to the 'unsubstantial ideas and non-present grounds of justification

[*Berechtigungsgründe*]' that are a feature of abstract philosophical systems.[80] The rationalist position wants to establish that there are real conditions which make plausible the demand that agents may be asked to explain themselves. A society of such agents assumes that its members will live according to certain norms of self-control. This is not only the act of not surrendering to impulse—that is, to spontaneity—but of countermanding the promptings of impulse with actions based on a range of supportable reasons.[81] This is a society of order, no doubt, but also one in which the very scope of an acceptable action is circumscribed in advance, with the state itself, Wagner's critical thought implies, authorized to corral those impulses that do not conform to what is held to be reasonable. In the variety of freedom he promotes, justification rests on 'involuntary human feeling'.[82] Feelings are a reliable basis for justifiable action 'in a human society that is essentially at one with itself'.[83] It might be important note at this point, though the issue will become clearer in the next chapter, that that society is not one governed from the centre and therefore not some anticipation of a modern state in which the loyalty of citizens is assured by their affection and not by their rational consent.

In the aesthetic model of freedom, Wagner, we see again, reaches for the analogy with creation. The right action comes from reliable feelings, just as the artist simply intuits what is right and finds no inspiration through rules. This is, to give it a name, the Walther von Stolzing paradigm, the 'involuntary' yet necessary space of free creativity.[84] And in this sense, right free action is sui generis, 'justified only from the feeling from which it arises'.[85] When Wagner speaks, therefore, of the downfall of the state, he is not simply interested in what we might call the surface problems: the unacceptable distribution of wealth and opportunity, although these clearly prompt his outrage. Of deeper significance is the transformation of the human community by removing the structures of control. The abolition of the state, in short, opens up the possibility of freedom's legitimacy as involuntariness. Social accounting, built as it is on the principle of rational self-control, is annulled. It should, however, be acknowledged that what Wagner has in mind here invokes the prospect of a kind of irrational cohesionism in which societal membership rests on supposedly wholesome intuitions that cannot be challenged by reason. That point perhaps echoes the question raised earlier about the peculiar danger that Wagner's open model of the future risks, indeed, closure of the future. The intuitive model is pursued by Wagner on the basis that it alone aligns directly with the notion of aesthetic spontaneity. Its realization necessarily entails the renunciation of anything that can be considered a separating identity. Such identities represent spaces of experience and expression that mark one group off from another, even if not essentially or prejudicially. Their ongoing existence makes it necessary to have in place well-understood, reasonable, and contestable systems of social coordination. But it is those very systems that stand in the way of an intuition-led society and ipso facto, to follow the train of Wagner's idea, an aesthetic community. The notion of individuality may seem to disappear into a negative, as that which is left over when everything we regard as a source of social antagonism is subtracted. However, Wagner maintains, as we shall see in the chapter to which we turn next, that individuality and community can exist without the subordination of one to the other or loss to the vitality of either.

4

Freedom as Social Emancipation

IT IS not unusual to find philosophers struggle to reconcile what they identify as the ideal freedom of the individual with their notion of freedom in society. Individual freedom might be a good in itself or a vital condition for the most important things of all, for example, the right of the individual to realize themselves to the fullest of their capacities. That set of concerns may, though, find itself confronted by the realities of social life, where compromise is required as individuals are obliged to curtail the scope of their choices. One kind of response to the tension between individual and social freedom is to abolish one of its terms with the declaration that we must learn to do without organized society altogether, an entity which, by its very nature, is injurious to individuality. Claims of this sort are produced essentially by a narrow conception about what freedom is. The starting point determines the path to the conclusion. It may in some cases be that individual freedom is conceived in isolation from the ineliminable contexts in which life takes place, resulting, quite predictably, in the view that societal obligations are secondary, mere impositions. The history of political thought has produced a number of positions marked by this perspective. The divergence between the two spheres, alternatively, might be down to the different normative registers that prompt the analyses. Personal freedom could, for example, be conceived along the lines of moral thinking, where the individual must do only what is right according to some demanding standard of virtue they have chosen to live by. Adjacent to this is the register of action in which a relationship to others under broader social norms is the focus. A paradigmatic case of this kind of divergence is found in Kant, whose interpreters continue to offer a range of criticisms of and solutions to the differing kinds of obligations he places on the person in his moral and political philosophies respectively. These two registers are not logically complementary, but nor are they mutually exclusive in practice. They leave the individual who takes both dimensions of freedom seriously (personal and societal) with practical challenges about which one to weigh more heavily in different situations. Realism might declare that this flexibility is an intrinsic feature of societies willing to tolerate significant manageable differences among their members.

Wagner contests the notion that these divisions are intractable. The conflict between the individual and the community is indeed real, but it is not final or rooted in the dispositions of human nature. Philosophy makes that conflict into something essential. The critique of the forms of freedom produced by a fragmented and unfree society can, Wagner believes, contribute to the realization of a community in which individuality and social intercourse are mutually enforcing and reciprocally enabling. This kind of holistic thinking may sound well and good in principle, but without some specific account of the various elements encompassed within its view of freedom, it threatens to have the character of a magical conclusion. What is required of Wagner, among other things, is plausible identification of the connections that supposedly pertain between the freedom that is instantiated in 'individual involuntariness' and the freedom of individuals among others, where others are a positive condition of individual freedom, not a hellish nuisance or mere potential partners in beneficially transactional exchanges. And, importantly, the theory has to affirm individuality in a genuine sense, where difference is valid and diversity not a problem that needs to be resolved.

Wagner's holistic intent in some respects echoes the fervid romanticism found in Germany in the decade or two before his birth. He shares with so-called 'Frühromantik' a rejection of reason as an appropriate way of either organizing or understanding human communities. In no small degree, this position was originally prompted in response to ever-growing scepticism about the revolution in France. Enthusiasm for the destruction of the old order gripped German intellectual circles, but the failures evident in the inhumane abstract ruling principles that replaced it motivated new thinking on the place of affection and religiosity in cohesive communities. Alongside that concern there is also, though in varying measures, an emphasis on the nonnegotiable significance of free individuality—in its uniqueness and diversity—and, vitally, community is identified as an indispensable condition for its fulfilment.

As we shall see, Wagner's political theory shows sympathy for the broad ideals just mentioned, even if they never appear by name. But there is much also that separates him from the romantic strain of thought. The first, most significantly, is time and place. The bucolic Germany which was home to the early romantics lay sixty years or so in the past. The shimmering beauty of the Thuringian landscape, the melancholic remnants of a Christian feudal world were not necessarily the primary visual stimulants to the critical intellect. Wagner lived in Saxony as it emerged as an industrial region. It boasted the first long-distance railway in Germany, connecting Leipzig, the city of Wagner's birth, with Dresden, the place in which his revolutionary disposition would ultimately express itself in action. That modernization is no incidental fact in Wagner's biography. He attests to it through imagery that brings Friedrich Engels's Manchester to mind. His social analyses are never clouded by nostalgia for a premodern world saturated with an uncorrupted German spirit. As a class-conscious revolutionary, he was suspicious of the true objectives of images of a national past. He did not, at that time, endorse the medievalism that had crept into German romanticism, even if it is a feature of some of his prerevolutionary dramas, not least because of its attachment to a stratified and constraining Christian social order.

The project Wagner begins in *Art and Revolution* is sustained to a significant degree by an idealized image of freedom in the social world of ancient Greece. Very importantly, though, that image should not be interpreted as the product of aesthetic yearning for that reality. For Wagner, Greece is, rather, an encouraging example which allows him to develop a conception of freedom that can be critically relevant to contemporary society and, in a new form, attainable in the future. His conceptual approach is holistic, and hence the absence of those tensions that typically arise within theories of freedom whose bias lies either on the side of the individual or of the societal. Wagner endeavours to conceive individual and community together, never in isolation. This means that the individual cannot be reduced to a social function, as that diminishes rather than recognizes the particularity of each person. Equally, society is no collection of individuals externally connected to each other through laws.

This chapter will begin with the lessons Wagner thought we could take from the Greeks and their intuitively developed societies. A repeated commitment throughout the trilogy is to the exemplarity of 'the natural customs of all peoples'. They can guide us to 'recognize the truth of human nature in its full nobility, its real beauty', as Wagner puts it.[1] However, it is the Greeks who can be credited with the most humanly appropriate forms of social life yet established. Their accomplishments, he maintains, should serve as valuable precedents for us. What needs to be understood is how a model that emerged somehow naturally can be relevant to the age of self-conscious politics. That salience is perhaps at its most effective where Wagner employs the Greek model to generate his diagnoses of the pathologies of modern society, that is, those behaviours that are ingrained in us through suffocating socialization—habit, as Wagner labels it—but which are independent of the ends of freedom and well-being. The chapter concludes with a consideration of the affective dimensions of freedom, its significance for interpersonal life and for the happiness of individuals themselves.

The Greek Ideal

The Greek ideal infuses an array of Wagner's key theses, not least, as we have seen, the aesthetic model of the Gesamtkunstwerk. The appeal of their world is founded in what Wagner regards as the highly differentiated forms of individuality their societies actively sustained. It was not until *German Art and German Politics*, a piece from 1867, that Wagner made his first published observation on J. J. Winckelmann. He, together with Lessing, is praised for allowing the modern world a glimpse of the superior and spontaneous reality of the Greeks: 'Hail to you, *Winckelmann* and *Lessing*, who, even beyond the centuries of your own German glory, found and recognized the ancestral relatives, the divine Hellenes', whose exemplary ideas of human beauty contrasted with the decadent 'powder-dusted' model given to Europe by French civilization.[2] Winckelmann's influential work, *The History of Art in Antiquity* (1764), was dedicated primarily to the genius that gave rise to the artforms of the ancients. He also provided, albeit briefly, a number of thoughts on the political conditions that were uniquely conducive to their exceptional creativity. He maintains that their democratic system in which 'the entire nation never recognized a sole ruler' meant that the Greeks had no debilitating social distinctions.[3] Each person was equally empowered in politics, and the freedoms provided by the 'constitution and government of Greece' are 'the chief reason for their arts' superiority'.[4] The principle that Wagner evidently extracted from Winckelmann, at some point, was that flattened structures of power alone can provide individual freedom not just for a special class, but universally. Those structures must be robust if over time they are to sustain spaces of creativity, self-realization, and voluntary social cooperation. The notion of a differentiated individuality is derived from the extraordinary creativity of the Greeks, a reality that could not have been possible in socially and aesthetically underdeveloped or conformist communities.

The Greece we are presented with here is manifestly a romanticized version, purified of the bloody events placed on record by those classical historians of whom Wagner could hardly have been ignorant. This is typical of a general prejudice of that dreamy German Hellenism to which Wagner subscribed, where contrasting Rome is identified as the repository of all we can count as disordered civilization: brute law, joyless living, carnage, ugliness, and the absence of a communal or general spirit. It was, Wagner writes, a world of 'self-contempt, disgust with existence, dread of community'.[5] Unlike the Romans, the Greeks lived without inhibition, with restless creative energy, willing to give their all to protect their achievements and producing in themselves, as he puts it, 'the most unceasing, freest development'.[6] That vibrant precedent suggests that individuality and freedom are fully compatible with social order once that order is willing to reinvent itself as required by developing human talents. A repressive society may justify itself in the name of stability, but its capacity to reproduce itself will be limited since it is indifferent to the ultimately ineradicable need each individual has for fulfilment. It is precisely because a tumultuous and richly varied society provides the ideal conditions for individuality that its members, Wagner claims, willingly protect it from all existential enemies. They share, in a sense, a spirit that appreciates the value of the very variety their social arrangements uniquely permit.

Wagner also points to the Greek's special capacity to perceive the internal threat of the 'tyrant'. Capturing their vigilance in terms coinciding with republican theory, he notes that the people would never lapse into 'soft trust' in a ruler who could never ultimately be contested and under whose whims they would have to live.[7] Power was diffused among the citizens with freedom a responsibility falling to all. The Greeks perceived tradition as an even more insidious danger than that of the autocrat. No norm, Wagner claims, could gain enduring influence with them simply because it was 'venerable'.[8] What mattered, rather, was the compatibility of a norm with free development. Traditional practice could be summarily nullified by the people whenever it was perceived to be life stifling.

The society portrayed here was not preserved by coercion, caution, or by fear of disagreement or plurality. It had its grounds, supposedly, in the fortuitous 'success of natural development' which was to the Greeks 'a half unconscious gift'.[9] If that is the case, however, the Greeks might seem to serve, quite difficultly, as both an encouraging yet impossible precedent: we would prefer not to think of ourselves as naive about the kind of societies in which we want to live. A free society will emerge, if at all, only through a conscious project of renewal rather than by way of the good fortune enjoyed by the Greeks. Wagner insists, nevertheless, that such a society can be informed by what we know of the Greek precedent. As a programme for political development, this must sound dissatisfyingly vague.

Arguably, however, rigorous theory is not the only source of political motivation. Indeed, it may even by itself be rather puny as the basis for prompting social renewal. There is also the value of the force of example. It invites some level of imitation though not reproduction. Exemplary models encourage us to believe that human beings are capable of more than they have come to see in themselves. Wagner's turn to the Greeks is based on that principle: to recognize that life today, with its pains and disorders, is not the final word on social relations. And that is motivating even if we acknowledge that the Greeks' path to their society was an unconscious one: their societies were human, as ours too can be, he maintains. Across the texts, Wagner is in fact consistent in holding that our relation to the Greeks is to be one of informed and critical learning rather than replication.

The Greek model, then, largely has its place within Wagner's philosophy as a critical comparator. He does not invite us simply to worship the past and has no inclination, therefore, to glorify it in all its aspects. Its exemplarity is not to be confused for perfection. Hence Wagner is anxious to highlight a fundamental rupture between our age and the Greeks where right, in fact, falls in our favour. We abhor slavery, and its prevalence in the ancient world does nothing to give it redeeming moral value. It rested on what Wagner decries as an exclusionary view of humanity. The Greeks erred in finding dependence upon slavery for basic labour perfectly consistent with the highest ideals of their own society.[10] Wagner, in this way, does not align himself with those apologists who might regret the Greek institution of slavery but insist that it was not an intrinsic property of Greek culture, but rather an unfortunate side practice, a forgivable lapse shared with all ancient cultures but one without which—we should not forget—the Greeks could never have managed to bequeath the world all kinds of unparalleled splendours. Wagner is rigorously free of a relativism that would leave the Greeks to their own strictly internally defensible web of norms. The Greeks should have recognized, as we do, the antinatural and therefore arbitrary basis of human bondage.

No person, he declares, has enslavement as 'his nature'. It is inflicted by others as 'his destiny, the sin of history against his nature'.[11] The Greeks—Aristotle included, we can add—deluded themselves with the notion that the 'slave, by his mere existence as a slave' was a slave by necessity.[12] This deformation, however, cannot be sustained because nature itself does not ultimately accommodate itself to what is contrary to it, and for Wagner slavery is a violation of our nature as human beings. The affectivity of human beings is distorted in the creation of a class of people who supposedly do not need to be loved. That distortion is characteristic of all societies up to the present time, albeit in differing ways. And it is the reason why those societies must inevitably fail. In the case of the Greek state, he writes:

> No, we do not wish to become Greeks again; for what the Greeks did not know, and precisely because of which they had to collapse, 'we' know. That very fall, the cause of which we now recognize after long misery and out of the deepest universal

> suffering, shows us clearly what we must become: it shows us that we must love all people in order to love ourselves again, in order to be able to regain joy in ourselves.[13]

The end of slavery is not conceived as a moment of liberal progress where new ideas about who should be respected broaden the application of freedom. The normativity of our natural dispositions is, ultimately, the source of that respect. Without it, we rely mistakenly on those very 'ideology-first', or 'primacy of the intellect' approaches that hover above human connection. (We might wonder, though, how reliable such an approach might be, not least because Wagner himself was so certain that aversion towards a particular group of people, as we saw in chapter 2, was natural and therefore understandable.)

Wagner attempts to extend the slave paradigm by using it to characterize the modern order. Its presence in a new form is 'the sin of society and civilization'.[14] Slavery exists in any situation in which the freedom to use one's energies for expressive and affective action is precluded. Another way of putting this deficit is to say that a state of slavery prevents a community from being responsive to needfulness. This is a reality even where a formal guarantee of equality under the law exists, since that bare guarantee, of itself, expresses no interest in what sort of activity is possible for individuals. Not only is there the relentless necessity of toil, Wagner suggests, there is no system of law that prohibits that necessity. Hence Wagner's declaration that 'the free man has become a slave'.[15] The legal existence of minimal equality can, he argues, confuse us about what it is we are equal in. We are equally free to work or perish, operating, as he puts it, under the misleading 'comfort of knowing that we are all slaves . . . slaves who are now taught by bankers and factory owners to seek the purpose of existence in manual labour for our daily bread'.[16] This arrangement—sufficiently similar, in Wagner's view, to the Greek disfiguration of some human beings into chattel—is essentially unnatural and is therefore, for Wagner, vulnerable to a revolutionary transformation carried forward by the real—that is, affective—promptings of need.

Wagner's image of the Greek world turns out, then, to be a qualified one. He offers no blind 'back to Hellas' fantasy, in that he recognizes that the Ancients developed their forms of living without reflection and without moral sensitivity. That is not open to us. Reflection should take us not in the direction of spirit but towards an understanding of the natural basis of our moral and therefore intrinsic worth. At the same time, the Greeks demonstrate certain human capacities that have been suppressed by the conditions of modern life. They provide us with a critical vantage point rooted in human experience.

The Political State

A truly human society, Wagner maintains, will overcome in all respects the demands of the political state. The latter is condemned as the overarching institution that in varying ways constricts the lives of all who are forced into its dependence. Wagner is, as noted above, sympathetic to the ideal of authority held directly by the people themselves and therefore shared equally by them. Authority, in this form, has a special dynamic vitality in that it will not settle for custom nor ever bind itself with laws that are designed to limit the present and the future. In its traditional forms, political authority is a matter of ancient privilege, while the contemporary 'rational-legal' state, to use Max Weber's categories, is mere external authority. Wagner worries about both. The rational-legal state is held by its proponents to be a special achievement—perhaps culminating point—of the modern world. Indeed, in the early phases of the developments of 1848, Wagner, as we have seen, partially sympathized with that progressive ambition, even if with a notably untechnical interest in its details. But the course of the revolution converted him, like many others, into a radical who had to think of existing models as doomed compromises with an intrinsically hostile system.

Wagner's thinking falls a half century beyond the brilliantly crafted arguments for a constitutional order found within classical German philosophy. Although not shared in identical ways, there was a prevalent view among those earlier thinkers that history is purposeful, a process itself, and not simply the name for the chronological set of human actions. Its tendency is progress. The perception of progress is always linked to some phenomenon of special interest to the observer, as discussed in chapter 2. In this case, the interest is political freedom, and nothing, it was thought, could equal the capacity of a state to bring that about. The rational state is a democratic institution marked by a constitution which guarantees fundamental rights while correlatively setting out the limits of governmental power. Ancient privileges would finally be overcome by liberal historical forces. In the constitutional state, the citizens' adherence is gained through the reasonableness of its provisions, never naked obedience or inherited customs. A weighty philosophical argument that has sometimes attached to the idea of the constitutional state is that the highest form of freedom is social and exists, properly speaking, only in societies with rational practices. Freedom in the state of nature—a place with no laws and no institutions—is therefore an ungrounded fantasy. The state of nature thesis has, nevertheless, a lasting if fuzzy appeal. It somehow survives the devastating criticisms that it projects socialized needs and competences on to a nonsocialized situation, misinterpreting the demands of incomplete social freedom as a persuasive cry for the abandonment of society. There is nevertheless something the state of nature thesis tries to tell us that cannot be eradicated without converting the very idea of freedom into a concept contrary to its meaning. And that is that freedom must have no element of social conformity, cannot be grounded in the rules of institutions, and is irreducible to the notion of the 'good citizen'.

Viewed from the loaded vantage point of 'progress', the constitutional state seems a compelling ideal. A rival vision of human communities, one that emerged at roughly the same time as statist philosophy—the romanticism discussed above—is suspicious of what it takes to be the life-crushing frameworks of formal law, that is, of 'right'. Its preference, rather, is the 'spirit' of the people, their affective connection with each other, their predecessors, and their traditions. This intuition gave rise to a range of imaginative alternative communities. One could find, at perhaps the most extreme, premodern communities petitioned to speak against the rational-legal state. The Teutonic tribes, it was fancifully thought, had required no laws, so profound was the sense of honour with which they regulated themselves. Wagner was instead, as we have seen, drawn to the intuitive yet organized civilization of the Greeks, a civilization which, unlike the legendary and mythologized Germans who instilled fear and respect in the Romans, is relevantly similar to ours, not least because of Wagner's concern with the precedent they provide for an aesthetic ideal. It is from that vantage point that 'the political state' is criticized.

Wagner speaks of 'the shattering of the natural Greek state and its dissolution into the political state',[17] a form of regulating social organization that is necessarily oriented against creative and affective human powers. The familiar logic of Wagner's normative perspective—we have already observed it in his criticism of rationalist freedom—is put to work here. The 'essence of the political state', precisely as something removed from nature, is, he maintains, 'arbitrariness, while that of free individuality is necessity'.[18] And, as we have also seen, arbitrariness is a characteristic of any norm which does not respond to genuine need. I have mentioned the appeal of the constitutional state among Wagner's predecessors and indeed among those who in Wagner's time sought, through the Frankfurt parliament, a constitutional Germany. With a backdrop of the reserved privileges of the ruling nobility, of individuals fixed in the asymmetrical role of 'subject', the clamour for rights and articulated laws on the limits of government would seem unexceptionable. Wagner, however, takes a sceptical view and rejects the claim that we must celebrate the system of rights given to us by the modern state. The state has provided, he alleges, only a 'complete distortion' of 'a truly human concept of right'.[19] This is because, he holds, the political state is geared towards one predominant right, namely the right to property.

Wagner tells us in his autobiography that he had grappled in early exile with the text of Pierre-Joseph Proudhon's *What Is Property?*, though he had previously taken in a more digestible form of that work through conversations with Röckel.[20] However, typically enough of Wagner's way of engaging positively with the ideas of certain thinkers, we find hardly any evidence of familiarity with the refinements of Proudhon's detailed system. What he added to the view of Proudhon's general theory about the interference of property in the 'social instinct and moral sense'[21] of human beings was the positive corollary of a people who work socially for the satisfying accomplishments of personal and communal ends. Property, Wagner holds, corrodes human freedom in that it is protected by laws that are designed 'to order future life with the laws given by the present'.[22] The future, in other words, is determined by property arrangements established in the present. The law will, as he puts it, hold 'on to property, the property that is to be nailed down for all eternity', but that is antagonistic to the dynamism of 'the self-shaping life drive' which alone supports human freedom.[23] Hence 'right' is indexed primarily to ownership, he alleges. As he argues in 'The Artistry of the Future', property is an 'irrational relationship' since it is based on a contradictory combination of the supposed ideal grounds of entitlement to ownership and some quality of the object itself, that is, the opaque quality of being ownable.[24] The latter, however, is a projection of the former on to things, that is, it constructs the world in such a way that it aligns with the desire for possession: to hold without affection, one-sidedly and possessively. It is therefore quite the reverse of those original human communities characterized by Wagner as 'the natural union of those in equal need . . . a beneficent protective contract of all' in that it removes objects from their availability to need.[25] The modern state—again, the institution that exists to protect property—is a notion that comes 'from above'—like the supposed ideal laws of reason identified by rationalism and idealism—not from life. It exists to protect and enshrine the interests of bourgeois society.[26]

In *Opera and Drama,* Wagner advances those views through a powerful reinterpretation of the Antigone story.[27] He evidently draws on Sophocles's *Antigone,* and perhaps Aeschylus's adjacent drama, in his portrait of the heroine's motives. Euripides's *The Phoenician Women* provides him with the background to the dispute between her two brothers. Wagner sees this story as a mythic depiction of the original intentions that would give rise to the political state. Creon is characterized as the representative of state power and of the life-crushing customs with which it justifies itself. His 'cruel edict'[28] forbidding Polyneices's burial, which Antigone defied, was, Wagner holds, motivated by a preference for the rigid institutions of state, whatever the surface of his actions might otherwise say. Polyneices's aggression may seem to justify Creon's decision, but behind it lay a deeper concern, one with which Wagner is in sympathy. Polyneices had insisted on receiving his agreed share of a fraternal inheritance—power and wealth—only to be met with refusal by Eteocles. Creon's judgment on the cause of the violence that followed showed that he was sympathetic to Eteocles and, in this way, gave legal authority, now as king, to the very possessiveness that, as Wagner puts it, is 'the essence of property, which everyone happily enjoyed alone, but did not want to share with anyone else'.[29] He protected the fixity and exclusivity of possession. This was a profound corruption of a properly human community, Wagner holds, in that hardened laws now came to override agreements among people. It is against this rigidification of human action that Antigone's response must be understood. She is an instance of what Wagner describes as the 'sensualized power of involuntariness in the unconscious, naturally necessary action of the individual'.[30] This means that she could not accede to the arbitrary authority of the state, because as an artificial entity, it has no natural right to defeat agreements made through intuitive familial affectivity. Antigone, then, acted on the necessity that comes from life, doing what is naturally obligated by the situation in defiance of the manifest arrogation of right by the state. Wagner describes her situation in this way:

> Antigone's love was a *fully conscious one*. She knew what she was doing, but she also knew that she had to do it, that she had no choice and had to act according to love's necessity; she knew that she must, *out of sympathy*, obey this unconscious compelling necessity *of self-destruction*; and in this consciousness of the unconscious she was the perfect human being, love in its highest abundance and omnipotence.[31]

Mere positive law required her to subject her impulses to control, and because of her unwillingness to do so she is a figure of resistance against whatever destroys the vitality of the human community.

Wagner's thoughts on the limitations of the political state are consonant with his implicit criticisms of the autonomy of reason (considered in the previous chapter). The state, like the philosopher's 'reason', is 'an abstractum' which, as Wagner puts it, has never 'entered into reality'.[32] Of course, both exist—they are influential notions, powerful enough to have deep affects on human behaviour—though their authority comes not from involuntariness but from 'external compulsion'.[33] In other words, their position as norms places them 'above' or 'outside' life and need, and that means that they are not grounded in necessity. The philosopher and politician, he maintains, are involved in artificial reconstructions that misrepresent the involuntary life processes.[34] A further similarity between autonomous reason and the state is that they share, in spite of their self-perception as expressions of enlightened humanity, a picture of human beings as yearning to lapse into depravity. This is the pessimistic thesis that the human being is, Wagner writes, 'fundamentally weak' and 'forever to be mistrusted'.[35] Because each of those systems lays exclusive claim to order, those convinced by the importance of order—those, in effect, socialized to do so—are amenable to its strictures despite personal cost (self-guided by principles, not affections, the citizen is suborned to the laws, whatever they happen to be). This reality, Wagner writes, is experienced by 'free individuality' as 'its negating destiny'.[36]

According to Wagner, the state identifies itself as the general and only true object. Truth claims are assessed against their consistency with the state. And 'the particularity of individuality', as he puts it, in what could almost be a pointed reference to Hegel, exists only insofar as it is derived 'from its essence'.[37] That essence supposedly 'predetermines the individual—thus shall you think and act!'[38] The notion of a particular individual whose essence is independent of the state is thereby undermined.

This metaphysical-sounding relation of individual to state is the structure which validates the state's right to model a version of individuality whose primary function is the state's own perpetuation. Rather than allowing that unbounded expressivity that marked out the world of the Greeks the political state, Wagner suggests, requires habit. Habit fixes individuals in repetition, not self-renewal. 'Habit' here is intended in a charged sense: the repetition of narrowed behaviour that is congenial to the limited processes of the state. In this way, the state colonizes our dispositions. As Wagner explains: 'The life instinct of the individual expresses itself *ever anew and directly*, but the essence of society is habit and its view is a *mediated* one'.[39] The relative simplicity of habituated behaviour aligns the individual with the rigorous structures that define the state. They follow a 'state-political morality' that is 'completely hostile to the development of individuality'.[40] 'Habit', then, is the word Wagner uses to capture the inculcation of everyday behaviour which is emptied of spontaneity and marked by unthinking acquiescence.

Wagner inventively connects habit with egoism, a condition we have seen him ascribe to the occlusion of our aesthetic and affective dimensions. His approach is structural in that the form of organization that is specific to the political state produces, he holds, a kind of societal egoism. The analysis is focused on the disconnectedness of individuals which comes about when their interrelations are mediated through the state. In this context, the immediacy which is an essential property of affectivity is eliminated. That is, as Wagner believes, their 'habit', their way of acting without the spontaneity that is characteristic of sensitivity to the needs of others. Hence, as he awkwardly puts it, individuals habituated by the political state form a 'communism of egoism, the unyielding bond of communal, needless self-interest'.[41] As should now be clear, such action—egoistic action—has no necessity: it is arbitrary from the point of view of the real needs of human beings. Wagner captures this with the phrase '[e]goistic arbitrariness'.[42] It may seem strange to claim both that individuals are egoistic and that they are deeply entrenched in conventional society (habituated society). Wagner is not in this instance guilty of losing track of his thoughts, however. He describes such individuals as the 'self-sufficient submissive'.[43] The contradiction, in other words, lies in the very nature of those narrowly socialized individuals. Wagner's criticisms here are antecedents to the efforts of twentieth-century critical philosophy to expose the illusions of individualism that have been necessitated by the modern state's desire to preserve itself.

Wagner appears, though, to be in two minds about the degree to which conscience is subdued by the state. He is largely committed to the view that there is still that space where the individual may 'think silently to himself'.[44] Hence, the miseries of state life are not entirely mysterious to its members. However, he also holds the more radical notion that the state is so effectively influential that individuals confuse their spontaneous decisions and actions for the product of their own personal intentions. Wagner puts it this way: 'the individuality which the state instils in him is taken by our involuntary feeling as his real essence'.[45] At that point, any sense of the limits of the state becomes impossible because the individual cannot set up a critical vantage point from where they, even if only notionally, separate themselves, somehow, from immersion in the processes of state life. Life is, for that purpose, stifled and replaced with the 'uniform of class', its hold being such, Wagner argues, that 'people today cannot grasp the human being in any other way' than as a creature who belongs to some fixed social grouping that determines what is appropriate and proper for thought and action.[46]

We have seen the broad claims Wagner makes for the deformations of individuality found in the political state. His critique does not end there. He develops a set of analyses of pathologies that are peculiar to that form of social organization. In using the term 'pathology', I am drawing on more recent social criticism rather than Wagner's own language. It seems quite apt, nonetheless, since Wagner is attempting to bring to the surface practices that are socially endemic, barely noticed as having the influence they have, and yet which narrow the scope of freedom to a concern with values that lie outside the supposedly real need of individuals. And since those practices are not spheres of self-realization, they serve, as we shall now see, only to constrict individuality and community.

The Pathologies of Modern Life

A widely held tenet of classical liberal theory is that the state has no obligation to attend to the happiness of its citizens. Happiness, as it is intended in this context, occurs when the individual experiences a contentment that comes about only when they feel themselves actualizing parts of their humanity, particularly through the development of skills of various kinds. Its pursuit is left to each person, as they choose or not, while the state, with the usual provisos, takes no view on how a life might be satisfyingly led. A philosophical entailment of this neutrality is the exclusion of perfectionism. A just society, according to the restricted view of the state, is found where there are no institutional hindrances placed in the way of any individual's personal happiness-directed projects. That, at least, is the theoretical picture, as it is unlikely that a state where no one was successful in achieving happiness would last very long, in that form at least. The state will limit itself to equipping individuals with what is required for social effectiveness. That minimalism, in Wagner's view, amounts to the state's abjuration of an interest in genuine freedom. It is the mere freedom of rights and economic agency. Rather, happiness, in his view, is the fundamental end of human beings precisely because it is the very property of the most developed human life. A freedom which does not also involve an interest in that development is unworthy of the name. In 'Man and Existing Society'—which as I have already suggested is the most speculative of the philosophical works which precede his trilogy—Wagner sets out that proposal in a series of rhetorically structured principles:

> It is man's *end* to reach an ever higher, purer happiness, through the ever higher perfection of his spiritual, moral, and corporeal capacities.
>
> It is man's *right* to reach the pleasure of an ever growing, purer happiness, through the ever higher perfection of his mental, moral, and corporeal capacities.
>
> Hence the *end* of man arises from the *right* of man, *end and right* are *one,* and the right of man is simple: to obtain his *end*.[47]

Happiness is the condition which accompanies the free pursuit and realization of essential human potentialities. This very process falls within the sphere of freedom since its achievement necessarily requires action. But it is action of a very different kind to the restricted sphere of the liberal state since it is supported by a community which is active in eliminating any societal condition which inhibits individuals' ability to reach that form of happiness—the only genuine happiness—that is grounded in the experience of growing ('ever higher') perfection. The community in this way must be assistive, not neutral.

Because the state of mere rights has no interest in the realization of human beings, Wagner argues, individuals are left vulnerable to goods that either merely counterfeit opportunities for perfection or provide only shallow forms of happiness. The neutral state's indifference is the background condition for, as Wagner puts it, 'every vice, every crime against nature'.[48] These so-called crimes—acts without necessity—are exemplified in the obsessive pursuit of false needs. False needs corrupt our capacity for freedom since they direct us towards ends that are unsympathetic to our natural being, the source of all genuine freedom. The most prevalent among them, Wagner seems to believe, are fashion, money, work, and luxury. In differing ways, each of them has the effect of reducing the actions of individuals to interests that leave the state untouched and without challenge. And at the same time the individual makes no advance in their freedom, happiness, or development. Wagner does not propose in their place some form of antimodern asceticism. That would hardly be consistent with his commitment to validating the sensuous dimensions of human life. Furthermore, his expressions of admiration for the supposed simplicity of the daily lives of the Greeks is not to be mistaken for a conventional rebuke to the material excesses of the contemporary world. The perniciousness of false needs consists in their power to draw us away from those real needs which, if realized, would give life to a society entirely unlike that of the contemporary world. Wagner approaches these questions with primarily critical intent as he draws attention to the hidden though enervating presence of the pathologies of contemporary society.

Fashion

On first reading, we might believe that Wagner's comments on fashion are exclusively guided by a desire to promote the idea of artistic authenticity and, correlatively, to expose the shallowness of what passes modishly, and with no little success, for true art. Meyerbeer, lionized in Paris as the master of grand opera, is never far from his thoughts. That motivation is certainly significant, but the basis of Wagner's analysis, in *The Artwork of the Future* in particular, is concern with the effects of fashion—or fashionableness, perhaps less misleadingly—on everyday life. He opposes fashion to that family of forces which he consistently connects with freedom: namely, nature and the necessity of needs as the basis of what is truly human. Subjection to fashion therefore means taking guidance from heteronomous influences. Fashion is an 'illness' and 'weakness'[49] in that it detaches us from that which is necessary and therefore vital: it is 'unnatural need'.[50]

Wagner recognizes that fashion asserts itself as a social force. It secures normative authority within contemporary society through rules that eventually gain control: it is, as he puts it, the 'most insane tyranny' over the preferences of individuals.[51] He explains: 'It must therefore make arbitrary systems for itself, to put its intention into rules, to make itself known in unnecessary presuppositions and assumptions so that it can be understood and executed by its disciples'.[52] The force of this normative distortion is subversion of our understanding of what human beings require, making what is necessary—nature—seem 'ridiculous'.[53] These rules have the inevitable effect of producing 'absolute uniformity' among individuals, of shaping all according to a limited model of life. Fashion has no interest in individuality as such, but it does, according to Wagner—in that distinctive concept we have seen before—support a form of living that is marked by 'egoism'. In this case, egoistic concern is self-conscious adherence to whatever fashion serves up. This is, to put it another way, the relation of the individual to a transient social phenomenon rather than directly to other human beings. The individual's sense of needfulness is suborned to motivations that are secondary to life and detached from social concern.

Wagner speculates tenuously on a connection between the normative force of fashion and the state's grip over individuals. Without being able to bring the point to completion, he thinks of the state as itself a place that rests on fashion—'life in the present, with its fashionable police-like uniformity, is, unfortunately, the all too faithful image of the modern state'[54]—but it seems that a number of lines cross each other. Wagner wants to portray the state as a place of indifference to true needs. Furthermore, the state is uniquely powerful in distorting our sense of what we need. Wagner's point rests on the rather broad similarities that might be drawn between the lack of independence of those who are governed by fashionableness and the requirement of the state to bring conformity to its citizens. His point is polemical and at one with his general effort to explain what turns out to be, in his accounting, the disappearance of individuality in the political state.

Money and Work

Wagner offers a set of interconnected observations on the adverse effects of money and industry on the scope of human self-realization. These are found primarily in *Art and Revolution,* where the Greek model stands in telling contrast with the present age. His critical claims derive some of their force from an implication, and certainly a questionable one, that the Greek world was innocent of commerce in inessential goods. His adherence, in broad terms, to the anarchist and utopian socialism of his times is also evident. Wagner's claims here are often conventional, lambasting as he does the worship of money, for example: 'but our god is money, our religion the acquisition of money'.[55] He maintains that money releases those who have it from 'public slavery' in that they enjoy options that are closed to those whose energies are directed almost entirely towards 'securing' their subsistence.[56] There are several ideas in play in this claim. First, money is a metonymous term for the wider world of capital in which labour is monetized and the worker's independence sold or surrendered. Second, there is an interest in what specifically is arrested through that process: namely, the ability of all affected individuals to engage in expressive activity. And since Wagner's notion of freedom, as we have seen, draws on the example of aesthetic spontaneity, any impairment of expressivity attacks freedom in its essence. This privation would seem to apply to the moderately wealthy too, since the financial autonomy they have gained must itself have required some level of ongoing commitment to the system of pecuniary reward.

However, as creatures of the system, they, no less than exhausted labourers, prefer to give their free time to restful entertainment, rather than to any aesthetic challenge.[57] Expressivity is damaged by the all-consuming intensity of work, Wagner maintains.

A more fundamental dimension that Wagner considers is the pathological effect of working to instruction. In this context, labour is narrowed to executing the preferences of others. This is 'toil . . . sad, sour work' which embitters because of its direct spiritual and physical consequences.[58] With pathos Wagner bears witness to the industrial conditions he finds around him. He speaks of factories as sites of 'the deepest degradation of humanity', where human beings labour to little purpose 'without air and love'.[59] He believes that work can be a good in itself, but will never be fulfilling where industry prevails. He envisages growth in expressive possibilities once the worker moves beyond what is existentially necessary. His point is conveniently facilitated by choosing the example of the craftsman—not, for example, the farmer or teacher—whose work has some obvious similarities with that of the artist. The freer the work, the more the worker or artist can invest the thing of their labours with their personality, that is, invest it with a uniqueness that refers distinctively to them:

> if the craftsman's immediate purpose is nothing more than the satisfaction of his own needs, e.g., the production of his own home, his own tools, clothes, etc., he will gradually acquire, thanks to the pleasure he derives from the useful objects that remain to him, the inclination to work the material in such a way as suits his personal taste. After the production of the most necessary things, his work, now directed toward less pressing needs, will elevate itself to an artistic one.[60]

The opposite of expressive work could be many things, of course, including sheer idleness, a way of being that Wagner, we can infer, would regard as an inexcusable waste of life. His ideal communities are, after all, characterized by vibrancy and restless renewal.

Wagner acutely connects the wretched circumstances of industry with a power generally thought to lie outside it, namely, Christianity. Christianity, he maintains, insists on the valuelessness and irrelevance of earthly pleasure, of sensuous enjoyment, and thus passes no judgment on the brutalizing conditions of labour. It does not promote the idea of a world oriented towards 'a happy, self-conscious existence', Wagner notes, and that is because it teaches human beings to believe that that form of contentment is an assertion of their fallen nature.[61] To defeat that corruption, the doctrine maintains, the senses must be subdued. The Christian thesis threatens to condemn any effort to liberate human beings from that misery, since we are, Wagner writes, 'obliged to preserve it until it pleases God alone to free us from its burden'. The absence of spontaneity which is demanded by Christianity is, he alleges, 'openly embodied in a cotton factory of today'.[62] Work may not be a virtue or an ethical practice, but it is somehow wrong, the religious view goes, to think we are entitled to live without its pains (as that would mean we had committed ourselves to its inverse, namely, pleasure). That binding misery—a condition of radical unfreedom—is ordained by Christianity. But, Wagner contends, Christian principles cannot ultimately exercise dominion over life since they in fact are themselves principles of lifelessness.[63] He anticipates the 'life for our future free man' as one no longer governed by the need to 'gain a living'.[64] That does not, again, mean that work should cease. Rather it will be detached from the mercantile system and, as we have seen in the discussion of the Gesamtkunstwerk, connected instead with creative needs that harmonize with the real needs of others.

Luxury

An abiding question for those social philosophers who speak about true needs is how they can reliably distinguish them from those they deem to be false. One form of demarcation is simple stipulation, a declaration of what is good indexed to some account of what human beings really are and require in order to be what they ought to be. That account might involve great elaboration but yet be suspected simply of pushing the question into another region, the question of what makes a true human being rather than one that merely seems to be. A more effective type of argument, one which in fact Wagner adopts, identifies some property of the false that prevents it from meeting its own criterion or criteria. This, if skilfully executed, shows that the need is incoherent. A need presents itself to us as a privation and is experienced as a form of discomfort. It should follow, in principle, that a need once fulfilled brings about some type of release which lasts as long as the need remains fulfilled. A criterion of a true need, then, is that it can be satisfyingly attained.

Conversely, a false need, Wagner writes, is 'itself just not a natural one that could be satisfied, and for precisely the reason that, as an untrue one, it also has no true essential opposite into which it could dissolve, and thus destroy or satisfy itself'.[65] Although Wagner did not realize it at the time of writing, his account of this pathology resembles Schopenhauer's notion of the painful impossibility of gaining the repose promised by the satisfaction of a desire. False needs, unlike our sensuous needs, do not, Wagner suggests, permit satiety. Their dynamic is towards superfluity, that is, of limitless gain. Wagner captures this phenomenon in ways that oppose the language of rest. A false need is pursued in a condition of emotional turbulence. As he puts it: 'It tortures, consumes, burns and torments always unquenched, lets the mind, heart, and senses languish in vain, devours all the air, contentment, and joy of life'.[66] Is it, though, the case that true needs, in contradistinction to false ones, can be satisfied? For example: aesthetic production is, in Wagner's view, quite certainly a true need. How then might we explain the artist's—not least Wagner's—need to continually create new things? Answers, in fact, are implicit in the material we have just reviewed. Aesthetic creation in this sphere is not prompted by a culminative urge, that is, to have created in quantity. And, indeed, it is free of that set of pains that Wagner ascribes to the desire for luxury.[67] Other real needs are more readily differentiated from the objects of the luxury-drive. The love for another person is enduringly satisfying: it is a significant dimension of a contented life. False needs are not just what we dislike, find uncouth, or facile. Rather, they contain characteristics that necessarily produce a restless dissatisfaction. Such needs are external and therefore arbitrary, failing to attach to what we somehow naturally require. Wagner's novel critique of false needs sits neatly enough, then, within his broader account of necessity.

Luxury, in common with all those dispositions that are not oriented towards necessity, is egoistic. There are two aspects to egoism in this context. First, Wagner offers his standard worry that a false need—in this case luxury—separates us from our affective, sensuous needs and therefore sets us 'egoistically' apart from others. The second aspect involves the use of others. Luxury, Wagner maintains, requires a readiness to exploit in the name of the satisfaction of one's own needs. He claims that those very systems of production that exist in order to fuel, indeed inflame, the desire for luxury, are exploitative. The enthusiast of luxury, Wagner charges,

> squanders, for the sake of a single yet unattainable moment of renewal, the activity and vitality of thousands of needy people; he lives on the unsated hunger of thousands of poor people, without being able for even a moment, to satisfy his own hunger; he holds a whole world in the iron chains of despotism.[68]

This despotic force has determining influence on the structure of society. Those who are gripped by the false need of luxury rely on social arrangements that ensure that the goods that would—however delusorily—fulfil that need are available. Thus they grant special value to production and only secondarily to those human beings who are obliged by their circumstances to serve it. This system commits its subjects—egoistically—to indifference to what Marx calls the forces of production, or 'vital force', as Wagner himself puts it.[69] Those workers are the mere 'accidental material'[70] in the system 'which kills man in order to use him as a machine'.[71]

A different point that might be worth noting here is Wagner's acerbic view of the hypocrisy of those whose altruistic sentiments towards those they consider their inferiors are roused only through art. In *Art and Revolution*, for example, he ridicules Louis XIV's passion for 'skilful verse' that, through Corneille and Racine, gave voice to the Greek's hatred of the tyrant.[72] He observes likewise that the 'fattened gods of our industry' may indulge in momentary pity at the sight of 'the starving proletarian' in theatrical productions, but they are in no way disposed to changing the order of things to bring about the satisfaction of real 'need' in the world.[73] Images of the poor and the exploited may move a saccharine tear or two, but sentimentality is a hollow form of sympathy if it leaves the normalized world of social fracture and atomization as it is. In similar vein, Wagner contends that the egoist may appear capable of altruism, as witnessed, as he sees it, in the performative language of Christian brotherhood or in ostentatious acts of charity. Because these impulses stem from a non-affective disposition—a disposition not sensitively attuned to the community of all—they are, in reality, acts of self-satisfaction.[74]

Freedom and Reconciliation

Wagner's thoughts on the social nature of freedom are connected with his views of interpersonality. We have already seen what he takes to be the implications of the capacity to perceive needfulness in others and in ourselves. We might say that in that respect there is for Wagner a recognitive element to social freedom. It is the mechanism by which we develop self-esteem, a sense of our distinctiveness, and any number of human goods. Freedom is secured where needs are met, a situation in which individuals gain the space to realize themselves and their projects among others. That idea is aligned with the aesthetic materialism that marks out both Wagner's social theory and his account of human nature.

Since, then, individuality is enabled through an essential and ongoing interpersonal development, we can, Wagner argues, dismiss that 'wretched misconception' which makes freedom equivalent to 'loneliness'.[75] This is the fantasy freedom of the 'egoist' for whom, as he puts it, there is 'the isolation of the individual, in which each isolated nothing is supposed to be something, and the entire universal [*das ganze Allgemeine*] nothing'.[76] In other words, the egoist's conception of freedom rejects the holistic context—'the universal'—and elevates what is in principle inseparable from the whole into properties that supposedly stand on their own. Wagner supports this thought with the speculative though once commonplace thesis that everything in nature is interdependent. Given that human beings are part of nature, occupying the world in accordance with their own distinctive characteristics, they too are interdependent (not in some bare ecological sense, but in the sense appropriate to the complex of human need). In an uncharacteristically dialectical turn of thought, the latter thesis leads Wagner to conclude that freedom as isolation must therefore be a self-annihilating project. He maintains, in effect, that part of our self-identification lies in our ability to distinguish ourselves from others. However, that act of differentiation does not warrant any basis for autonomy construed as perfect independence. To put it another way, differentiation is negation grammatically, but not existentially. Indeed, though Wagner does not express it quite this way, differentiation might also entail complementarity. And that is because self-identification necessarily references others. Total independence means superseding those references, thereby necessarily depriving the individual of an identity condition. In that case, Wagner argues, if the individual 'wished to separate from himself that which is different from himself, he would then no longer be anything distinguishable, thus no longer recognizable to himself'.[77] Alienation from others through an isolating act of self-determination leads, then, to self-alienation, that is, to becoming a self which has become a stranger to itself. By contrast, as Wagner puts it, it is only through 'the fullest communion [*Gemeinsamkeit*]' with what is different from each individual that they can become what they are, 'ought to be and reasonably' only wish to be.[78] That is, realization of oneself is possible only within a community.

One might reasonably worry here that Wagner is making the mistake that some before him and many more after have also made. It is that of conflating the conditions of psychological individuation, where Wagner has plausible views, with the conditions of freedom which, at times, will necessarily involve separation from others: 'loneliness'. Without the possibility of the latter, freedom would be perhaps claustrophobic, where private spaces, both mental and physical, were somehow perceived as vicious. However, it is clear from everything we have seen that the particular type of freedom at issue for Wagner is anti-individualism of a specific kind, directed in principle against such notions as that of 'ownness' argued for by his contemporary Max Stirner (in which the self is a sheer and irreducible particular whose motives and interests are to be hermetically isolated from all supposedly external factors).[79] And its theatre of operation is not detached reflection on moral dilemmas or anguished questions of self-determination. It is a social conception of freedom rooted in a reformed community which does not suffer from the pathologies of modern life: selfishness, abstract state mechanisms, and so on. It is freedom within a community of sensibly liberated human beings. The presence of a community is essential to the realization of needs and the affirmation, indeed, of our self-defining projects. By contrast, the rational-legal state—the political state—narrows the scope of action. Importantly, the state is incompatible with 'involuntariness' because its own processes have priority over individuals who must operate under the control of habit. That, Wagner maintains, is a society without reconciliation. In a letter of 1849, he expresses his rival thesis in the following way: 'the only thing that makes us free is a loving association with others'.[80]

5

The Drama of Revolution

A CENTRAL concern of this study has been Wagner's efforts to give intellectual substance and systematic form to his perceptions of the limits of freedom within the peculiarities of a world governed by feudal authority and Christian asceticism yet shaped by commercial forces. His project is not exclusively critical. In Wagner's aesthetic materialism, we have found innovative concepts that capture what he understands as the form that authentic and untrammelled experience must take in a truly expressive and affective community. He addresses his criticisms to the present and much of his theory of experience to the future. This body of thought emerged almost entirely from Wagner's responses to the events of 1848–1849, first as a political activist and finally as a philosopher. An obvious avenue of enquiry is the relationship between the ideas we find in Wagner's theoretical writings from that time and the dramatic works of the same period.

Even before his philosophical phase had begun, Wagner put into dramatic form the idea that human beings are gifted with a natural capacity for freedom that is suppressed by the excrescences of our determining social institutions. Those characters who allow their actions to be aligned with their spontaneous and unbidden urges are marked out for tragedy, finding themselves in destructive conflict with the expectations of what is considered to be respectable human behaviour. A chronological review of Wagner's dramas reveals a formative process in which his relatively simple framing of the primacy of passionate human instincts—hardly without precedent in the operatic tradition—grew in complexity. During the period in which he was developing his ideas of revolution, however, we can see a productive cross-fertilization of the interests of his dramatic and philosophical work. And yet neither collapses into the other: the dramas are never aesthetic pretexts for theoretical ideas—though they at times make use of such ideas—and the philosophical work largely depends on the discipline's conventions of persuasion to make its points. Wagner was notably strict with himself in abandoning projects without dramatic potential, either because of the limitation of their plots or, more saliently in this context, an excess of discursive philosophical content.

This chapter begins with a consideration of Wagner's earlier musical projects and the first canonical dramas, that is, those of his works that he permitted to be staged in the Festspielhaus in Bayreuth. No attempt will be made to offer full-scale interpretations of the philosophical meaning of the work considered here. Rather, there will be a concentration, with some occasional further reflections, on what we can see in them that reveals something about Wagner's commitment to a distinctive version of affective, involuntary human action and his belief about its inevitable conflict with authority. Before concluding with some observations on the illustrative nature of several of the characters of the *Ring*, I will look at a range of pieces Wagner had drafted during the revolutionary period.

Early Work and the First Canonical Dramas

This partial study of Wagner's creative work starts with that period in which Wagner had begun to emerge as a developed artist, that is, in 1840, when he had completed the composition of *Rienzi, der Letzte der Tribunen* (*Rienzi, the Last of the Tribunes*). Although *Rienzi* is not among the works that Wagner later included within the Bayreuth canon, he was anxious, for some years after its first production in

1842, to see it performed in various opera houses across Europe. There was a financial dimension to that desire, certainly, but Wagner recognized its enduring qualities, even after the radical transformation of his compositional ideals. The story of *Rienzi* is taken over from another author, Wagner's usual creative practice in that period.[1] Of all his dramatic works, *Rienzi* is the most explicitly and conventionally political, but it is far from clear that it represents Wagner's worldview. The version of the historical Rienzi we find in the opera is taken in large part by Wagner from a book by the English writer Edward Bulwer-Lytton. Cola Rienzi is a Roman public figure of the fourteenth century who, enraged at the lawlessness and clannish rivalries that have afflicted his city, determines to restore it to a magnificence it had formerly enjoyed as the *caput mundi*. Rienzi is declared tribune of the people after successfully suppressing the warring nobles whose sponsorship of street violence lay behind the city's disorder. The central dramatic interest lies in Rienzi's fall from favour among ordinary Romans. His conciliatory clemency towards his noble enemies is initially admired, but the abuse of that graciousness by those he had spared sees renewed conflict, leading to the people's growing distrust of Rienzi's use of power. The people are portrayed as a fickle mob, easily turned by emotive events and manipulative rhetoric. Rienzi's commitment to the autonomy of Rome leads him into dispute with the Church and the Holy Roman Empire as he seeks to establish a separation between the interests of his city and those of both external authorities. In the opera's final scene Rienzi and his devoted daughter perish in the burning Capitol.

Some notable worries have hovered over this opera, the least accomplished of Wagner's works still performed and recorded. One is induced by the apparent though disputed claim that what Adolf Hitler had perceived in a 1905 production of *Rienzi* inspired him to take a similarly salvational mission to a failing Germany. A musical friend reported that thought from meetings in 1905 and 1939. If this is true, and there is reason to believe it is nothing more than the product of the friend's fervour, it looks like yet one more instance of Hitler's penchant for self-aggrandizing affinities, in this case latching onto Wagner's relatively simple tale and imposing on it a purpose that lay entirely outside Wagner's and indeed Bulwer-Lytton's (a Whig politician at the time of his historical novel) intentions.[2] A different kind of association is found in Adorno's contention that *Rienzi* contains an abysmal political vision: fascism. Although rejecting the view, in 1934, that *Rienzi* can be connected with 'current German events',[3] he later suggested that the opera contains traces of 'anti-feudal authoritarianism'.[4] Adorno eventually moved to declare Rienzi 'the first bourgeois terrorist', a 'dictator' who abolishes factionalism but concentrates power in his own office.[5] Adorno, it appears, was unaware of the connections drawn in Hitler's circles between Cola Rienzi and Hitler's messianism, but his observations coincide, albeit with critical intent, with the notion that the opera is a lionizing portrait of the future *Führerprinzip*. This innovative line of interpretation is sustained by a transhistorical perspective, with less interest in the political environment within which Wagner was working and the political views he was known to have held at the time. Of additional relevance is a relatively deflating motive behind the selection of the theme of *Rienzi*—alongside genuine artistry—namely, Wagner's desire to gain a reputation within the field of Parisian grand opera, something the maligned figure of Meyerbeer had achieved long before him.

Der fliegende Holländer (*The Flying Dutchman*) (1841) draws on a range of existing sources, including a story by Heinrich Heine. It is the first of the Bayreuth canon, and in it we find prefigurations of the idea of involuntariness, albeit in a heightened and exaggerated form. Senta's compulsive, steadfast love for the Dutchman, a figure whom she has never met, is supernatural in origin. Its inexorable power leads her towards death, a climactic moment that is somehow to be understood as the worthy price of her final connection to the Dutchman. The quality of her drive is grotesquely mirrored by the motives of her father, Daland, who is coarsely in favour of the Dutchman as a match for his daughter for no other reason than the inestimable riches promised to him. Senta dies by drowning, pushed by a curious involuntary willingness to allow herself to be enveloped and extinguished by the dark primal energies of nature. Wagner was clearly taken with the romantic idea of an alluringly melancholic nature as he drafted out the idea for a further drama, drawn from E.T.A. Hoffmann, called *Die Bergwerke zu Falun* (*The Mines of Falun*). It is one of several projects that fall between *Der fliegende Holländer* and *Tannhäuser*. Falun's mines are mysterious places, and although they contain great wealth, they do not anticipate the toilsome misery of *Das Rheingold*'s tyrannically governed and all-too-human depths. Elis, a simple worker, deems himself unworthy of Ulla, who loves him, and suffers unbearable pain as he sees her prepared to marry the wealthy Joens. He seeks solitude in the mine, where he encounters Torbern, its forbidding spirit. Elis is instilled with an irreversible and identifiably romantic desire for his own death in the deep comforts of the earth. We see then in these two Scandinavian tales—set in Norway and Sweden respectively—a climactic moment where the individual renounces not only their ego in response to 'oceanic feelings', to borrow Sigmund Freud's notion, but also their lives as they yearn for eternal connection with obscure nature. Those pieces mark both the beginning and end of Wagner's interest in this thanatotic aspect of romanticism, with his work returning decisively to the processes of life and pointing increasingly in the direction of politics.

Wagner took a fuller creative role in the preparation of a text for a drama he called *Die Sarazenin* (*The Saracen Woman*). Set in the era of the Holy Roman Emperor Frederick II, its vibrant blend of hot-headed infatuation and sword violence operates within a broader story about the control of an Italian kingdom under threat of disintegration. Manfred, son of the emperor, is opposed by the viciously rivalrous Burello, who is supported by the Church in the matter of who should inherit the crown. The main character, however, is the Saracen woman, Fatima. She is central to both the romantic passion of the story—she is beloved by two men—and the mission to save the kingdom for the Hohenstaufen. She devotes herself entirely to encouraging Manfred, a reluctant prince as well as one of her suitors, to take up that mission. What is especially noteworthy about this compact drama is Fatima's reverence for—as she sees it—the legacy of Frederick, who held no religious prejudices and under whose governance Christian and Muslim thereby united.[6] This thought hints for the first time in Wagner's artistic work at the universalism that would later underpin his revolutionary ideals, though it is a different sort of universalism to that which is envisaged in the trilogy and not least in the controversial 1850 essay. What is proposed there is the overcoming of all identities, whereas Fatima here celebrates a reconciliation of peoples as they are.

We have seen Wagner's undiluted rejection, in the trilogy, of Christianity. As a dramatist, however, he evidently believed that it contains truths that rise above the doctrinal precepts that had made it inimical to human self-fulfilment. A choral work, *Das Liebesmahl der Apostel* (*The Apostles' Love Feast*), first performed in 1843, calls for the unity of the oppressed and emphasizes the overarching value of universalism. Wagner's setting is a meeting of the apostles following the death of Jesus. A Christian sect, now persecuted, has been established. A 'choir of disciples' urges strength through unity. The assembled group understands its purpose as preaching the word around the world, not merely locally. Wagner's sympathetic representation of Jesus's original followers rests primarily on the supposed desire of the disciples for a morality that embraces all of humanity. Here, and in other places, Wagner is drawn to what he perceives as Christianity's commendable unwillingness to remain within the culture in which it first emerged. It understood itself to be a system whose appeal is clear to every human being who hears its message, particularly those in need, that is, those who thirst and hunger in both the literal and figurative (spiritual) senses. The text speaks of *Noth,* in the sense of adversity, with little anticipation of that specific sensibility as the founding impulse of a humane community.

The first completed music drama to follow *Das Liebesmahl der Apostel* is *Tannhäuser*. That work explores a range of different ideas of love through the perspective of its eponymous character on the brotherly bond of the minnesingers, the carnal life of Venus, and the chaste purity of the unbearably pious Elisabeth. Its drama is created by the oscillating appeal of each of these forms of life. Wagner went on, in *Art and Revolution*, to ridicule the 'abyss between real life'[7] and the disembodied idea of love like that promoted in the beautifully wrought yet strangely self-reverential lyrics—the lover's virtue is foregrounded—of the courtly singers. The chivalric ideal became 'the genuine hypocrisy of fanaticism', that is, a sincere but inhuman life of self-deception.[8] Tannhäuser memorably confronts that hypocrisy when he loses patience with the airy ideals of the minnesingers and reveals the disgraceful truth that he has illicitly enjoyed the uninhibited sensuality of Venusberg. (Wagner's early and first performed opera, *Das Liebesverbot* (*The Ban on Love*) (1836), considers, by contrast, the naked and in no sense naive hypocrisy of those who rail against sensuality while secretly pursuing their lustful pleasures.) His subsequent efforts to atone for his sinful past are a failure. A gruelling pilgrimage of penitence to Rome ends with the pope's heartless damnation. He is effectively homeless in the world. It is not, however, Wagner's intention to promote carnality as the overriding truth of human needs. After all, Tannhäuser begs Venus, at the beginning of the work, for release from her world, a world to which he has somehow become captive. What he seeks is not a life of renewed virtue. Indeed, his reentry into the courtly brotherhood of singers is the result of an accidental encounter. Rather, as he implores Venus, he wishes to experience pain, sadness, unpredictability, and restless movement: to become, in effect we might say, a creature of needfulness, of *Noth*. His time in the Wartburg—the home of Elisabeth and the singers—is ill-fated, as he cannot divest himself, as the pope would clearly perceive, of the knowledge of another kind of living. Tannhäuser is a tragic figure in that he is never at peace with the three forms of authority which variously govern him: Venus, the Wartburg, and Rome. *Tannhäuser* was an opportunity to give extended reflection to the question of what kind of existence is closest to what is properly human. None of the three, in the extreme forms they take in the text, provide satisfying answers.

In July 1845, just a few months after completing the score of *Tannhäuser*, Wagner wrote the first prose draft of *Die Meistersinger von Nürnberg*, a work he brought to completion some twenty-two years later. Interpreters in recent decades, more alive to Wagner's antisemitism (the figure of Sixtus Beckmesser has already been mentioned) and the reckless excesses of German cultural nationalism, proclaimed here by its everyman hero, Hans Sachs, increasingly position it as Wagner's most controversial musical work.[9] Together with those worrying dimensions is the work's endorsement of cosy provincialism, with bullying, humiliation, and low domestic plotting all part of what Wagner himself called a comic opera. And it is possible—as I have implied through my invocations of the Beckmesser and Walther von Stolzing paradigms—to see elements of its central drives as representing in dramatic form some of the key philosophical ideas found in the trilogy. This is arguably evident in the contrast between regulation and spontaneity that finds expressions in both places. However, the 1867 version rests on several other crucial elements, not least the idea of a supposedly Schopenhauerian renunciation that is instantiated in Sachs's decision to suppress his love for Eva.

What is already strongly present in the first draft is a belief in the cultural power of music, that is, its capacity to bind a community. Taking his lead from the example of the Greeks, Wagner later amplified this theme to encompass the art of drama. The art of song is valued here above the usual virtues, as implicitly it alone qualifies the winner of a particular contest to marry the daughter of an old man. The latter two are without proper names but are recognizable as the figures Eva and Veit Pogner of the later version. The competition for the prize of Eva's hand is between an individual known dryly as the Marker—he is qualified to score performances and undertakes his business with dead academicism—and the poor son of a knight (later Beckmesser and Walther respectively). The Marker abuses his authority by declaring mistake after mistake as the young knight auditions for admission to the guild of mastersingers. The Marker himself has two set piece opportunities to display his musical prowess, the first of which is spoiled by Sachs, the sardonic cobbler and singer, who disruptively hammers on his last as the Marker sings, and the second—at the contest—which he himself destroys by using a verse without understanding its metre and melody. (In the final version, the second occasion is additionally affected by the Marker's lack of composure on foot of a nasty beating he was set up to receive just the night before.) The gifted knight, by contrast, is encouraged by Sachs to believe that he is a kind of warrior, equipped with the aesthetic weapons needed to take on the good fight which will run alongside those who use the sword. The verse used to disastrous effect by the Marker is, in fact, the creation of the knight. As the contest's winner, he wants only the prize of the daughter, dismissing from a position of artistic superiority the accompanying honour of membership of the rigid guild.

This text of 1845 evidently displays little of the political commitments of revolutionary emancipation Wagner was soon to adopt. It leans towards a story which celebrates aesthetic culture above all else. But without the counterbalance of universality, that story slides towards a tumescent nationalism. Indeed, its very location, old Nuremberg, taps into a nostalgia that Wagner shared with some of his contemporaries for a golden age of luminous German figures.[10] Perhaps it is important to bear that point in mind in that, as we shall see in a discussion of aspects of the *Ring*, Wagner's dramas gained a capacity to align themselves with progressive politics by abandoning concrete times and places and adopting in their stead mythic settings or real places, such as the Rhine, unbound from history.

In contrast with *Tannhäuser*, *Lohengrin* offers fewer obvious themes of a philosophical kind. Of some significance, however, is the dramatization of a thesis about knowledge. A central element of Wagner's story is Lohengrin's demand that he is never to be asked to reveal his name. The tragic Elsa gladly accepts ignorance of his identity as a condition of their marriage until poisonously influenced to insist that he utter it. She is, in effect, committed to the purest love because it is love without knowledge and therefore outside the space of evaluation. Wagner, in a later and clever piece of retrojection (in *A Communication to My Friends*), associates Elsa with the 'involuntary' in human nature. Lohengrin, by contrast, is the 'conscious' force who seeks redemption through her, clearly indicating the elevated status of the unconscious condition.[11] As Wagner puts it, 'Lohengrin sought the woman to whom he did not need to explain or justify himself but who loved him unconditionally'.[12] Even if the language of involuntariness was unavailable to Wagner at the time of the *Lohengrin* text, he was evidently aware of the closely related romantic idea of irrationalism: the sentiments have priority over concepts or judgments in leading us to truth. His opposition to rationalism was declared in the name of the suppressed capacity for experiencing and responding to aspects of our humanity that are more important and essential than whatever can be aligned with reason in its efforts to reveal every aspect of what is valuable to us. Knowledge as such shatters the connections that we can only intuitively recognize. In his skilful plot, Elsa's intuitive trust in Lohengrin—both as her saviour and husband—is a condition of bliss. She speaks of the happiness that is given *nur durch Glauben* (only through faith). That state is lost when she is manipulated by base claimants to her late father's title into importuning Lohengrin to tell his story, that is, to leave the space of what is sacred and unsaid and enter instead into discursivity, stories, and justification.

From the Revolutionary Years

Lohengrin, as Thomas Grey points out, occupies a 'position on the brink of Wagner's private aesthetic revolution, which coincided with the political upheavals of 1848–1849 and with the early genesis of *Der Ring des Nibelungen*'.[13] His next developed text would be *Siegfrieds Tod* (*Siegfried's Death*), which was eventually to become *Götterdämmerung*, the fourth part of the *Ring* tetralogy. Wagner had begun an intensive phase of research into the legends of the Nibelung, determined to craft them into a dramatic form whose mythic content would give expression to the unthematizable complex of human experience. Indeed, this is an extraphilosophical motivation behind the antihistorical perspectives we saw above. In a piece of 1848, suggestively titled 'The Wibelungen: World-History as Told in Saga' (Die Wibelungen: Weltgeschichte aus der Sage), Wagner maintains that the myths passed down by the people are more reliable guides to their experiences than the narratives of the 'learned historian' who merely assembles the surfaces of what they find through detached research.[14] Nevertheless, what emerged in Wagner's work was also in part shaped by the contemporary political ideas he embraced first intuitively and then reflectively during the revolutionary years. His pivot away from inspirational feudal settings crystallized in his decision in 1849 finally to discontinue a project on Friedrich I (Barbarossa) which he had begun in 1846. It exists as a sketch of several acts with its most interesting element a momentous discussion between a papal legate and the emperor in which each side competitively claims that the other depends on it: the Church legitimizes the empire—gives it a spiritual unity—whereas the emperor protects the worldly institution of the Church. Curiously, in light of Wagner's dawning Hellenism, the emperor warns that his power is necessary to prevent the Church from meeting the same fate as that of the Greeks. They lacked a cohesive central power and were therefore vulnerable to external disruption. (We recall that Wagner was soon to idealize the Greeks as possessing a quasi-natural cohesion that, in fact, was at its strongest whenever threatened by outsiders.) We do not know what conclusion Wagner had conceived for this piece, but we can infer that no resolution of the tensions between two overbearing temporal powers would have been attractive to the political sentiments he had developed during the revolutionary years.

The Nibelung project—the *Ring*—which Wagner, as just mentioned, had initiated at this time will be examined below in a separate section. Alongside that venture were two further projects, *Jesus von Nazareth* (1849) and *Wieland der Schmied* (*Wieland the Smith*) (1849–1850). No dramatic work attempted or completed by Wagner foreshadows or contains as many elements of his philosophical writings on revolution as the *Jesus* text. It deserves extended attention. The voice of the main character, Jesus, is largely indistinguishable in intent from that of Wagner's. The text is didactic and arguably thin in dramatic potential. Its ideas are formed in a manner that is more treatise than dialogue. One possible, though not specified, plot line might have been built around the two versions of Jesus that are visible in Wagner's draft. The more prominent of them portrays Jesus as a teacher of love who sees the existence of positive law as indicative of a corrupt, failed, and unfree society. Alongside that characterization, though in smaller measure, is a quite severe Jesus mercilessly preaching the law of God and the rigours of faith.[15] Its tone, often established by direct scriptural quotation, bears some of the harshness of the contemporaneous 'The Revolution'. The first of these two perspectives articulates some of the most fundamental revolutionary elements of the trilogy: the primacy of love over institutions, the disavowal of property, and a cooperative community that is free of hierarchy.

Wagner's Jesus is, in the main, a prophet—an ethical teacher—urging the renewal of all humanity. He is contrasted with Barrabas, whose view of emancipation is limited to freeing Judea from Roman rule. Jesus is described as a descendent of Adam with 'all men' therefore 'his brothers'.[16] His popularity and charisma mark him out as the natural king of Judea at a time of national liberation. However, he repudiates the role since he takes the scope of his concern to be, rather, humanity as a whole. He lovingly acknowledges socially disvalued individuals. In Wagner's version of the story, Barrabas's rebellion ends in failure because, under his leadership at least, it is not widely favoured by his people. The people, however, find themselves disappointed by Jesus's response to their support for him. He invokes a universalism they neither understand nor desire. His mission is the redemption 'of all peoples of the earth . . . not of the Jews alone'.[17] Later, when an apparently judicious Pilate has the opportunity to spare Jesus's life, the crowd, inflamed by the Pharisees, demand that that special act of clemency be granted instead to Barrabas, the unsuccessful insurgent. They believe that they had been deceived into thinking of Jesus as their king only to see him prove worthless in the fight against 'contemptible Roman tyranny'.[18]

Throughout the text, Jesus speaks against 'oaths' which, identically to laws in this context, are symptomatic of a world which cannot bind itself through trusting affection, a thought that echoes the tragic logic of Elsa's loss. Love, contrastingly, is the basis of freedom, since it is through love that we act rightly and without constraint. It is the sole basis of morality, overriding all considerations of lawful strictures and traditional practice.[19] As Wagner puts it, the disposition of love alone permits the 'moral pleasure of freely doing what is right'.[20] He is without obvious precedent when he includes 'the flesh' within the forms of love ordained by Jesus.[21] Hence any moral precept which sees the body as sinful in essence is dissolved by a Jesus who will redeem us from fear of our own embodiment. That sensualistic thesis—a commitment Wagner, as we have seen, unconvincingly claimed he did not exactly hold—means that marriage has no basis if it is maintained solely by oaths and not by love in all its forms. The text makes the notable claim that procreatively oriented sexual love is a wholly positive act of self-externalization. It involves 'a giving of one's own life force' to a process greater than oneself in the reproduction of the species. In this respect, it is profoundly anti-egoistical, and contrasts with the isolating affirmation of the ascetic's version of self-renunciation.[22] All love is, in the view of Wagner's Jesus, characterized as a divestment of egoism, and it alone can bring about a return to a true self. Furthermore, that loving self is not guided by the constructions of rigid morality. This is what a return to innocence means. Sin, as Wagner dialectically conceives it, creates its own wrong by stipulating some unnatural boundaries of appropriate human behaviour.[23] Jesus will end sin in that sense by invalidating the strictures of law which assault our sensuous and affective needs. In Wagner's complex and elusive thought, Jesus's death is to be understood as a loving and redemptive act in which humanity is liberated from the very lawfulness that validates the idea of our sinfulness.[24] That act is the perfect yet symbolic supersession of the very egoism which depends on the regulatory systems that oversee and perpetuate atomized social relations.

An equal offence against our capacities is the grip of the institution of private property over our deeper instincts. This thesis is dramatized in the stories of a prospective follower, a young nobleman, who is told by Jesus that he must dispose of all his wealth and of Jesus's anger at the merchants who defile the temple. Jesus preaches against property under the general category of possession (*Besitz*). The negative phenomenon of possession gives rise, though, not only to private property but also to the laws governing family relations in which some elements are said to belong only to specified others. In thinking of the family as a case of disfiguring possession, Wagner's Jesus is primarily concerned, of course, with marriage. But the unfreedom experienced by children under the ownership of their parents is also decried. Those who break away from the institutional constraints of the family are likely to be acting out of the need for love in its purest and most innocent forms. This is vividly represented in Wagner's dramatic work in the bond between Sieglinde and Siegmund. These twins, separated early in life, enjoy a wholly natural love that, no matter how socially scandalous we might at first perceive it as being, surpasses Sieglinde's cold though lawful relationship with her gruesome husband, Hunding. The twins, it might be suggested, exemplify those who, as it is put in *Jesus von Nazareth*, are responsive to 'the free and eternal movement of love' rather than its reification within its legally protected form.[25] This truth is characterized by Wagner as the law of God, but this God is simply an avatar for what Wagner regards as proper to the natural and happy disposition of human beings. Hence when social institutions are condemned for conflicting with God's will, the justification he offers is intelligible in terms of human need, rather than an inscrutable transcendent design. This is vividly captured in the provocative claim that we worship God not through prayer and sacrifice but through all acts of love for other human beings, acts which are specified as the embodied expressions of heartfelt desire.[26]

A community built on a liberated affectivity is, the text maintains, one of interdependence and mutual support. Jesus offers a defence against the accusation that what he proposes is implausible (resembling Wagner's direct response, in *Art and Revolution*, to the charge that he is entangled in utopianism). His teachings, in fact, capture a more realistic human arrangement than the tawdry laws of morality and society which, as constrictions that are alien to genuine need, are ceaselessly and inevitably violated or ignored. Although *Jesus von Nazareth* was developed in the midst of the Dresden turmoil, it is, perhaps surprisingly, indirect in its assessment of secular authority (unlike Wagner's political pieces from this time). In the final few pages of the draft, however, Wagner refers, quoting from Ephesians 6:12, for the first time to the 'princes and powers' who 'rule in the darkness of this world'.[27] A line from that same text adjuring the obedience of slave to master (6:5) is not of course cited by Wagner, demonstrating the constructive selectivity of his use of scripture. There is also use of an apt passage from Acts 4:26 regarding the conspiracy of kings and the princes 'of the earth . . . against the Lord and against his Christ'.[28] Much of what Wagner assembled in *Jesus von Nazareth* self-evidently foreshadows core principles of his theoretical writings on revolution. A reason for abandoning this project, he later explained, was a struggle to manage the 'contradictory' realities of his Jesus, a figure who was, in the text, historical, symbolic, and of relevance to the very world Wagner was attempting to change. He was also concerned that a work about Jesus would simply be too controversial given his intention to impose his 'modern consciousness' on the meaning of Jesus's teaching, an imposition that was led more by 'philosophical than artistic intentionality'.[29]

A more symbolically driven vehicle for elements of Wagner's revolutionary thinking is found in *Wieland der Schmied*, which he worked on over the winter of 1849. A short prose sketch is appended to the first edition of *The Artwork of the Future*. Wieland is a preternaturally gifted smith of elaborate jewellery and fine weaponry who has fallen in love with a swan maiden, whom he saved from the sea, and whose power of flight is given to her by a magical ring. As an act of total self-giving she surrenders the ring to Wieland so that she might never fly from him. Their world is suddenly broken when he is cruelly captured by a king, Neiding, who desires the exclusive use of his talents, not least to equip his conquering army. Wieland's ability to walk and therefore escape is destroyed by an injury intentionally inflicted on him. From that point onwards, he is forced to labour according to his captor's demands alone. He eventually realizes, inspired by his memory of the swan maiden, that his abilities extend to creating wings which he will use to flee his bondage, though not before dispatching the king. The symbolism of the story obviously lies close to the surface, with Wieland's liberation representing the overcoming of the slave-like system of production. It contrasts free artistic creation with the subjugation of that capacity to the will of another. The narrative may also encompass the idea of the political self-emancipation of one group, which has gained some sense of its own hidden powers, from an outside entity.

Wagner subsequently developed the Wieland story into the form of a drama. It differs in some significant respects from the first version, not least in an expanded range of characters who interact in complex and changing ways. The ring's magic is no longer that of flight but the power to enchant those who approach its wearer into a lost infatuation of the greatest intensity. Wieland falls in love with Schwanhilde, but when she reveals that she believes it is the ring which has given rise to the surge of feeling within him, he begs her never to wear it again. Wagner affirms the primacy of authentic human attachment by having Wieland insist that the source of his love must be his involuntary humanity, which is in this instance greater than the feeling artificially induced through the ring. The symbolism of the destruction caused by forced creation is evident in this version of the story too, as Wieland laments that his captivity—analogous we might say to that of the worker who enriches others to his own disadvantage—sees him 'forge his own chains'.[30] Also of significance in this story is Wieland's reply to the infatuated Bathilde (King Neiding's daughter), who uses the ring to possess him. She sees him as a god, but he insists that he is, rather, 'A man! A man in the highest distress [*Noth*]!', a cry that generates, appropriately to its message of vulnerability, a profound and reforming sympathy in Bathilde, now finding that she loves him for his suffering.[31] Another suggestive element is found in Wieland's creative reshaping of weapons of war—the very things he has been forced to make—into a featherlike thinness which form the wings he uses for his escape. The few themes that are echoed in the prose writings are set here within an austere drama whose energy perhaps lies as much in conflict and revenge as in reconciliation and love.

The *Ring*

In 1848 Wagner sketched out *Der Nibelungen-Mythus* (*The Nibelung Myth*), the original prose resumé for what was to become *Der Ring des Nibelungen*. It tells of the gods' wish to bring about an order of the world through the establishment of moral consciousness. By stealing the hoard of gold from Alberich—who had himself taken it from the Rhine, its ordained place—in order to pay for the construction of their stupendous world, they have become, they realize, illegitimate. They want human beings, who up until now have been of little significance, to gain a capacity for self-governance which will allow them to reign over the world. Wagner expresses that extraordinary intention as follows:

> [The gods] therefore seek to transfer their divinity into man in order to raise his power so high that he, in becoming conscious of this power, will reject divine protection in order to do, of his own free will, whatever his mind inspires him to do. The gods now raise man to this lofty destiny, to be the nullifier of their own guilt, and their design would be achieved if, in this creation of man, they annihilated themselves, that is, if, in the freedom of human consciousness, they had to surrender their direct influence.[32]

The implication in Wagner's phrasing that the obscure causation of indirect influence might not disappear, in fact, is not accidental. He produced this text in the autumn of 1848, and he may have envisaged the German princes surrendering power through moral necessity and a recognition of the capacities of their subjects to govern themselves. The parallel is not perhaps strong, since Wagner's gods give to human beings a freedom they—as far as we are told—have never sought. And furthermore, it is not entirely motivated by the gods' sense of their own unworthiness for absolute sovereignty. Human beings will somehow take on and expiate the guilt of the gods.[33] That expiation has something to do—Wagner is not very specific—with the recovery of the gold. The complexity of the gods' purposes here is obvious: the development of human moral consciousness seems to be both a higher end in itself and, at the same time, the instrument, granted to human beings, by which the gods' greater scheme is to be accomplished. In the process of running their own affairs—a privilege that cannot be annulled once granted—human beings will also become the strangely free executors of a project that is beyond their understanding.

Wagner's composition of the texts of the four parts that would eventually grow into the *Ring* cycle began in 1848 and was completed several years later. Those texts therefore overlap with Wagner's writing of the trilogy. Although self-evidently a work of extraordinary symbolic and thematic complexity, in which some commentators find a cohesive mythologization of the deepest determining forces of human life, elements of Wagner's published political and philosophical ideas are not difficult to discern within it. Wagner had no wish to glut his dramas with a stated politics, leaving that act of self-clarification to his theoretical writings. It is consistent with his great artistry that those ideas are at the service of a larger drama, not the other way round. That implies, however, a recontextualization of those ideas. As they are transposed to the unique world of the *Ring*, they cannot quite have the same normative force or meaning as that which attaches to them in the trilogy where they represent Wagner's overriding philosophical commitments. They sit alongside a huge range of additional narrative elements, which means they do not enjoy the same foregrounding necessarily given to them in the theoretical work. And because these elements are part of the complex of spaces and characters that make up the *Ring*, they are not attached to the sufferings of those human beings whose plight had excited Wagner's revolutionary passions. We cannot say, therefore, that the ideas found in the writings and the dramas are simply aspects of a single thing. They belong to separate modalities of experience and reflection, notwithstanding some common elements. The *Ring* is not, then, a sort of grand parable of Wagner's politics. It occupies its own quasi-historical, quasi-natural space. As myth, it takes place in a time of pastness that Wagner wants us to appreciate is ever present in the now. Its principal characters possess human traits in varying ways and measures, with their experiences sometimes powerful enough to provoke strong reactions of sympathy or dislike. They may in places be read as allegorical figures who draw attention to some general emotional or moral qualities rich in human significance without, at the same time, being one-dimensional embodiments of those qualities.

It would, though, be quite stipulative to place cordons around the theoretical and dramatic work and declare that neither is reflected in any way in the other. Interpreters who reject political readings and indeed stagings of the *Ring* as alien impositions on a much grander project may find some success in developing ambitious narratives that connect the diverse elements of the tetralogy without reference to Wagner's context. The text becomes a space unto itself and the interpreters our guides to a world which they have themselves to no small degree constructed. My objective is the relatively modest one of identifying the presence of ideas in the text of the *Ring* that originated in Wagner's revolutionary experiences and subsequent reflections and to do so without claiming that those ideas frame the work as a whole.

The four parts of the *Ring*—*Das Rheingold, Die Walküre* (*The Valkyrie*), *Siegfried,* and *Götterdämmerung*—were originally conceived in reverse order to the sequence that forms the cycle. Wagner began with *Götterdämmerung* which, at first, he titled *Siegfrieds Tod.* Because of the prior detail of events alluded to in the text, he decided that an entire drama on the early history of the figure of Siegfried was required. To that end he developed *Der junge Siegfried* (*The Young Siegfried*), later simply *Siegfried.* Realizing the enormous potential of the space he was working within, he moved on to *Die Walküre,* and then the work which sets up the cycle, *Das Rheingold.* The music was added to each part in the order in which the *Ring* is to be performed, a task that took Wagner many years to complete, stretching out long after his revolutionary political commitments had faded away.[34] Some adjustments to the texts were inevitably required as the compositional task unfolded and as Wagner reflected on the effectiveness of the narrative as it took shape across its four parts. The most discussed of those changes is to the final scene of *Götterdämmerung.*[35] In the original version, in short, the gold is returned to the Rhine, the gods recover their power, and all is well. This may at first strike us as a surprising conclusion when considered in the context of Wagner's revolutionary politics, but that version is from November 1848 and hence predates the Uprising and the theoretical work that followed. A new ending was written in 1852—sometimes referred to as the Feuerbach ending—and here Brünnhilde not only envisages the fall of the reign of Valhalla but also offers emancipatory proclamations about private property, the cruel nature of law, and the preeminence of love that resonate both with *Jesus von Nazareth* and the trilogy's philosophical theses. 1856 saw the 'Schopenhauer ending' in which Brünnhilde declares the end of the world and of all suffering through her renunciation of Valhalla, desire, and illusoriness. Wagner's final version returned to something close to the Feuerbach ending. The domain of the gods is destroyed, though the Wagner of 1874 was not inclined to include within the text the rousing anarchist avowals of 1852.

The chronology of Wagner's relevant output at this period is as follows, with the date of completion rather than publication noted.[36]

Siegfrieds Tod, later retitled *Götterdämmerung*, first version of the libretto, November 1848
Art and Revolution, completed in July 1849
The Artwork of the Future, completed in November 1849
'Jewishness in Music', August 1850
Opera and Drama, completed in February 1851
Der junge Siegfried (later, *Siegfried*), first version of the libretto, June 1851
Die Walküre, first version of the libretto, July 1852
Das Rheingold, first version of the libretto, November 1852

A philological approach to this series of works might focus on the first utterance of key ideas and then trace their reappearance in, or significant omission from, subsequent texts. What I intend here, however, is the more direct task of identifying those theoretical concepts that play some role in the dramas. This will not involve, for reasons already mentioned, a wholescale interpretation of the *Ring* as the working through of those concepts. I will, rather, undertake an examination of some of the work's principal characters insofar as their qualities or actions embody ideas, both positively and negatively, found in Wagner's revolutionary philosophy. As we shall see, the range of relevant concepts is not confined to those of politics.[37]

Wotan

Although there may have been few in the audience of the first performance of *Das Rheingold* in 1869—or, for that matter, of the entire *Ring* cycle in 1876—who had read Wagner's trilogy, those who did would have sensed some of Wagner's once ardently held commitments. And in the drama surrounding the figure of Wotan, several of the younger Wagner's precepts lie close to the surface. Wotan is the highest god, and among his responsibilities is that of guarantor of contracts and law. His powers are not inherited or purloined but were created ex nihilo by himself alone. That itself symbolizes something that is typically rebarbative to anarchist thought: the invention of power over others which validates itself only through its continual exercise. Those familiar with the trilogy would immediately and rightly conclude, therefore, that Wotan must be something considerably less than a perfect being. Furthermore, the very business of lawful contract is, for Wagner, a sign of a deficient society, which, in place of the bonds of confraternity, requires cold agreements protected by a higher force. Wotan's very existence, then, is a flawed one. His essence is to guarantee what ought not to be guaranteed. And he acts with the use of authority which comes from above—that is, from the position to which he has elevated himself—which, as we recall from Wagner's philosophy, is an essentially illegitimate form of governance. Wotan's person furthermore embodies a contradiction from whose consequences he can protect himself by virtue of his authority: he stands for a principle—draws his very meaning from a principle—that he does not consistently apply to himself. He steals for his own ends and is unfettered by any oaths, not least that of marriage, as he confesses to his daughter, Brünnhilde. He defines himself, nevertheless, as a being who is bound by his own laws.

Wotan, through his own genius, has created power. Although secured by the possibility of violent force, it has somehow gained a kind of—often grudgingly recognized—preeminence which places him effectively beyond challenge. He oversees an order of a certain manner. His spear is both a symbol of his position—a type of sceptre—and a weapon which he fashioned from a particular limb that was part of the world ash tree. On it are recorded all the contracts of which the gods approve and which Wotan consequently must protect. The troubling significance of this object is plain enough when we learn that the tree, a thing of primal vitality, was effectively destroyed when sundered by Wotan, thereby ending the reign of nature and supplanting it with worldliness, albeit of not quite human order. Another obvious metaphor of Wotan's imperfection is his blinded eye. He freely chose to mutilate himself in order to secure a special capacity for wisdom, a capacity he possesses in greater share than many of the *Ring*'s other protagonists but whose narrowness leads him to designs that prove to be self-defeating. Wotan, then, is a precariously positioned deity. He has gained his sovereignty through a destruction of innocence, his vision is figuratively and literally impaired, and he cannot live up to the very function he has given himself and guarantees for others. Each of these deficits resonates with what we have seen in Wagner's criticisms of what he understands as the essence of the normative power that structures the contemporary state and its governance. Wotan, as he put it to Röckel, is 'the sum total of present-day intelligence'.[38]

Wotan's failings are also manifest in the vulgarity of his ambition for the splendour of Valhalla. It is an expensive extravagance, motivated by nothing better than a desire for luxurious and imposing circumstances.[39] Moreover, it is an embarrassing reality that he is unable to pay the giants who have built that palace. He had insincerely promised them Freia as their fee, knowing that the community of the gods could not survive without her. His foresight is limited, with the day of reckoning coming as some surprise to him. He rashly solves the immediate problem of that debt by offering the giants enormous amounts of gold in place of Freia. Fatefully, for the narrative that unfolds across the cycle, this is gold he does not actually have but which he will cunningly acquire through theft from Alberich. At that moment he further diminishes his divinity by adopting, if not inventing, yet another form of violence, that of finance. He is able to convince the giants that Freia is fungible and can be appropriately expressed as dead bullion.

Wotan's scheming fails at essential points as he attempts to bring about ends that lie either beyond his powers or his self-definition. He is contradicted in his desire to return the gold to its natural place, the Rhine, from which it was taken by Alberich. Somehow realizing, rather late, that he forbids himself to steal from the giant to whom it now belongs, he attempts indirect influence, investing his own issue and the next generation (Siegmund and Siegfried respectively) with the task of restoring the gold. He perhaps sees himself, as those with deific delusions often do, as an invisible hand who can move others in ways they take to be their own will. However, they have their own purposes and evidently do not advance Wotan's plans. What Wotan does not himself appreciate is that he is, in fact, a piece of a larger process that is at work. We have seen Wagner maintain that there is an inevitability to the reassertion of nature over all the distorting forces of convention. Wotan's rise is the very beginning of the process of both his own and his world's destruction, at the end of which there will be no more gods. Significantly and through the most unplanned of developments, the gold is reclaimed by the Rhine in the final moments of the cycle, though the primal world is not itself restored.

Wotan is not, for all that, without a certain magnificence. The music that represents him is mighty, perhaps hintingly bombastic. He is a figure to be respected. His forceful presence holds our attention at every moment. Nevertheless, he is essentially a deficient entity, as any being who seeks dominance must be, who has created an unstable though functional order.

Brünnhilde

Brünnhilde's part in the conclusion of the *Ring* is momentous. It is through her that the gold, or rather the cursed ring that has been forged from it, is returned to the Rhine. She is given, furthermore, as noted above, the culminating voice across different versions of the cycle's ending. It is, however, her role in *Die Walküre* that is of the greatest significance to the philosophy of the trilogy. She is characterized there by her responsiveness to the affective needs of others. In this respect, she is, notwithstanding her divine status as a Valkyrie, an essentially human character, possessing a sensibility that Wagner elsewhere envisages for the community of the future. The key moment in her downfall is her disobedience to Wotan when instructed by him, in the name of the protection of marriage, to see to the death of his son, Siegmund. Siegmund and Sieglinde, the long-separated siblings, have become lovers. Sieglinde's husband appeals to Fricka for vengeance, and she in turn reminds Wotan of his obligations as the protector of contracts. Brünnhilde, however, believes that Wotan is acting against his deep paternal feelings. She recognizes that he is a tormented prisoner of his very own categorical imperative. Her form of interaction represents a competing version of necessity: to act on the emotional truth she finds in any given situation. She believes that Wotan too recognizes that form of necessity but has unnaturally suppressed it in the name of the authority of invariant law. She takes it upon herself to become the agent of a freedom he does not himself, it seems to her, have the strength to exercise. In this respect she, like Antigone, is a revolutionary figure, seeing beyond the destructive constraints of artificial order. Her sense of necessity is also evident in her reaction to Siegmund's distressful need, his *Noth*. In an intensely emotional exchange, she learns from him that if he must die, then so too must Sieglinde, whom he cannot bear to leave alone in the wretched circumstances from which he had almost rescued her. Brünnhilde's secret attempt to save them both fails when Wotan suddenly intervenes to ensure Siegmund's designated end. Wotan understands his own unfreedom as the result of an entanglement of coldly affirmed oaths and commitments. He cannot see in Brünnhilde the greater nobility that allows her, unlike him, to react spontaneously yet rightly to the particular needs of individuals.

The contrast between Wotan and Brünnhilde takes on an additional dimension as the drama moves from competing ideas of what is to be done about Siegmund to the consequences of her defiance. Wotan hides behind the language of necessity—of the ineluctable logic of the situation, of what 'must' happen—when he sets out the penalties for Brünnhilde's disobedience. He is not wrong in principle to declare that Brünnhilde has effectively determined her own sentence, not he. In expelling her from the sisterhood of the Valkyrie, he is reducing her to what he considers the lowliness of mere humanity. That aptly confirms her in what has been implicit in her actions: her ungodly and humanlike sympathies. The punishment does not stop with that. Wotan's further stipulation reveals his lofty ignorance of the complexity of human feeling. The world, at least at this point in the drama, is divided for him between law and whatever stands in opposition to it, namely, the contemptible morass of mere animal sentiment. The bizarre and apparently condign fate he initially conceives for Brünnhilde—but soon moderates on appeal—is of a piece with that thinking: since she has allowed feelings of care to defeat the command of duty, she must in turn endure the full and not selective reality—the freedom to feel—of being human. She is to be left as a thing of coarse pleasure for the first passing man. And the duty her father expected of her as an expression of higher love will be replaced by servile and fearful obedience to an inferior. Wotan does not anticipate that the human condition will allow her to experience anything but degradation.

Brünnhilde is the victim of a horrible scheme which not only takes her beloved Siegfried from her but converts her into a commodity to be traded for the hand of Gutrune. Furthermore, she is deceived into conspiring—of swearing an oath, no less—to bring about the innocent Siegfried's death. This is suffering produced by circumstances: it is a personal catastrophe. The wider and perhaps metaphysical tragedy of Brünnhilde's situation, though, is that she is equipped with a sensitive intelligence that her world—as administered by her father—is not ready to accommodate.

Alberich

Alberich's character and actions nakedly illustrate much of what Wagner rails against as the distinctive norms of modern society. Perhaps this is the essence of the affinity drawn by Wotan himself when in *Siegfried* he refers to himself, with some degree of insight, as Light Alberich as opposed to the original, Dark Alberich. Both might be seen as the symbolic authors of those practices and institutions that Wagner criticizes throughout the trilogy.

When told by the Rhinemaidens that only those who renounce love can ever gain the gold they playfully watch over, Alberich declaratively sunders himself from the possibility of any affective connection. He has risen to their challenge and in this regard might be thought to have acquired the gold on their terms, terms they never imagined any being willingly accepting. The circumstances in which he later fathers Hagen are explained by his cold-hearted seduction of a noblewoman with gold alone. Hagen is born to serve as little more than an instrument of Alberich's ongoing obsession with the ring, paralleling Wotan's intentions for his own progeny. Alberich's loveless connection with things quickly evolves into what looks very much like the invention of capital. As Mark Berry observes, 'Alberich definitively changes the world'.[40] He fiercely works his enslaved people to create added value to the gold, and that is the form, we might suggest, in which Wotan finds it when stealing it from him. In this regard, he contrasts both with the giant, Fafner, who lets the gold he and his brother have received from Wotan lie idle in his lair, and with Siegfried, to whom it transfers when he kills Fafner. Other than the ring that has been forged from the gold and the magic *Tarnhelm*, Siegfried leaves the hoard, literally without interest, where he found it.

A curious element of the *Ring*'s extended plot is Alberich's disappearance from the action. What is most disturbing is that it seems that he survives the ending of the story. In the final moments of *Götterdämmerung*, men and women, as Wagner puts it, watch in shock the conflagration in which Brünnhilde perishes.

That marks the end of one phase of the world: it is the death of the gods. With the continuing existence of Alberich—if that is Wagner's intention—the evils associated with capital have yet to be negotiated.

Siegfried

Wotan and Alberich bear the pathologies of power and greed to which Wagner gives theoretical description in his writings. As we have seen, Wagner's thoughts about revolution are not confined to questions of social transformation. Transformation of society will be impossible if there is not also a change in human beings themselves. What is required is an emancipating relationship—one that is sympathetic to their nature—through which individuals fully inhabit and express themselves in their actions. The figure of Siegfried is where, it seems to me, some of Wagner's thoughts about action are explored in drama. He wanted Siegfried's essence to be understood through ideas that he had already prepared in his theoretical writings. It was his hope, he wrote in 1854, that

> my hero should not leave behind the impression of a totally unconscious individual: on the contrary, in Siegfried I have tried to depict what I understand to be the most perfect human being, whose highest consciousness expresses itself in the fact that all consciousness manifests itself solely in the most immediate vitality and action.[41]

The execution of this idea sits uneasily, however, with Wagner's stated philosophical principles. The two dramas in which Siegfried appears bookend chronologically the composition of the trilogy, but he is no exemplar of the kind of free humanity Wagner sets out in those works. He is manifestly without that sensibility that is required to respond to the needfulness and vulnerabilities of others. Of the figure of Siegfried Nietzsche wrote that he might be the 'strangest thing that Richard Wagner created' precisely because he is 'that *very free man*, who may in fact be too free, too hard, too cheerful, too healthy, too *anti-Catholic*.'[42] This description challenges in us the adverse reaction that we are likely to experience as we witness Siegfried's blunt dynamism and unpleasantness. With the exception of the sorrow he feels when told of his mother's death—she died as he was born—and the clownish scene where he is overwhelmed by the sight of a woman's body when he removes the sleeping Brünnhilde's armour, he is limited to a happy and mindless virility.

Siegfried possesses nothing resembling an internal life. If he is a precursor to the Nietzschean *Übermensch*, as George Bernard Shaw has maintained, then the elusive idea of overcoming humanity looks as though it can take form only as regression, regardless of the philosophemes in which it is justified.[43] Adorno, for his part, sees Siegfried as 'the man of the future . . . a bully boy, incorrigible in his naivety, imperialistic in his bearing, equipped at best with the dubious merits of big-bourgeois self-confidence as contrasted with petty bourgeois pusillanimity'.[44] And many are disturbed by the merriness with which he physically and verbally abuses his adoptive father, Mime. The latter's duplicitous nature is itself repellent, and some might take Siegfried's particular response to it as therefore understandable.[45] A great violence against Mime is to deprive him of interiority when, having accidentally ingested the blood of Fafner, Siegfried gains, even if without cognizance, the magical ability to hear Mime's thoughts. This may be a useful power, in view of Mime's malevolent intentions, but it is nonetheless one which in principle reduces anyone with whom Siegfried comes into contact to his own simple level: creatures for whom there can be no reflective space between thought and action. The thought, voided of privacy, is taken to be an action since it is pulled, by Siegfried's sudden new ability, into public space.

Siegfried's contribution to producing the next phase of the world is, nevertheless, essential, intriguing, and unwitting. In Act III of *Siegfried*, he is intercepted by a stranger, his grandfather Wotan, at this stage under the guise of the Wanderer, as he attempts to find his way to the mysteriously alluring Brünnhilde (of whom he knows nothing other than that she should be his bride). In an exchange of words, he finds Wotan to be little more than an unhelpful blatherer. This is partially true of the weary god, but it is also the case that his elevated perspective is lost on Siegfried. Temperatures rise and a challenge is made. Wotan's spear, once powerful enough to shatter the sword now used by Siegfried when in the hands of Siegmund, is itself destroyed in the clash of weapons. We may infer that the sword which Wotan himself had originally created for Siegmund is even stronger in the form in which it has been reforged by Siegfried. A new hierarchy of creative potency is implied. The theme of wider significance, however, is the destruction of the spear, the manifest representation of Wotan's power, and also the register of oaths. Siegfried in a moment of spontaneous force—a literal force of nature—thereby opens up a space in which there will be no more Wotans, no more Creons. A consciousness in Siegfried of what he has done and of the consequences of his simple-looking act is entirely absent. When we think of Wagner's idea of history as the effort to project the present into the future, we might see Siegfried as acting for antihistory, that is, for an unfolding of things that is not to be controlled by intellect. The more immediate effect of sweeping Wotan aside is to reaffirm a condition that Siegfried has always instinctively adopted, namely, his freedom to roam as a powerful and situational actor in a rule-free world.

That freedom is opposed in principle, even if not in effect, by the reality that he is supposed to play some role in returning the gold to the Rhine, a relatively simple task that Wotan himself cannot perform without stealing it (for a second time) and thereby contaminating the restoration. Siegfried has inherited this mission from his father, Siegmund, whose very existence, as Wotan's unknowing son, was brought about for that purpose. He is perfectly unaware that the gold should be returned to its natural place. If he is a transparent puppet, then Wotan has effectively engineered a theft. For that reason, Siegfried must act with utter freedom. Indeed, as we have seen, the freedom that is possible only through involuntariness is lost when it is delayed and processed through reason. Wotan's hope is ill-conceived—in fact, it is groundless—as nobody can realistically be the unwitting vehicle of some external purpose while also correctly seeing every act as their own, that is, as free. His own impulses alone drive him forward, and without reflective compromise (though his independence is lost when the calculating Hagen who, in league with the Gibichung court, drugs him into actually taking on a mission that is not his own).

The final act of *Siegfried* is driven by Siegfried's determination to reach Brünnhilde, an intention as intuitive and opaque as Senta's desire for the Dutchman or Elsa's anticipation of Lohengrin. It is love, nevertheless, and as a behavioural motive stands above the strictures demanded by external authority. Siegfried in this respect may perhaps point towards the spontaneity of a revolutionary world. He is troublingly, nevertheless, an adventurer, seeking his own pleasure, free of awareness of the needs of Wagner's community of all (*Allgemeinheit*). As Nietzsche puts it in another observation, Siegfried represents 'the innocence of the utmost selfishness'.[46] In *Götterdämmerung*, in the fateful hunting scene, he wanders off from the main party and indulges in empty frolics with the Rhinemaidens (whose warnings he is incapable of appreciating). The hunt is not for him a joint enterprise. Likewise, his departure from Brünnhilde's rock, notwithstanding lavish avowals of eternal love, is spurred merely by his restless need for daring enterprises. He is an extraordinary contrast with his affecting father, a passionate creature of *Noth*. (The famous sword that Wotan created for Siegmund bears the resonant name, *Nothung*.) Siegmund readily imperils himself to rescue the vulnerable from the hands of brutes. It is more than difficult to imagine that even a version of him overcome by a philtre could undertake something like Siegfried's mission to secure Brünnhilde—pitilessly and against her will—for the pathetic Gunther (and with Gutrune as his reward). Siegfried is activity without reflection and, contrary to Wagner's claim, will be difficult to perceive as anything much more than an 'unconscious individual'. Wagner is closer to the truth, though, when he has Brünnhilde say, in the Prologue to *Götterdämmerung*, that Siegfried is, in fact, *des Wissens bar* (bereft of wisdom). Siegfried's incapacity for fear might be part of his reflective deficits. As Aristotle suggests, fear can 'be defined as a pain or disturbance due to imagining some destructive or painful evil in the future'.[47] Ideation, in which pictures of the future may be formed, is not part of a life of pure immediacy.

And yet Siegfried's death is marked with towering music of monumental loss. Something is to be grieved, but what exactly that might be is an open question. The figure of Siegfried does not appeal to the heart, notwithstanding the shabby circumstances in which he is killed. His unknowing contribution to the ending of the reign of the gods, however, with his contemptuous and aggressive dismissal of Wotan, representing a triumph of natural spontaneity over scheming control, is evidently of huge significance to the drama as Wagner constructs it. The interpretative point noted above—that drama and philosophy are not straightforwardly interchangeable in Wagner's work—has application here: an assessment of Siegfried cannot rely predominantly on the terms of the trilogy. By that measure, he is an asocial and profoundly limited creature of immediacy, no ideal citizen of the future, nor even a heroic holdover from the past. We might more naturally take as our primary interest his role in the unfolding development of the world of the *Ring* itself. Wagner's lofty description of Siegfried (in the 1854 letter) will in that case begin to appear as a complex tangle of the spaces of philosophy and drama.

6

The End of the Revolution—Schopenhauer

THE CRISIS of the Dresden Uprising was the culminating point of Wagner's involvement with radical political activism. Subsequent work on the theory and drama of revolution, which began to appear very soon after his exile began, took him to a level of philosophical reflection that was unparalleled by anything he had previously written. At some point in the 1850s, he began to retreat from his revolutionary commitments. He did not, however, cease to be thoughtfully engaged—sometimes with infamous polemics—with issues of contemporary interest. The story of that phase of his life, lasting up to his death in 1883, lies outside the scope of this study. In purely philosophical terms, the difference between the revolutionary Wagner and what came after is sometimes considered to be marked by Schopenhauer's impactful influence. There are differing opinions about how much of Schopenhauer Wagner incorporated into his view of the world, and a useful examination of that issue would also take us beyond the period of interest here.[1] An overlooked question, though, is what might have predisposed him to consider Schopenhauer's philosophy—only one of many Wagner had attempted to negotiate—as the new direction he apparently believed he had to follow.

Wagner claimed that he was immediately captivated by Schopenhauer following his first reading in 1854 of *The World as Will and Representation*. There are three principal reasons for this. The first, as Wagner himself declared, was the appeal of Schopenhauer as a writer.[2] Accessibility played no incidental role in steering Wagner's philosophical choices. We recall his initially favourable response to the 'stimulating' and 'lyrical' prose of the first of Feuerbach's books that he had studied. Schopenhauer's lucid and forceful style stood in contrast with the texts of the idealist tradition of official German philosophy, whose daunting complexity had too often confounded him. Wagner was not alone in being overwhelmed by the power of Schopenhauer's gifts for the use of dramatic description and metaphor in leading his readers towards the extraordinary, if not unlikely, substance of his theories. He wrote breathlessly to Liszt to relate his newfound enthusiasm for Schopenhauer, a figure shabbily neglected, he alleged, by a conspiracy of professors. He simultaneously and faithfully denounced the school of Hegel, deeply loathed by Schopenhauer, as a bunch of charlatans.[3]

A second reason is that Schopenhauer effectively absolved humanity of the burden of political engagement.[4] This was particularly salient in the wake of the failure of 1848, since it gave dignity to disillusionment. Radically modifying what Kant meant by the phenomenal world, Schopenhauer maintained that all experience in space and time is mere appearance and therefore somehow unreal in a particular sense when compared with the fundamental reality that lies behind it. This has obvious implications for the supposed value of politics, since it is within the phenomenal world that individuals compete, attempt to make peace, and build their institutions. Schopenhauer's philosophical mission was not driven by a primary interest in dismissing politically oriented life as futile or counterproductive. His philosophy nevertheless gives justification to those who might wish to set themselves above societal concerns. We cannot of course know the exact time at which Wagner finally abandoned his commitment to the ideas that had led him to radical activism and, subsequently, the theoretical work of the trilogy. However, he claimed that by 1855 he was no longer in sympathy with his revolutionary philosophy, disavowing with 'irritation', under 'the influence of Schopenhauer', the optimistic proposals for social reform he had expressed in *The Artwork of the Future.*[5]

Wagner was alarmed at first by what he found in Schopenhauer, correctly perceiving its inhospitality to the very assumptions of the kind of political thinking he still believed in at that time. Instead of the redemption of all Wagner sought through revolution, Schopenhauer recommended renunciation of the self.[6] Those acts, he maintained, could contribute to the alleviation of suffering, essentially by suppressing it at its source. No progress, no increase in lasting happiness in the world, however, was possible. The negation of misery was the most that could be achieved. Hope was without foundation simply because we lacked free agency, that is, the capacity to alter the course of things through our own choices. Any assertion to the contrary, he believed, was a naive utterance generated from the phenomenal standpoint. Wagner was still wedded to the image of vitality and attracted to that special attunement to human nature found among the Greeks, whereas Schopenhauer's work stimulated a glowing contempt for and perhaps even fear of life.[7]

The notion of self-renunciation gave Wagner pause, but he believed that Schopenhauer's philosophy otherwise contained ideas which helped to ground some of his own existing intuitions. He discerned in Schopenhauer a way of understanding the complexity of his very own creation, the figure of Wotan.[8] He has primarily in mind, and with no small degree of retrojection, the discussion of, in effect, the manifest and true will that takes place between Wotan and Brünnhilde, a parallel he stretches to excess.[9] Many scholars, perhaps guided by Wagner, have detected a pre-Schopenhauerian pessimism in Wotan's words. This may suggest either that Wagner already had, when he was writing *Die Walküre,* some inkling of *The World as Will and Representation* or that he coincides uncannily with Schopenhauer's point of view. Some hesitation, however, is called for on this point. Wotan's state of mind is one of defeat, a realization that he is trapped by the very status he has created for himself. This is certainly a gloomy thesis, but it is one born of experience and not, in contrast with Schopenhauer's elaborate variety of global fatalism, of theory. And in the discussion of the dialogue between Wotan and Brünnhilde in chapter 5, I suggested that Wotan had destroyed his capacity for free action by governing his will through a categorical imperative of his own making. That contrasted with the affective and spontaneous will of Brünnhilde. In short, Schopenhauerian concepts are a distraction as an explanation of Wotan's plight.

A third thing that may have drawn Wagner to Schopenhauer (in addition to the appeal of the writing style and the apolitical perspective it justified) is identifiable, perhaps counterintuitively, in the partial amenability of Schopenhauerian ideas to what remained of Wagner's philosophy once divested of its political commitments. In other words, Wagner did not need to abandon all his philosophical beliefs in order to move in Schopenhauer's direction. Amenability should not be confused with the hermeneutically unlicenced notion of 'anticipation'.[10] Rather more straightforward is the claim that Schopenhauer's ideas on the significance of music, his theory of compassion, and his weakening of the *principium individuationis* have approximate equivalences in Wagner's mid-century thought, even if produced through a significantly different theoretical framework.[11]

We can quickly consider, as Wagner himself recognized, Schopenhauer's exceptional exaltation of music.[12] It is tied in with a metaphysical theory about the basic form of the world which lay at a huge distance from Wagner's materialist orientation at the time. As we have seen, he held that the preeminence of drama—which included music as one of its elements—lay in its special capacity to afford humanity an elevating sense of totality and inclusion. Nevertheless, Wagner appreciated Schopenhauer's unique positioning of the supremacy of music among human activities even without, at first, endorsing the many remarkable conceptual entailments one had to understand for the theory to work on Schopenhauer's own terms. His fullest effort to align his work with Schopenhauer's aesthetics appears much later, in *Beethoven* (1870).

It is curious that although Wagner had a well-articulated view that a capacity for *Noth* will underpin a truly human society, he did not appear, at first, to be struck by Schopenhauer's resonant claim that compassion is 'pure love'.[13] Both needfulness and compassion refer similarly to a disposition which responds to the vulnerability of others, and acknowledges our own fragility, but can become possible only when we overcome forms of life that falsely insist on the basic fact of human separateness. It is an act, in Schopenhauer's theory, in which we no longer see ourselves as creatures exclusively of the phenomenal world.[14] He takes the alleviation of suffering as the central question for ethics (as opposed, say, to the meaning of the good). As we have seen, Wagner produced his ideas about needfulness without the use of a theory that drew on metaphysics or anything approaching a complex ethical theory. It was, for him, a given affective capacity in human beings that is too often repressed by social practices. All truly benevolent action is undertaken for the sake of the love of others and never as a fulfilment of mere law or duty. Without quite realizing it, then, Wagner found himself drawn within a philosophical theory which complemented his own concern with suffering. That concern played a significant role in motivating his political activism, which of course had life-altering consequences for him. Wagner's view about our capacities for benevolence may look unworldly when compared to Schopenhauer's unromantic thesis about the violence and 'suffering that is essential to human life'.[15] Yet Schopenhauer, unlike Wagner, displayed something approaching naivety about the effects of social forces on the circumstances of suffering, treating it as an unalterable given which lies beyond the political and moral question of human responsibility.[16] And there is arguably a further advantage to Wagner's original position. Schopenhauer's simultaneous theories of the renunciation of life and of compassion are not easy to reconcile, since the latter must require a living and feeling self to be the kind of response we expect it to mean. Wagner, by contrast, grounded our capacity for *Noth* in a fully affective human being who was drawn to others, as one always just like them, in their specific need.

Schopenhauer used the term *principium individuationis* for the phenomenal and therefore divisive idea of individuation. Taken as agents in the phenomenal world, we are mere appearance. We wrongly take ourselves to believe that we possess a personal will that is utterly particular to us. There are as many wills, the rejected thought goes, as there are entities capable of exhibiting will. But behind that appearance, Schopenhauer contends, lies a single and, in effect, cosmic will, and it alone is fixed reality. Again, Wagner held no view of that type when he first encountered Schopenhauer, nor does any phrase referring to the principle of individuation appear in his writings (other than in a late unpublished fragment). Indeed, as noted above, he was disconcerted by Schopenhauer's demand for personal renunciation since it was incompatible with a programme for the freedom of the individual qua member of a new community. Furthermore, by rejecting the power of the individual will to act in freedom, since the individual will is mere appearance and we are driven without knowing it by the cosmic will, Schopenhauer's position has the effect of implicitly undermining one of the key pillars of Wagner's philosophy. Wagner, as we have seen, maintains that freedom consists in aligning our desires with our nature. That alignment produces reliably free spontaneity or involuntariness, that is, action which is immediately expressive of our natures rather than action mandated or generated by some form of rational deliberation or social control. Schopenhauer, though, rejected all models of free agency, framing it as an illusion of the phenomenal world in which things are individuated.[17] The restless power of the will over which we have no control, other than the ascetic power to renounce it, prevents us from achieving tranquillity or equilibrium. It compels us to become dissatisfied with whatever we have achieved regardless of how long or intensively we have pursued it. (As noted earlier, Wagner had independently developed, in *The Artwork of the Future,* a claim about the insatiability of certain kinds of inauthentic needs.) Schopenhauer ridicules the notion of blissful happiness, a state in which no further effort or new desire is required, since what we know, in the main, is only the misery of further wanting. The implications of that thesis for Wagner's philosophy are considerable. If Schopenhauer is right about the obscure motivating power of the will, then Wagner's notion of involuntariness must seem to be the product of deep innocence: the will is not after all prompted either by an inner benevolence or tendency towards freedom. It is, rather, restless activity with no intrinsic interest in value.

In the unhelpful editorial addition to his collected works, already discussed in this study, Wagner addressed the issue of where he had stood on the question of the will when compared to what he had discovered in Schopenhauer's theory. He continues to maintain that *Willkür* is an inferior form of the will to *Unwillkür,* the latter necessarily expressive of what we truly are. However, Schopenhauer's 'instruction', as he puts it, had changed the meaning of this opposition. In the revolutionary period, *Willkür* designated an arbitrariness of action not rooted in real human needs, and among the false needs are those contrived by the kind of rational reflection that distances us from ourselves. That remains his meaning in his later thinking, but *Willkür* is opposed in a new way by *Unwillkür,* which has taken on, Wagner believes, Schopenhauer's sense of the will. It means, as Wagner's gloss puts it, the 'truly productive qualities' of human beings.[18] In other words, nonrational involuntariness which underpins the capacities for freedom, creation, and affectivity—the position of the trilogy—is officially superseded by the involuntariness of the Schopenhauerian will. But given that Wagner highlights the productive dimensions of the latter, obvious similarities between the early and later varieties seem hard to ignore, even as Wagner takes pains to distinguish them. Here, it appears, the philosophical framework of the trilogy directs his thinking, preventing him from making good on his self-effacing intuition that he now belonged to a drastically new system of philosophical thought.

The Wagner of 1854 may have been unnerved by the implications of Schopenhauer's particular line of attack on the *principium individuationis*, but it is useful to set that concern in the context of his own efforts to develop a notion of decentred subjectivity. He did not understand the object of his criticism as an illusion of phenomenal experience. There is in Wagner's theory no true reality hidden behind what has come to be called the 'modern subject'. Rather, the limitations of individual development—which, ironically, give rise to the delusion that the self is at its most impressive when self-contained and wholly self-constituted—must be superseded. It is to be replaced with an ideal of a socially imbricated self, one in which the very idea of individuation takes on a more complex and relational meaning. Wagner has two broad models for thinking of this. The first is his perfectionism—apparent as early as the 'Man and Existing Society' essay—which entails a hierarchy of social development which has as its ideal those individuals who realize themselves among and with others. Their actions possess an elevated quality and value solely because they exist within those involvements. This model is nowhere more evident than in Wagner's thoughts on the Gesamtkunstwerk. Not simply an artwork of all the media, it is, as we have seen, a collective endeavour in which individuality is not erased, certainly, but achieves its greatest possible realization as part of a collective aesthetic project which necessarily requires the flattening of competitive and hierarchical social roles.

The second model is found in *Jesus von Nazareth*, where individuality is presented as having its full significance only within a transhistorical context. For obvious reasons, that text cannot safely be regarded as a vehicle for Wagner's settled philosophical convictions. It is, however, difficult to ignore as a source of ideas given its discursive structure, not least when we find long prose passages which read as philosophy in the guise of religious teachings. What we find there goes beyond the claim that we are constituted as social beings. Jesus instructs us, Wagner writes, that we must understand ourselves as elements of a larger reality. We have already noted the idea found in that text that intentional and loving reproduction—the creation of family—can be characterized as 'a giving of one's own life force'. The egoistic perspective is surrendered through that act of self-externalization. It contrasts with the repressive act Wagner was later to encounter in Schopenhauer but which he aptly labels here as the egoism of 'monkish renunciation'.[19] In the latter case, the individual foregoes all pleasure in the name of a higher virtue but must exclude the world of others from experience. It is that exclusion which marks it out as egoism. *Jesus von Nazareth* voices the idea that the deaths of those who have lived without egoism—in Wagner's sense—are never perceived as terrible since they are appreciated as individuals who have undertaken an essential role in the natural perpetuation of life. Egoists stand in a different position, however, fearing death since the loss of their lives is a total loss: nothing of value in their contracted world endures after them, since they have never sought to create anything of worth that extends beyond their own immediate self-interest. It is also suggested that patriotism is an expansion of that renunciation of egoism found in the familial situation. But patriotism is itself surpassed in scope, we are told, by what Jesus teaches us about the possibility of 'universal human love'.[20] The more my own needs are given to 'the satisfaction of a universal love of humanity', Jesus instructs, 'the more I destroy my egoism through merging myself into the universal'. Furthermore, 'the most complete—as well as necessary—destruction of this individual self is attained in death, the surrender of myself brought about by my life'.[21] What is emphasised here is not the cessation of the individual—that is to think within the frame of egoism—but the global process of continuing regeneration.

These claims are made, obviously enough, from a grand perspective which, like that of Schopenhauer (in his case, life viewed from the perspective of the logic of the cosmic will), is concerned with the most fundamental processes of life. We are encouraged to understand our actions through a truer or higher framework that rescues us from the limiting perspective of finitude. What is to be cultivated is an existential sensibility in which each person understands themselves to be essentially diffused across the totality of human connections: within their families and nations, over generations, and, most importantly of all, within the universality of humanity. The picture that emerges is intended as a reassuring one. It conceives death as a necessary part of a magnificent process—life and its renewal—which must not itself be allowed to perish. It combines the renunciation of egoism by means of self-externalization with an affirmation of the species. In a variety of differing ways, and across the trilogy and at least some part of the dramatic work, Wagner, then, exposes delusive notions of individuation which are oblivious to the wider processes of community (perfectionism) or life as a meaningful process (the transhistorical perspective). His field was not metaphysics but the interactive complex of feeling, needful, and creative human life. Wagner would remain a politically engaged thinker, though no longer of the left, who never, on this point in particular, subscribed to the extreme demands of Schopenhauer's philosophy. He returned in later writings to patriotism, and that again required an anti-individualist notion of the person but hardly the abolition of the self. However, he went as far as he could to interpret his own thinking through Schopenhauerian categories, with his focus largely on the dramas rather than his existing political and philosophical theories. But potential for alignment with Schopenhauer was nevertheless latent in the theoretical ideas of his revolutionary writings. It required considerable adjustment but not, after all, a rupture with his earlier work.

Wagner's contribution to the discussion of individuation, together with his more radical ideas of antihistory, spontaneity, and needfulness, has been largely lost to the history of ideas. The trilogy is usually read, if at all, as background to Wagner's compositional endeavours with an untested assumption that it has little intrinsic value of its own. This simply misses the overmastering importance that Wagner himself saw in philosophical work during his revolutionary period. His brief though intensive engagement generated, this study has tried to show, a system that is relatively cohesive and distinctively new. Across its diverse theses, Wagner demonstrates varying levels of original philosophical ingenuity. But what might be of even greater significance, in the end, is the individual perspective from which his ideas emerged. By that I mean not just Wagner's moral or political judgments on the world. I am referring primarily, rather, to the unique productivity of a sublimely artistic mind within the field of philosophy. He was perfectly aware, as the careful wording of his dedication in *The Artwork of the Future* suggests, that he was drawing on the experience of creation—his artistic personality, in effect—in reconceiving and devising ideas that he believed could be realized in a future unimpaired by the exigencies of modern society. The perspective of the artist is an alternative to those philosophical viewpoints which, as Wagner saw it, are merely amplifications of concepts—an intraconceptual activity—and not responses to the most important and satisfying human experiences.

In spite of Wagner's protestations, we are as likely as the sceptical contemporaries he confronts to find the idea of an aesthetic future, with all its entailments, charmingly utopian. But it is not of course necessary that we adopt his vision in order to see the critical salience of his ideas and approach within the context of the rationalism of the German thought he found around him both in philosophy and in state life. Those achievements place him in opposition to certain formal ideals that have been defended ever more starkly in the wake of the devastation of European life in the twentieth century by an ideology that attempted to lay claim to him. Wagner's universalism, not always adequately expressed, envisaged, though, the very opposite of sentimental division among people, urging instead a human community of individuality and commonality, where the natural capacities for aesthetic and affective sensitivity could be developed and deployed against egoism and alienation. There are many reasons to regret that Wagner did not continue to expand on this view of things, since it is rich with unfulfilled philosophical possibility and free of the intolerant ideas that would, after the revolutionary period, overtly assert themselves in his thinking. The trilogy itself nevertheless has left us with a substantial set of distinctively framed contentions which together should give us reason to reappraise Wagner as a philosophically enterprising theorist of revolution.

NOTES

Introduction

1. ML 429 / SSD XIV, 283.

2. For instance, Wagner, without any particular agenda, had attempted to read Hegel just a few years prior to the revolutionary events, though he never claimed to have made much sense of what he found there. See Richard H. Bell, 'Teleology, Providence and the "Death of God": A New Perspective on the *Ring* Cycle's Debt to G.W.F. Hegel', *The Wagner Journal* 11, no. 1 (2017): 32.

3. Wagner, it is claimed by one of his confidants, had anticipated revolution several years earlier, declaring in 1846 that 'national institutions were only outwardly intact'. Quoted in Mark Berry, *Treacherous Bonds and Laughing Fire: Politics and Religion in Wagner's 'Ring'* (Oxford: Routledge, 2016), 39.

4. Richard Wagner, Letter to Theodor Uhlig, 16 September 1849, in *Richard Wagner's Letters to His Dresden Friends*, trans. J. S. Shedlock (Cambridge: Cambridge University Press, 2015), 10 / SB III 123.

5. The title pages of these books note 1850, 1850, and 1852 respectively as their years of publication.

6. No single English word captures the range of significances of the German original. And I am using the older orthography, *Noth*, to ensure it is not confused for the English adverb 'not'.

7. Certainly, many lightweight pieces designed to elevate Wagner appeared in the controversial *Bayreuther Blätter*. It might be indicative of the Bayreuth circle's curation of Wagner's reputation that its leading figure, Houston Stewart Chamberlain, produced a lengthy and ideologically twisted study—*Richard Wagner*, the first edition of which was published in Munich in 1895—that includes just a handful of pages on Wagner's revolutionary and universalist ideas. Among the more engaged studies from the period are Hugo Dinger, *Richard Wagners geistige Entwickelung* (Leipzig: E. W. Fritzsch, 1892); Rudolf Louis, *Die Weltanschauung Richard Wagners* (Leipzig: Breitkopf und Härtel, 1898); and Arthur Drews, *Der Ideengehalt von Richard Wagners 'Ring des Nibelungen' in seinen Beziehungen zur modernen Philosophie* (Leipzig: Hermann Haacke, 1898).

8. Not to be overlooked, however, are Bryan Magee, *Wagner and Philosophy* (London: Penguin, 2000); and Julian Young, *The Philosophies of Richard Wagner* (Lanham, MD: Lexington Books, 2014), which with differing interests both from each other and the present study proceed insightfully on the basis of the philosophical significance of Wagner's thought.

9. Ernest Newman, *Wagner as Man and Artist* (New York: Alfred A. Knopf, 1924), 270; Michael Tanner, 'The Total Work of Art', in *The Wagner Companion*, ed. Peter Burbidge and Richard Sutton (London: Faber and Faber, 1979), 148; R. J. Hollingdale, *Nietzsche: The Man and His Philosophy*, 2nd ed. (Cambridge: Cambridge University Press, 1999), 58; Anthony Winterbourne, *Speaking to Our Condition: Moral Frameworks in Wagner's 'Ring of the Nibelung'* (London: Associated University Presses, 2000), 22; Philip Kitcher and Richard Schacht, *Finding an Ending: Reflections on Wagner's 'Ring'* (Oxford: Oxford University Press, 2004), 6.

10. This observation does not refer to the group of sceptics named in the previous footnote. John Deathridge notes: '[p]hilosophers in the postwar Anglo-American tradition, too, were for a long time skeptical or simply ignorant about Wagner (often both)' ('Waiting for Wagner: Reluctant Musicology, Radical Philosophy, and the Rescue of a Fraught Legacy', *The Opera Quarterly* 30, nos. 2–3 [2014]: 267). Within German-speaking academic departments, by contrast, Wagner has certainly been a marginal figure, but not one who is superficially considered.

11. John Deathridge, *Wagner Beyond Good and Evil* (Berkeley: University of California Press, 2008), 241.

Chapter 1. The Practice of Revolution

1. ML 40 / SSD XIII, 54.

2. Much of the historical material for this section is drawn from the following sources: Christopher Clark, *Revolutionary Spring: Fighting for a New World 1848–1849* (London: Allen Lane, 2023); Manfred Görtemaker, *Deutschland im 19. Jahrhundert. Entwicklungslinien* (Opladen: Leske und Budrich, 1983); Dieter Hein, *Die Revolution von 1848/49*, 6th ed. (Munich: C. H. Beck, 2019); Robert W. Lougee, *Midcentury Revolution, 1848: Society and Revolution in France and Germany* (Lexington, MA: D. C. Heath and Company, 1972); Douglas Moggach and Gareth Stedman Jones, eds., *The 1848 Revolutions and European Political Thought* (Cambridge: Cambridge University Press, 2018); G. H. Müller, *Richard Wagner in der Mai-Revolution, 1849* (Dresden: Oscar Laube Verlag, 1919); Lewis Namier, *1848: The Revolution of the Intellectuals* (Oxford: Oxford University Press, 1992); Wolfram Siemann, *The German Revolution of 1848–49* (Basingstoke: Macmillan, 1998); Jonathan Sperber, *The European Revolutions, 1848–1851*, 2nd ed. (Cambridge: Cambridge University Press, 2005); Rolf Weber, *Die Revolution in*

Sachsen 1848/49. Entwicklung und Analyse ihrer Triebkräfte (Berlin: Akademie Verlag, 1970).

3. Görtemaker, *Deutschland im 19. Jahrhundert*, 96.

4. See Clark, *Revolutionary Spring*, 317–324.

5. Ernest Newman, *The Life of Richard Wagner*, vol. 1, *1813–1848* (Cambridge: Cambridge University Press, 1976), 403, 484–487.

6. Weber, *Die Revolution in Sachsen 1848/49*, 14.

7. SSD XII, 227.

8. See *Der Aufruhr in Dresden am 3, 4, 5, 6, 7, 8 und 9 Mai 1849* (Dresden: Adler und Dietze, 1849) by Dr. Karl Krause, a virtually contemporaneous compilation of events.

9. Görtemaker, *Deutschland im 19. Jahrhundert*, 116.

10. Clark, *Revolutionary Spring*, 649.

11. PW 8, 216 / SSD XII, 359.

12. This piece does not appear in the *Prose Works* collection.

13. SSD XII, 221.

14. Ernest Newman, *The Life of Richard Wagner*, vol. 2, *1848–1860* (Cambridge: Cambridge University Press, 1976), 9.

15. Rüdiger Krohn, 'The Revolutionary of 1848–49', in *Wagner Handbook*, ed. Ulrich Müller and Peter Wapnewski, trans. ed. John Deathridge (Cambridge, MA: Harvard University Press, 1992), 161.

16. A wide-ranging study of the ideological complexity of the Vaterlandsvereine in Dresden and across Saxony can be found in Weber, *Die Revolution in Sachsen 1848/49*. Also of help are Manfred Botzenhart, *Deutscher Parlamentarismus in der Revolutionszeit 1848–1850* (Dusseldorf: Droste Verlag, 1977); and Dieter Langewiesche, 'Die Anfänge der deutschen Parteien. Partei, Fraktion und Verein in der Revolution von 1848/49', *Geschichte und Gesellschaft* 4, no. 3 (1978): 324–361.

17. K.H.L. Pölitz, *Die Staatswissenschaften im Lichte unserer Zeit*, vol. 1 (Leipzig: J. C. Hinrichs, 1823), 423. See Wolfgang Mager, 'Republik', in *Geschichtliche Grundbegriffe*, ed. Otto Bruner, Werner Conze, Reinhart Koselleck, vol. 5 (Stuttgart: Klett-Cotta, 1984), 619.

18. SSD XII, 220.

19. SSD XII, 225.

20. SSD XII, 226.

21. SSD XII, 228.

22. SSD XII, 224.

23. SSD XII, 227.

24. SSD XII, 226.

25. SSD XII, 227.

26. Weber, *Die Revolution in Sachsen 1848/49*, 115.

27. Weber, *Die Revolution in Sachsen 1848/49*, 332.

28. SSD XII, 223.

29. SSD XII, 223. The peculiarities of this passage are discussed in Eckart Kröplin's comprehensive study, *Richard Wagner und der Kommunismus: Studie zu einem verdrängten Thema* (Würzburg: Königshausen & Neumannn, 2013), 53–54.

30. A typical utterance occurs in 'The Artistry of the Future', PW 8, 345–346 / SSD XII, 256.

31. SSD XII, 224.

32. PW 4, 7 / SSD VIII, 5.

33. And nor does this piece appear in the *Prose Works* collection.

34. SSD XII, 415.

35. SSD XII, 415.

36. SSD XII, 415.

37. SSD XII, 416.

38. SSD XII, 417.

39. This essay appears in PW 8 with the title 'Man and Established Society'.

40. PW 8, 228 / SSD XII, 241.

41. PW 8, 228 / SSD XII, 241.

42. PW 8, 229 / SSD XII, 242.

43. PW 8, 230 / SSD XII, 243.

44. PW 8, 231 / SSD XII, 244.

45. ML 385 / SSD XIV, 225.

46. ML 386 / SSD XIV, 225.

47. ML 407 / SSD XIV, 254: 'The tears of a philistine are the nectar of the gods' are the words Wagner attributes to Bakunin.

48. PW 8, 232 / SSD XII, 245.

49. Michael Bakunin, 'The Reaction in Germany', in *Selected Writings*, ed. Arthur Lehning (London: Jonathan Cape, 1973), 58. I am grateful to Fred Rush for drawing my attention to this.

50. PW 8, 236 / SSD XII, 249.

51. See Newman, *Life of Richard Wagner*, vol. 2, 54–57.

52. PW 8, 236 / SSD XII, 248.

53. See Curt von Westernhagen, *Wagner: A Biography*, trans. Mary Whittall (Cambridge: Cambridge University Press, 1978), 133; and Martin Gregor-Dellin, *Richard Wagner, His Life, His Work, His Century*, trans J. Maxwell Brownjohn (London: Collins, 1983), 190.

54. Carl Friedrich Glasenapp shows how far from accuracy zealous loyalty can go with his risible claim that 'Man and Existing Society' was intended primarily as a contribution to discussions about theatre reform. Carl Friedrich Glasenapp, *Life of Richard Wagner*, trans. William Ashton Ellis, vol. 2 (London: Kegan Paul, Trench,

Trübner & Co., 1902), 314. William Ashton Ellis's main contribution is found in a passionate yet analytical work with the self-explanatory title, *Wagner Sketches: 1849, A Vindication* (London: Kegan Paul, Trench, Trübner & Co., 1893).

55. Richard Wagner, Letter to Eduard Devrient, 17 May 1849, in *Selected Letters of Richard Wagner*, trans. and ed. Stewart Spencer and Barry Millington (London: Norton, 1987), 150 / SB II, 666.

56. ML 40–41 / SSD XIII, 55–56.

57. PW 4, 136.

58. PW 1, xviii / SSD I, vi.

59. ML 389 / SSD XIV, 231.

60. CF 355 / SSD IV, 309.

61. ML 390 / SSD XIV, 231.

62. Glasenapp, *Life of Richard Wagner*, vol. 2, 358.

63. ML 395 / SSD XIV, 238 (translation changed).

64. Richard Wagner, Letter to August Röckel, 2 May 1849, in *Selected Letters of Richard Wagner*, 145 / SB II, 652.

65. ML 392 / SSD XIV, 234.

66. ML 394 / SSD XIV, 237.

67. See, for example, Gregor-Dellin, *Richard Wagner, His Life, His Work, His Century*, 171.

68. ML 372 / SSD XIV, 208.

69. ML 398 / SSD XIV, 242.

70. ML 400 / SSD XIV, 245 (translation changed).

71. Gregor-Dellin, *Richard Wagner, His Life, His Work, His Century*, 175.

72. Glasenapp, *Life of Richard Wagner*, vol. 2, 347.

73. Glasenapp, *Life of Richard Wagner*, vol. 2, 347.

74. Richard Wagner, Letter to Franz Liszt, 9 July 1849, in *Correspondence of Wagner and Liszt 1841–1853*, ed. Francis Hueffer, vol. 1 (Cambridge: Cambridge University Press, 2009), 37 / SB III, 89.

75. See Newman, *Life of Richard Wagner*, vol. 2, 62–64.

76. This is noted in one of the police alerts seeking his arrest. See Müller, *Richard Wagner in der Mai-Revolution, 1849*, 62.

77. Richard Wagner, Letter to Theodor Uhlig, 18 September 1850, in *Richard Wagner's Letters to His Dresden Friends*, trans. J. S. Shedlock (Cambridge: Cambridge University Press, 2015), 58 / SB III, 411.

78. Richard Wagner, Letter to Franz Liszt, 18 June 1849, in *Correspondence of Wagner and Liszt*, vol. 1, 27 / SB III, 81.

79. Richard Wagner, Letter to August Röckel, 6 March 1862, in *Richard Wagner's Letters to August Roeckel*, trans. Eleanor C. Sellar (Bristol: J. W. Arrowsmith, 1879), 165 / SB XIV, 96–97.

80. Quoted in Westernhagen, *Wagner: A Biography*, 133.

81. Richard Wagner, Letter to Minna Wagner, 14 May 1849, in *Selected Letters of Richard Wagner*, 146 / SB II, 653–654.

82. Richard Wagner, Letter to Eduard Devrient, 17 May 1849, in *Selected Letters of Richard Wagner*, 146 / SB II, 660. See also Richard Wagner, Letter to Hermann Brockhaus, 2 February 1851, in *Family Letters of Richard Wagner*, ed. and trans. William Ashton Ellis (Cambridge: Cambridge University Press, 2015), 160 / SB III, 506.

83. Richard Wagner, Letter to Franz Liszt, 19 June 1849, in *Correspondence of Wagner and Liszt*, vol. 1, 31 / SB III, 86.

84. Richard Wagner, Letter to Eduard Devrient, 17 May 1849, in *Selected Letters of Richard Wagner*, 146 / SB II, 660.

85. Richard Wagner, Letter to Eduard Devrient, 17 May 1849, in *Selected Letters of Richard Wagner*, 150 / SB II, 665.

86. Richard Wagner, Letter to Eduard Devrient, 17 May 1849, in *Selected Letters of Richard Wagner*, 150 / SB II 665.

87. CF 355 / SSD IV, 308–309.

Chapter 2. The Revolution as Future

1. Richard Wagner, Letter to Franz Liszt, 5 June 1849, in *Selected Letters of Richard Wagner*, trans. and ed. Stewart Spencer and Barry Millington (London: Norton, 1987), 171 / SB III, 74.

2. CF 256 / SSD IV, 310.

3. PW 8, 345 / SSD XII, 256.

4. OD 173 / SSD IV, 49.

5. AF 206 / SSD III, 171.

6. OD 175 / SSD IV, 51.

7. OD 175 / SSD IV, 51.

8. PW 8, 344 / SSD XII, 255.

9. AR 55 / SSD III, 31.

10. AF 84 / SSD III, 56.

11. AR 50 / SSD III, 26–27.

12. In this way, Wagner is quite at odds with the view among nineteenth-century German thinkers who, as Raymond Geuss points out, disfavoured the idea of civilization while remaining confident in the life-enhancing qualities of *Kultur*. Wagner evidently conflates these two ideas and condemns in culture—or at least in modern culture—what others see as mere civilization. See Raymond Geuss, 'Kultur, Bildung, Geist', in *Morality, Culture, and History: Essays on German Philosophy* (Cambridge: Cambridge University Press, 2008), 29–50.

13. Friedrich Nietzsche, *On the Genealogy of Morality and Other Writings*, ed. Keith Ansell-Pearson, trans. Carol Diethe (Cambridge: Cambridge University Press, 2017), 24.

14. AF 206 / SSD III, 171.

15. OD 205 / SSD IV, 75.

16. OD 204 / SSD IV, 75.

17. AR 56 / SSD III, 32–33.

18. AR 57 / SSD III, 33.

19. AR 64 / SSD III, 40.

20. AF 207 / SSD III, 172.

21. AF 75 / SSD III, 48.

22. Necessity, as we shall see in the following chapter, is a quality that Wagner ascribes to any action that is grounded in what he thinks of as properly human. It will be found in several contexts, including authentic freedom and genuine creativity. And it is always employed by Wagner alongside its objectionable opposite, namely, what is arbitrary. In the context of 'the people', what is necessary are social arrangements that are needs sensitive, and the arbitrary is what has egoistic purpose.

23. AF 81 / SSD III, 53.

24. PW 8, 348 / SSD XII, 259.

25. AF 81 / SSD III, 53.

26. AF 81 / SSD III, 54.

27. Hartmut Zelinsky interprets *Noth* as a version of Hegel's 'unhappy consciousness' and then aligns it with racial exclusion (*Richard Wagner—Ein deutsches Thema* [Berlin: Medusa, 1983], 19).

28. AR 75–76/ SSD III, 48.

29. AF 76 / SSD III, 48.

30. AR 59 / SSD III, 36.

31. AF 79 / SSD III, 52.

32. AF 83 / SSD III, 56.

33. OD 175 / SSD IV, 50.

34. OD 204–205 / SSD IV, 75.

35. With regard to spontaneity as a phenomenon of social liberation, see Dieter Henrich, 'Gesamtkunstwerk und Partialkunstwerk', in *Fixpunkte. Abhandlungen und Essays zur Theorie und Praxis* (Frankfurt: Suhrkamp, 2003), 43.

36. Udo Bermbach maintains that Wagner acquired some familiarity with and sympathy for the main outlines of anarchist theory during the years he had previously spent in Paris. He plausibly presents illuminating lines of influence as they bear on the *Gesamtkunstwerk*. *Der Wahn des Gesamtkunstwerks: Richard Wagners politisch-ästhetische Utopie*, 2nd ed. (Stuttgart: Verlag J. B. Metzler, 2004), 213. It is

important to note, however, that Wagner himself rarely mentions any anarchist thinkers in his writings.

37. Wolfgang Schild, *Richard Wagner recht betrachtet. Vierzehn Beiträge* (Berlin: De Gruyter, 2020), 96.

38. Wagner tends to spell the word with a double 'm': *Gesammtkunstwerk*. Although the term is almost exclusively associated with Wagner, it is not, in fact, his invention. See Alfred R Neumann, 'The Earliest Use of the Term *Gesamtkunstwerk*', *Philological Quarterly* 35 (1956): 191–193.

39. AF 77 / SSD III, 50.

40. AR 52 / SSD III, 28.

41. Friedrich Nietzsche, *The Gay Science, with a Prelude in German Rhymes and an Appendix of Songs*, ed. Bernard Williams, trans. Josefine Nauckhoff (Cambridge: Cambridge University Press, 2001), 96.

42. AF 162 / SSD III, 113.

43. AF 182 / SSD III, 149.

44. As, it seems, did Wagner too until confronted by the realities of the Parisian scene he had hoped to penetrate. In reaction, he took on the readymade identity, as Nicholas Vazsonyi puts it, of the unworldly German: 'In this tale, to be German was to be honest, genuine, to do things for their own sake, and not to be interested success or commercial gain. To be a German artist was to be willing to suffer that art, to martyr oneself for it. Wagner was all of these; thus he and the produced were "truly" German' ('Marketing German Identity: Richard Wagner's "Enterprise"', *German Studies Review* 28, no. 2 [2005]: 333).

45. AF 126 / SSD III, 96.

46. AF 127 / SSD III, 97.

47. AF 127 / SSD III, 97.

48. PW 8, 353 / SSD XII, 264.

49. AR 47 / SSD III, 24.

50. CF 276 / SSD IV, 237.

51. AR 35 / SSD III, 12.

52. AR 35 / SSD III, 12.

53. AR 52 / SSD III, 29.

54. AR 35 / SSD III, 13.

55. SSD III, 3. This line comes from a motto that Wagner decided not to use for the original edition of *Art and Revolution*.

56. The form of higher human self-expression that eventually emerged was Christianity, a form of life which Wagner sees as perfectly appropriate to a world in which the human being is split between body and soul—'incurably and irreconcilably divided within its deepest interior' (AR 39 / SSD III, 16). Without elaborating on the

thought, Wagner is suggesting that the fragmentation of the self is at one with the fragmentation of society.

57. AF 205 / SSD III, 169.

58. AF 208 / SSD III, 173.

59. PW 7, 233 / SSD II, 233.

60. AF 155 / SSD III, 122.

61. Olivier Schefer, 'Variations on Totality: Romanticism and the Total Work of Art', in *The Aesthetics of the Total Artwork: On Borders and Fragments*, ed. Anke Finger and Danielle Follett (Baltimore: The Johns Hopkins University Press, 2011), 32.

62. Michael Tanner, 'The Total Work of Art', in *The Wagner Companion*, ed. Peter Burbidge and Richard Sutton (London: Faber and Faber, 1979), 146.

63. AF 118 / SSD III, 89.

64. AF 173 / SSD III, 140. This is the particular 'redemption' referenced in Tanner's objections.

65. AF 145 / SSD III, 113.

66. AF 190 / SSD III, 156.

67. Wolfgang Marx, quoted in Schild, 83.

68. AF 153 / SSD III, 120. The following are further cases, from among many, of this accusation: 'In this way, our modern art of dance in *pantomime* takes on the aim of drama; it wants, like every isolated egoistic art form, to be everything for itself, to be able to do everything and to be capable of everything by itself' (AF 109 / SSD III, 80); or, '[t]his is the true egoism in which each individual art form would like to pose as a general art, while in truth it thereby only loses its real particularity' (AF 99 / SSD III, 71). In *Opera and Drama*, he continues to speak about 'egoistically isolated arts' (OD 120 / SSD IV, 2).

69. AR 41 / SSD III, 18.

70. AF 88 / SSD III, 60.

71. Howard S. Becker, 'Art as Collective Action', *American Sociological Review* 39, no. 6 (1974): 775. I am grateful to Jane Brennan O'Connor for suggesting this comparison.

72. AF 183 / SSD III, 150.

73. AF 192 / SD III, 162.

74. AR 60–61 / SSD III, 37.

75. OD 376 / SSD IV, 229.

76. CF 280–281 / SSD IV, 241.

77. Theodor W. Adorno, *In Search of Wagner*, trans. Rodney Livingstone (London: Verso, 1991), 28.

78. Adorno, *In Search of Wagner*, 109.

79. Adorno, *In Search of Wagner*, 102.

80. David Roberts, *The Total Work of Art in European Modernism* (Ithaca, NY: Cornell University Press, 2011), 70.

81. OD 46 / SSD III, 255.

82. Richard Wagner, Letter to Franz Liszt, 16 August 1853, in *Correspondence of Wagner and Liszt 1841–1853*, ed. Francis Hueffer, vol. 1 (Cambridge: Cambridge University Press, 2009), 318 / SB V, 401. In that letter, Wagner uses the term *Gesammtkunst*.

83. The artwork's 'opposition to' the present does not, strictly speaking, mean that it already anticipates the future (AR 52 / SSD III, 28).

84. PW 1, 24 / SSD III, 2.

85. Bermbach suggests that the *Gesamtkunstwerk* serves as a 'utopian model' in 'an anticipation of a community that represents the structural alternative to the status quo' (*Der Wahn des Gesamtkunstwerks*, 258).

86. Richard Wagner, Letter to Theodor Uhlig, 27 December 1849, in *Selected Letters*, 184 / SB III, 197.

87. The *Prose Writings* translates this essay's title as 'Judaism in Music'. *Judentum*, however, may refer both to Jewishness or Jewry and to the Jewish religion, but it is not the latter that is in view in Wagner's piece.

88. Paul Lawrence Rose, *Wagner: Race and Revolution* (New Haven, CT: Yale University Press, 1992), 2.

89. JM 79 / Richard Wagner, 'Das Judenthum in der Musik', *Neue Zeitschrift für Musik* no. 19/20 (September 1850): 101 (the older orthography was used in this publication). For an account of the contributions to this debate, see Jens Malte Fischer, *Richard Wagners 'Das Judentum in der Musik'. Eine kritische Dokumentation als Beitrag zur Geschichte des Antisemitismus* (Wurzburg: Königshausen & Neumann, 2015), 19–25.

90. That text will vary in important places from the version translated in PW 3.

91. SSD V, 2.

92. JM 85 / 'Das Judenthum in der Musik', 103.

93. Beckmesser's 'mangled speech patterns evoke *Mauscheln*, the bizarre travesty language attributed by Germans to Jews', argues Barry Millington in his *Richard Wagner: The Sorcerer of Bayreuth* (London: Thames & Hudson, 2012), 188.

94. And there is the reality that, notwithstanding his own powers, Wagner learned from both composers. There is the old quip that *Rienzi* was Meyerbeer's best opera, while the influence of Mendelssohn is discernible in *Der fliegende Holländer*. See, for instance, Thomas Gray, *Richard Wagner: Der fliegende Holländer* (Cambridge: Cambridge University Press, 2000), 47.

95. See Richard Wagner, Letter to Minna Wagner, 2 January 1844, in *Selected Letters*, 117 / SB II, 354.

96. JM 82 / 'Das Judenthum in der Musik', 102.

97. Fischer, *Richard Wagners 'Das Judentum in der Musik'*, 98.

98. JM 81 / 'Das Judenthum in der Musik', 102.

99. JM 87–88 / 'Das Judenthum in der Musik', 104.

100. This is implied by Hartmut Zelinsky: 'Der "Plenipotentarius des Untergangs", oder der Herrschaftsanspruch der antisemitischen Kunstreligion des selbsternannten Bayreuther Erlösers Richard Wagner. Anmerkungen zu Cosima Wagners Tagebüchern 1869–1883', *Neohelikon* 9, no. 1 (1982): 149. Rose makes the same claim explicitly (*Wagner: Race and Revolution*, 80). Rose, unfortunately, misquotes Wagner as saying '[all] is turned to money by the Jew' (80). In the original text, Wagner, though obscurely, claims something else: 'What the bondsmen of the Roman and medieval world paid in grind and misery to the masters, is nowadays turned into money by the Jew' (JM 82 / 'Das Judenthum in der Musik', 102).

101. AF 75 / SSD III, 48.

102. JM 89 / 'Das Judenthum in der Musik', 105.

103. And Rose here, once again, oversteps licit textual inference: 'Wagner's concept of revolution is, in fact, based here quite openly on his idea of the *Volk*: the revolution and the race are not only compatible with one another, but in fact inseparable' (*Wagner: Race and Revolution*, 80).

104. Dieter Borchmeyer, 'The Question of Anti-Semitism', in *Wagner Handbook*, ed. Ulrich Müller and Peter Wapnewski, trans. ed. John Deathridge (Cambridge, MA: Harvard University Press, 1992), 174.

105. JM 100 / 'Das Judenthum in der Musik', 112.

106. Saul Friedländer, 'Bayreuth und der Erlösungsantisemitismus', in *Richard Wagner und die Juden*, ed. Dieter Borchmeyer, Ami Maayani, and Susanne Vill (Stuttgart: Metzler, 2000), 10. Friedländer explains that as Wagner's antisemitism deepened that redemptive form gave way, successively, to ideas of 'redemption of the community of the people from the Jews; the redemption of the Aryan-Christian community from the Jews' (10).

107. JM 100 / 'Das Judenthum in der Musik', 112.

108. PW 8, 359 / SSD XII, 269.

109. JM 100 / 'Das Judenthum in der Musik', 112.

110. As Raymond Furness puts it: 'mankind as a whole must "die" to the modern world and its materialism to become reborn' (*Richard Wagner* [London: Reaktion Books, 2013], 86).

111. 'Das Judenthum in der Musik', 112. This passage is not part of the translated version in PW.

112. JM 100 / 'Das Judenthum in der Musik', 112.

113. AF 72–73 / SSD III, 45.

114. AF 172 / SSD III, 139.

115. OD 195 / SSD IV, 67. This term is also, for example, applied to Antigone, who is characterized as the annihilator of the state (OD 190 / SSD IV, 64).

Chapter 3. A Philosophy of Freedom

1. PW 3, 295 / SSD VII, 88.

2. PW 1, 25 / SSD III, 3.

3. PW 1, 24–26 / SSD III, 4.

4. CF 286 / SSD IV, 247–248.

5. See Mark Berry, *Treacherous Bonds and Laughing Fire: Politics and Religion in Wagner's 'Ring'* (Oxford: Routledge, 2016), 10–12, for the debate surrounding Feuerbach's influence on the *Ring*.

6. PW 1, 25 / SSD III, 3.

7. PW 1, 394 / SSD XII, 284.

8. See, for example, Arthur Drews, who observes that *The Artwork of the Future* 'of course makes no special claim to originality. It is merely the old naturalism' (*Der Ideengehalt von Richard Wagners 'Ring des Nibelungen' in Seinen Beziehungen zur Modernen Philosophie* [Leipzig: Hermann Haacke, 1898], 13). Drews, however, recognizes Wagner's work as a philosophical endeavour, even if not always, in his view, an especially novel one.

9. ML 430 / SSD XIV, 284.

10. Ludwig Feuerbach, *Thoughts on Death and Immortality from the Papers of a Thinker*, trans. and ed. James A. Massey (Berkeley: University of California Press, 1980), 10.

11. Feuerbach, *Thoughts on Death and Immortality*, 37.

12. Feuerbach, *Thoughts on Death and Immortality*, 38.

13. ML 431 / SSD XIV, 285.

14. PW 1, 25 / SSD III, 3.

15. Feuerbach, *Thoughts on Death and Immortality*, 162.

16. ML 430 / SSD XIV, 284.

17. Ludwig Feuerbach, *The Essence of Christianity*, trans. Marian Evans (aka George Eliot) (London: Trübner & Co, 1881), 13.

18. Feuerbach, *Essence of Christianity*, 207.

19. Feuerbach, *Essence of Christianity*, 73.

20. Feuerbach, *Essence of Christianity*, 111 et passim.

21. Feuerbach, *Essence of Christianity*, 111.

22. Louis thematizes Wagner's project around that notion of the purely human. See Rudolf Louis, *Die Weltanschauung Richard Wagners* (Leipzig: Breitkopf und Härtel, 1898), 70.

23. As Marx put it: 'Man, who has found only his own *reflection* in the fantastic reality of heaven, where he sought a supernatural being, will no longer be disposed to find only the *semblance* of himself, only a non-human being, here where he seeks and must seek his true actuality' ('A Contribution to the Critique of Hegel's Philosophy of Right: Introduction', in *Early Political Writings*, ed. and trans. Jospeh O'Malley with Richard A. Davis [Cambridge: Cambridge University Press, 1994], 57).

24. Mitchell Cohen, 'To the Dresden Barricades: The Genesis of Wagner's Political Ideas', in *The Cambridge Companion to Wagner*, ed. Thomas Grey (Cambridge: Cambridge University Press, 2008), 52–53. Cohen makes this suggestion on the basis of the extremely sparing employment of *Noth* in Feuerbach's *Principles of the Philosophy of the Future.*

25. Feuerbach, *Essence of Christianity*, 50.

26. Feuerbach, *Essence of Christianity*, 146.

27. Feuerbach, *Essence of Christianity*, 127.

28. Feuerbach, *Essence of Christianity*, 146.

29. Feuerbach, *Essence of Christianity*, 228.

30. Feuerbach, *Essence of Christianity*, 167.

31. Feuerbach, *Essence of Christianity*, 167.

32. Feuerbach, *Essence of Christianity*, 203.

33. Drews, *Der Ideengehalt von Richard Wagners 'Ring des Nibelungen'*, 12.

34. PW 1, 27 / SSD III, 4–5.

35. Friedrich Nietzsche, *Twilight of the Idols*, in *The Anti-Christ, Ecce Homo, Twilight of the Idols, and Other Writings*, ed. Aaron Ridley and Judith Norman, trans. Judith Norman (Cambridge: Cambridge University Press, 2005), 172.

36. See Laurence Dreyfus, *Wagner and the Erotic Impulse* (Cambridge, MA: Harvard University Press, 2010), for a detailed study of sensuality across Wagner's dramatic work.

37. In a footnote *to Opera and Drama*, Wagner rejects the accusation of a 'Saxon critic' that his use of *Sinnlichkeit* is to be conflated with 'crude' sensualism, but he cleverly avoids the question of whether 'sensualism' might be among its intended connotations: OD 121n / SSD IV 3n.

38. Ludwig Feuerbach, *Principles of the Philosophy of the Future*, trans. Manfred H. Vogel (Indianapolis: Bobbs-Merrill, 1966), 54.

39. Feuerbach, *Principles of the Philosophy of the Future*, 15.

40. Feuerbach, *Principles of the Philosophy of the Future*, 52.

41. Feuerbach, *Principles of the Philosophy of the Future*, 53.

42. Louis, *Die Weltanschauung Richard Wagners*, 73.

43. PW 1, 395 / SSD XII, 285.

44. Cosima Wagner, *Diaries*, vol. 1, *1869–1877*, ed. Martin Gregor-Dellin and Dietrich Mack, trans. with an introduction, Geoffrey Skelton (London: Collins, 1978), entry of 5 December 1869, 170.

45. SSD, XII, 362.

46. Immanuel Kant, *Groundwork of the Metaphysics of Morals*, in Immanuel Kant, *Practical Philosophy*, ed. and trans. Mary J. Gregor (Cambridge: Cambridge University Press, 1996), 55.

47. Immanuel Kant, *Critique of Practical Reason*, in Kant, *Practical Philosophy*, 161.

48. Kant, *Groundwork*, 67.

49. Kant, *Groundwork*, 67.

50. Kant, *Critique of Practical Reason*, 206.

51. Kant, *Critique of Practical Reason*, 206.

52. Kant, *Critique of Practical Reason*, 206.

53. We should note that in places Kant suggests that necessitation has its compensations. Interestingly, given his purism when it comes to reason, he finds this compensation in certain elevated feelings that are uniquely available to us as we contemplate 'the majesty' of the moral law and experience the relegation of unworthy motives: 'since this constraint [i.e. necessitation] is exercised only by the lawgiving of his own reason, it also contains something elevating, and the subjective effect on feeling, inasmuch as pure practical reason is the sole cause of it' (Kant, *Critique of Practical Reason*, 205). 'Self-conceit' gives way to 'self-approbation'. Kant believes this psychological dimension is operational in us all. Among the many examples he employs to confirm that is the case of the cheat who 'must despise himself as soon as he compares himself with the moral law' (Kant, *Critique of Practical Reason*, 170).

54. Immanuel Kant, *The Metaphysics of Morals*, in Kant, *Practical Philosophy*, 536.

55. Kant, *Groundwork*, 72n.

56. OD 193 / SSD IV, 66.

57. SSD XII, 362.

58. Friedrich Schiller, *On the Aesthetic Education of Man, in a Series of Letters*, trans. Elizabeth M. Wilkinson and L. A. Willoughby (Oxford: Clarendon Press, 1967), Letter XV, 107.

59. AF 201n / SSD III, 166n.

60. OD 179 / SSD IV, 54.

61. OD 165 / SSD IV 42.

62. Sixtus Beckmesser, from *Die Meistersinger von Nürnberg*, pedantically assesses the quality of singers against inflexible rules.

63. AF 83 / SSD III, 56.

64. AF 74 / SSD III, 46.

65. AF 83 / SSD III, 56.

66. AF 83 / SSD III, 55–56.

67. AF 83 / SSD III, 56.

68. AF 79 / SSD III, 52.

69. AR 33 / SSD III, 10. Parts of this passage are neglected in the *Prose Works* translation.

70. AR 35–36 / SSD III, 13.

71. Wagner's word *unerzwungen* has the stem *Zwang*, which, in fact, is the term Kant uses when speaking about necessitation's compulsion.

72. AF 73 / SSD III, 46.

73. AF 71 / SSD III, 44.

74. AF 71 / SSD III, 44.

75. AF 71 / SSD III, 44.

76. OD 193 / SSD IV, 66.

77. AF 82 / SSD III, 55.

78. AR 72 / SSD III, 45.

79. OD 205 / SSD IV, 75.

80. OD 210 / SSD IV, 80.

81. OD 195 / SSD IV, 67.

82. OD 210 / SSD IV, 79.

83. OD 210 / SSD IV, 80.

84. In *Die Meistersinger*, Walther defeats his rivals in the singing contest by going beyond the conventions of the existing musical form. As Christopher Kimbell puts it, Walther proves 'his musical worth despite his non-identity' with his judges' expectations (*Tradition, Community, and Nationhood in Richard Wagner's 'Die Meistersinger von Nürnberg'* (Oxford: Routledge, 2025), 50.

85. OD 210 / SSD IV, 79–80.

Chapter 4. Freedom as Social Emancipation

1. AF 89 / SSD III, 61.

2. PW 4, 43 / SSD VIII, 36. Lessing, however, is frequently referenced across Wagner's writings.

3. Johann Joachim Winckelmann, *History of the Art of Antiquity*, trans. Harry Francis Mallgrave (Los Angeles: Getty Research Institute, 2006), 187.

4. Winckelmann, *History of the Art of Antiquity*, 187.

5. AR 37 / SSD III, 14.

6. AR 34 / SSD III, 11.

7. AR 34 / SSD III, 12.

8. AR 34 / SSD III, 12.

9. AR 57 / SSD III, 34.

10. AR 50 / SSD III, 26.

11. AR 50 / SSD III, 27.
12. AR 50 / SSD III, 26.
13. AR 54 / SSD III, 30.
14. AR 50 / SSD III, 27.
15. AR 50 / SSD III, 27.
16. AR 51 / SSD III, 27.
17. AF 166 / SSD III, 133.
18. OD 193 / SSD IV, 66.
19. AF 89 / SSD III, 62.
20. ML 373 / SSD XIV, 270–271.
21. Pierre-Joseph Proudhon, *What Is Property?*, ed. and trans. Donald R. Kelley and Bonnie G. Smith (Cambridge: Cambridge University Press, 1994), 173. Barry Millington speculates that Wagner may actually have encountered Proudhon's work—again through conversation—in the early 1840s during his years of residence in Paris (*Wagner* [Princeton, NJ: Princeton University Press, 1992], 26).
22. AF 206 / SSD III, 171.
23. AF 206 / SSD III, 171.
24. PW 8, 344 / SSD XII, 255.
25. AF 80 / SSD III, 53.
26. OD 175 / SSD IV, 51.
27. E. M. Butler observes that in his characteristic approach 'Wagner was not creating myths, nor even recreating them, as the Greek tragic drama had done. He was merely adapting ancient legends to suit a philosophy of life they had not been created to express' (*The Tyranny of Greece over Germany* [Cambridge: Cambridge University Press, 1935], 312). Her accusation excludes the possibility that myths can have continuing vitality when reframed as illuminations of changed realities.
28. OD 184 / SSD IV, 58.
29. OD 185 / SSD IV, 59.
30. OD 180 / SSD IV, 54.
31. OD 189 / SSD IV, 63.
32. OD 192 / SSD IV, 65.
33. AF 203 / SSD III, 168.
34. This thought appears in 'The Genius of Commonality' (Das Genie der Gemeinsamkeit), a set of preparatory notes from the revolutionary period (PW 8, 358 / SSD XII, 268).
35. AF 206 / SSD III, 171.
36. OD 193 / SSD IV, 66.
37. OD 196 / SSD IV, 67.
38. OD 196 / SSD IV, 68.
39. OD 179 / SSD IV, 54.

40. OD 203 / SSD IV, 74.
41. AF 84 / SSD III, 57.
42. AF 131 / SSD III, 101.
43. AF 209 / SSD III, 174.
44. OD 196 / SSD IV, 68.
45. OD 199 / SSD IV, 70.
46. OD 199 / SSD IV, 70.
47. PW 8, 228 / XIII, 241–242.
48. AF 76 / SSD III, 48.
49. AF 84 / SSD III, 57.
50. AF 84 / SSD III, 56.
51. AF 84 / SSD III, 57.
52. AF 108 / SSD III, 79–80.
53. AF 84 / SSD III, 57.
54. AF 203 / SSD III, 169.
55. AR 51 / SSD III, 28.
56. AR 51 / SSD III, 27.
57. AR 44 / SSD III, 21.
58. AR 49 / SSD III, 25.
59. AR 49 / SSD III, 25.
60. AR 48–49 / SSD III, 25.
61. AR 37 / SSD III, 14.
62. AR 49 / SSD III, 25.
63. AR 59 / SSD III, 36.
64. AR 58 / SSD III, 34.
65. AF 76 / SSD III, 49.
66. AF 76 / SSD III, 49.
67. And as many of his biographies relate, Wagner himself had a fondness for the finer things that, more than once, led him into near ruinous debt.
68. AF 76 / SSD III, 49.
69. AF 78 / SSD III, 51.
70. AF 84 / SSD III, 56.
71. AF 76–77 / SSD III, 49.
72. AR 41 / SSD III, 18.
73. AF 87 / SSD III, 60.
74. AF 99 / SSD III, 70–71.
75. AF 98 / SSD III, 70.
76. AF 99 / SSD III, 71.
77. AF 98 / SSD III, 70.
78. AF 98–99 / SSD III, 70.

79. This thesis is found in Stirner's *The Ego and Its Own* (1844).

80. Richard Wagner, Letter to Theodor Uhlig, 27 December 1849, in *Selected Letters of Richard Wagner*, trans. and ed. Stewart Spencer and Barry Millington (London: Norton, 1987), 182 / SB III, 195.

Chapter 5. The Drama of Revolution

1. For instance, he had begun just a few years earlier a project named *Die hohe Braut* (*The High-Born Bride*), which was adapted from Heinrich König. While just prior to *Rienzi* he set out a text to a comic opera drawn from a story from *The Arabian Nights* called *Männerlist größer als Frauenlist oder Die glückliche Bärenfamilie* (*Men's Cunning Is Greater Than Women's or the Happy Bear Family*).

2. Jonas Karlsson, '"In That Hour It Began"? Hitler, Rienzi, and the Trustworthiness of August Kubizek's *The Young Hitler I Knew*', *The Wagner Journal* 6, no. 2 (2012): 33–47. See also Alex Ross, *Wagnerism: Art and Politics in the Shadow of Music* (London: 4th Estate, 2020), 427–428.

3. Theodor W. Adorno, *Gesammelte Schriften*, vol. 19 (Frankfurt am Main: Suhrkamp, 1984), 254.

4. Theodor W. Adorno, *The Psychological Technique of Martin Luther Thomas' Radio Addresses*, in *Gesammelte Schriften*, vol. 9.1 (Frankfurt am Main: Suhrkamp, 1975), 49n.

5. Theodor W. Adorno, *In Search of Wagner*, trans. Rodney Livingstone (London: Verso, 1991), 12, 13.

6. PW 8, 252 / SSD XI, 232.

7. AR 39 / SSD III, 17.

8. AR 40 / SSD III, 17.

9. Sachs's 'notorious passage', Dieter Borchmeyer claims, is an embarrassment even to the most ardent of Wagnerites; see his 'Schiller und Wagner oder die Entdeckung des Deutschtums', in *Wagner—Weimar—Eisenach: Richard Wagner im Spannungsfeld von Kultur und Politik*, ed. Helen Geyer, Kiril Georgiev, and Stefan Alschner (Bielefeld: transcript Verlag, 2020), 31. Earlier Adorno had made the even more consequential observation that *Die Meistersinger* had 'got a whole nation drunk on themselves, esthetically anticipating with their transfigured mirage, under the social conditions of liberalism, what the glorified ones would then inflict politically on mankind' (*Introduction to the Sociology of Music*, trans. E. B. Ashton [New York: The Seabury Press, 1976], 168).

10. Timothy McFarland, 'Wagner's Nuremburg', in *Die Meistersinger von Nürnberg: Richard Wagner*, ed. Nicholas John (London: Overture Publishing, 2011), 27–28.

11. CF 346 / SSD IV, 301.

12. CF 341 / SSD IV, 295.

13. Thomas S. Grey, 'Wagner's "Lohengrin": Between *grand opéra* and *Musikdrama*', in *Lohengrin: Richard Wagner*, ed. Nicholas John (London: Overture Publishing, 2011), 15–16.

14. PW 7, 267 / SSD II, 123.

15. Richard H. Bell rightly rejects the conventional view that Wagner portrays Jesus purely as a social revolutionary. There are certainly elements of Wagner's version of the story that are irreducible to the interests of 1848–1849. *Theology of Wagner's 'Ring' Cycle I: The Genesis and Development of the Tetralogy and the Appropriation of Sources, Artists, Philosophers, and Theologians* (Eugene, OR: Cascade Books, 2020), 34.

16. JN 298 / SSD XI, 285. It has been suggested that Wagner's Jesus owes something to the version found in David Strauss's *The Life of Jesus* (1835). Although the evidence is elusive, that possibility would be consistent with Wagner's sympathetic disposition towards the basic philosophical outlook of the Young Hegelians. See Ronald Taylor, *Richard Wagner: His Life, Art and Thought* (London: Paul Elek, 1979), 92; also Barry Millington, '*Der Ring des Nibelungen*: Conception and Interpretation', in *The Cambridge Companion to Wagner*, ed. Thomas S. Grey (Cambridge: Cambridge University Press, 2008), 77. A range of other possible sources for Wagner's revolutionary and evidently socialist Jesus are examined in Manfred Frank, *Mythendämmerung. Richard Wagner im frühromanischen Kontext* (Munich: Wilhelm Fink Verlag, 2008), chapter 6.

17. JN 291 / SSD XI, 279.

18. JN 298 / SSD XI, 285.

19. Frank detects the influence of Bakunin in this set of ideas—the rejection of oaths, the primacy of love—but surely goes too far in identifying Wagner's Jesus with such an apparently destructive spirit (*Mythendämmerung*, 153–154).

20. JN 299 / SSD XI, 287.

21. JN 300 / SSD XI, 287.

22. JN 315 / SSD XI, 300–301.

23. JN 311 / SSD XI, 297.

24. JN 303 / SSD XI, 290.

25. JN 302–303 / SSD XI, 289–290.

26. JN 305 / SSD XI, 292.

27. JN 340 / SSD XI, 324.

28. JN 338 / SSD XI, 322.

29. CF 380 / SSD IV, 332.

30. SSD III, 197.

31. SSD III, 201.

32. PW 7, 302–303 / SSD II, 158.

33. PW 7, 302 / SSD II, 158.

34. What Wagner had achieved in writing the texts for the *Ring* cycle was extraordinary. And it had taken years of research and labour to complete them. It was simply not realistic for him at a later stage to abandon any significant part of it or unstitch its intricate yet elusive interconnections through substantial revision. Now a post-revolutionary Schopenhauerian, he 'committed himself' in creating full music dramas based on those texts, Raymond Furness contends, 'to principles that were at odds with Schopenhauer's philosophy' (*Richard Wagner* [London: Reaktion Books, 2013], 112).

35. See Mark Berry and Nicholas Vazsonyi, eds., *The Cambridge Companion to Wagner's 'Der Ring des Nibelungen'* (Cambridge: Cambridge University Press, 2020), 19–22; H. F. Garten, *Wagner the Dramatist* (London: Overture Publishing, 2012), 93–96.

36. The sources for this chronology are Eckart Kröplin, *Richard Wagner—Chronik* (Stuttgart: J. B. Metzler Verlag, 2016); Barry Millington, *The New Grove Guide to Wagner and His Operas* (Oxford: Oxford University Press, 2022); Ernest Newman, *The Life of Richard Wagner*, vol. 2, *1848–1860* (Cambridge: Cambridge University Press, 1976).

37. This approach, which recognizes the presence of Wagner's normative commitments in dramatized form, does not exhaust the findings available through this kind of investigation. This seems pertinent in view of longstanding concerns about the visibility of Wagner's antisemitism in the presentation of at least one of the *Ring*'s characters, namely, Mime.

38. Richard Wagner, Letter to August Röckel, 25/26 January 1854, in *Selected Letters of Richard Wagner*, trans. and ed. Stewart Spencer and Barry Millington (London: Norton, 1987), 308 / SB VI, 69.

39. A desire that was later ironically paralleled by the building of Wagner's exceptional residence in Bayreuth.

40. Mark Berry, *Treacherous Bonds and Laughing Fire: Politics and Religion in Wagner's 'Ring'* (Oxford: Routledge, 2016), 82.

41. Wagner, Letter to Röckel, 25/26 January 1854, in *Selected Letters*, 308–309 / SB VI, 69.

42. Friedrich Nietzsche, *Beyond Good and Evil*, ed. and trans. Rolf-Peter Horstmann and Judith Norman (Cambridge: Cambridge University Press, 2002), (§356), 150.

43. George Bernard Shaw, *The Perfect Wagnerite: A Commentary on the Nibelung's Ring* (New York: Dover, 1967), 44.

44. Adorno, *In Search of Wagner*, 140. Wagner himself uses the phrase 'man of the future' in that letter of 1854 to Röckel that has already been cited here.

45. See Michael Tanner, *Wagner* (London: Harper Collins, 1996), 135.

46. Friedrich Nietzsche, *The Gay Science, with a Prelude in German Rhymes and an Appendix of Songs*, ed. Bernard Williams, trans. Josefine Nauckhoff (Cambridge: Cambridge University Press, 2001), 96.

47. Aristotle, *Rhetoric*, in *The Complete Works of Aristotle: The Revised Oxford Translation*, ed. Jonathan Barnes, vol. 2 (Princeton, NJ: Princeton University Press, 1984), 2202.

Chapter 6. The End of the Revolution—Schopenhauer

1. That question is succinctly addressed by Roger Allen. *Richard Wagner's Beethoven*, trans. Roger Allen (Woodridge: The Boydell Press, 2014), 15. See Mark Berry, 'Wagner and Schopenhauer', in *The Schopenhauerian Mind*, ed. David Bather Woods and Timothy Stall (Oxford: Routledge, 2024); and Julian Young, *The Philosophies of Richard Wagner* (Lanham, MD: Lexington Books, 2014), chapters 5 and 6, for insightful accounts of the presence of Schopenhauer's ideas in Wagner's later music dramas.

2. ML 509 / SSD XV, 81.

3. Richard Wagner, Letter to Franz Liszt, c. 16 December 1854, in *Correspondence of Wagner and Liszt 1854–1861*, ed. Francis Hueffer, vol. 2 (Cambridge: Cambridge University Press, 2009), 53 / SB VI, 298.

4. Jakob Norberg, making the novel case for a reconsideration of Schopenhauer as a political thinker, reports that one Bismarck supporter had contemptuously 'claimed that Schopenhauer had only become popular after the pan-European 1848 revolutions. For those disappointed and discouraged by the failure of 1848 Schopenhauer's philosophy of "misery" had proved congenial during a collective political "hangover", but it should be dismissed as Germans headed into a new epoch of great achievements' (*Schopenhauer's Politics* [Cambridge: Cambridge University Press, 2024], 5).

5. ML 606–607 / SSD XV, 212.

6. ML 509 / SSD XV, 82.

7. ML 509 / SSD XV, 82.

8. ML 510 / ML SSD XV, 82.

9. Magee suggests deep affinities not mentioned by Wagner himself between the dramatic work and Schopenhauer's philosophy; see *Wagner and Philosophy* (London: Penguin, 2000), chapter 8. However, Wagner, notwithstanding a change of politics, never became 'a rejecter of the world' (137).

10. William Ashton Ellis, JN 313n.

11. It is a long-established and continuing narrative that Schopenhauer utterly transformed Wagner's thinking. Hugo Dinger, for example, speaks of a 'complete inversion of his nature and world view' and of a Wagner 'fully changed' by that

encounter (*Richard Wagners geistige Entwickelung* [Leipzig: E. W. Fritzsch, 1892], xxi, 23). But the precedents in Wagner's thought, even though grounded in a different philosophical framework, are discernible.

12. ML 509 / ML SSD XV, 82.

13. Arthur Schopenhauer, *The World as Will and Representation*, ed. and trans. Judith Norman, Alistair Welchman, ed. Christopher Janaway, vol. 1 (Cambridge: Cambridge University Press, 2010), 402.

14. Schopenhauer, *World as Will and Representation*, vol. 1, 203.

15. Schopenhauer, *World as Will and Representation*, vol. 1, 369.

16. See Brian O'Connor, 'Melancholy and Pessimism: Adorno's Critique of Schopenhauer', in *The Schopenhauerian Mind*, ed. David Bather Woods and Timothy Stoll (Oxford: Routledge, 2023), 531–543.

17. Schopenhauer, *World as Will and Representation*, vol. 1, 317.

18. PW 1, 26 / SSD III, 4.

19. JN 315 / SSD XI, 301.

20. JN 316 / SSD XI, 302.

21. JN 316 / SSD XI, 302.

GENERAL INDEX

INDEX OF WAGNER'S WORKS

PROSE AND NON-DRAMATIC WORKS

Works cited by title are indexed here; abbreviated references can be found within the endnotes.

DRAMAS AND MUSICAL WORKS, INCLUDING PREPARATORY TEXTS AND SKETCHES

A NOTE ON THE TYPE

This book has been composed in Arno, an Old-style serif typeface in the classic Venetian tradition, designed by Robert Slimbach at Adobe.